IMAGES
of America

TREUTLEN COUNTY

I0792645

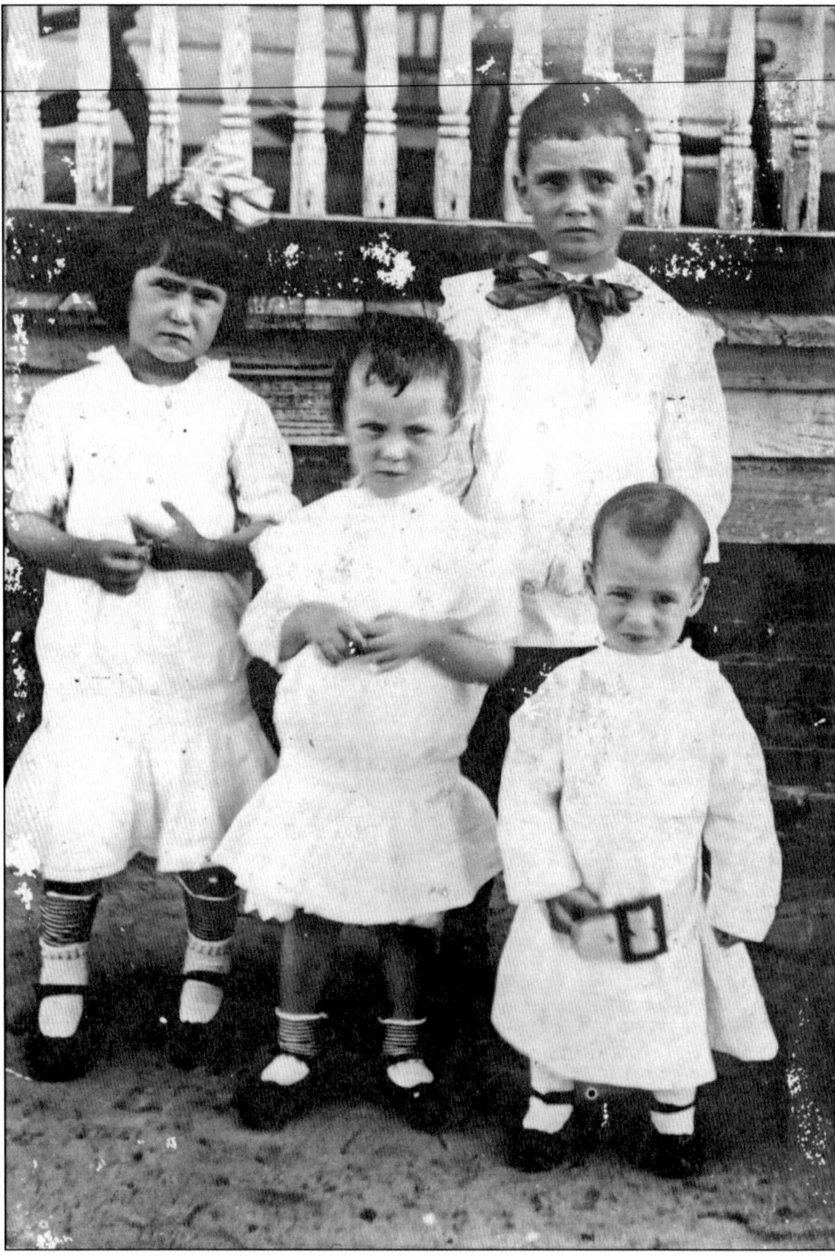

Shown in this c. 1915 picture are the first four children of James Tillman "Bud" Warnock (1875–1963) and his wife, Dora Braddy (1883–1963). From left to right are Mildred Warnock Hilton, Florence Warnock Overstreet, William Walton Warnock, and J. Carlton Warnock. They are standing in front of the home of their maternal grandparents, Moses Algerine and Florence Herndon Braddy. (Courtesy of Jane Warnock.)

ON THE COVER: The Daly Drug Store in Soperton is pictured here c. 1950. Bobbie Gillis Thompson, center, is shown with James Vance Daly and his wife, the former Pauline Pensy Wheeler. The Daly family was engaged in the retail drug business for 42 years. (Authors' collection.)

IMAGES
of America

TREUTLEN COUNTY

Larry Ronald Braddy and Olivia Williamson Braddy

ARCADIA
PUBLISHING

ISBN 978-0-7385-6742-6

Published by Arcadia Publishing
Charleston, South Carolina

Printed in the United States of America

Library of Congress Catalog Card Number: 2008929309

For all general information contact Arcadia Publishing at:
Telephone 843-853-2070
Fax 843-853-0044
E-mail sales@arcadiapublishing.com
For customer service and orders:
Toll-Free 1-888-313-2665

Visit us on the Internet at www.arcadiapublishing.com

Contents

ACKNOWLEDGMENTS

People who assisted us in this project are too numerous to name, and doing so could leave somebody out who made a large contribution to these pages. Therefore, we wish to thank all of the generous contributors who either gave or loaned us these cherished photographs and memorabilia, and we have noted them with a credit line following the captions; all other images appear courtesy of the authors. Also, the Treutlen County Historical Society gave tremendous support and encouragement to begin this project while materials were still readily available. We appreciate everyone for their help and generosity in making the publication of this book possible.

We would also like to acknowledge Hon. J. Clayton Stephens Jr., deceased, who, through his research, writing, and enthusiasm for local history, made such a tremendous contribution to the county of Treutlen.

INTRODUCTION

Treutlen County focuses upon the settlement of the geographical region of the state of Georgia that now comprises Treutlen County, including areas of Montgomery and Emanuel Counties. Located in southeastern Georgia, Treutlen County was part of the "pine barren" region of the state that was initially considered a wasteland, covered with wiregrass and pine trees. People from Virginia, North Carolina, South Carolina, and the piedmont region of Georgia originally settled the area that is now Treutlen County. Many of the early settlers were frontier subsistence farmers who produced only enough to feed their large families and purchase supplies for the next year's crops. These rugged frontiersmen cut the virgin pines to construct their dwellings and barns. In addition, they and their families labored diligently to clear the woods of this virgin pine timber so they could plant tobacco, corn, cotton, and vegetables for their livelihoods. Later these early settlers erected churches, schools, and towns from the yellow virgin pine timber that covered this entire area of what is now Treutlen County, Georgia. As European and Asian demand for virgin timber increased, strong, rugged settlers used broadaxes to fell, as well as oxcarts to transport, these huge yellow pines to the Ohoopee and Oconee Rivers, which constitute the eastern and western boundaries of Treutlen County. Eventually, these huge pine logs were tied together into large rafts that were floated down the Altamaha River to the port of Darien, where they were sawed into timber and shipped abroad. Later the pine tree served as the basis for the turpentine industry that originated in South Georgia. Treutlen County's economy has been intertwined historically with the production of the pine tree.

This volume provides pictorial documentation of the significance of the pine tree in the economy of Treutlen County and this region of Georgia. Subsequent to the depletion of the county's farmland through the production of cotton and other crops, and the lack of availability of commercial fertilizer, James Fowler of Treutlen County pioneered the reforestation of highly eroded and exhausted farms into the profitable production of pine trees. Fowler's partnership with Dr. Charles Holmes Herty at Georgia Southern College (now a university) led to the production of paper for newsprint and other purposes. This edition documents through photographs this county's technical and commercial contributions to the production of paper and the expansion of the state's timber industry, based primarily upon the reforestation techniques of a prominent Treutlen Countian. Thus, the memories of Treutlen County, the "Million Pines County," are interwoven historically with the pine tree. This book's content documents in pictures the evolution of the pine tree's production.

In addition, the county's agricultural development is documented through pictures, including the production of tobacco, corn, cotton, and other crops. The development of the livestock industry in the county is also traced pictorially, including cattle and swine production, from early strains to the purebred herds found in the county today. The installation of water mills on the creeks and streams of the county are likewise documented through photographs.

The wide divergence of early private and public schools throughout the county are traced through pictures provided in this edition. In addition, the history of some of the county's churches is documented through photographs. Pictures of a *c.* 1900 natural mineral spring, more specifically Gillis Springs, are included. Photographs of some of the county's cemeteries and historic monuments are provided, including Michael A. Troup's tomb at his Rosemont Plantation (Troup was a governor of Georgia). Pictures of early Soperton, Georgia, the county seat, are provided, including its founding as a railroad town at the beginning of the 19th century. Pictures of early homes, political and civic leaders, hotels, and town scenes are included in this publication. Images of historic homes throughout the county, including log cabins and ornate Victorian homes, are provided.

Portraits of prominent Treutlen citizens are likewise documented, including the founding fathers of Treutlen County and the early officials of Soperton, Georgia. The families of the county, including early settlers, have been portrayed—many of them posing in front of their family dwellings, on their horses, or in their automobiles. Pictures of prominent ministers, educators, and industrial leaders of the county have also been provided in *Treutlen County*.

One

The Way We Were

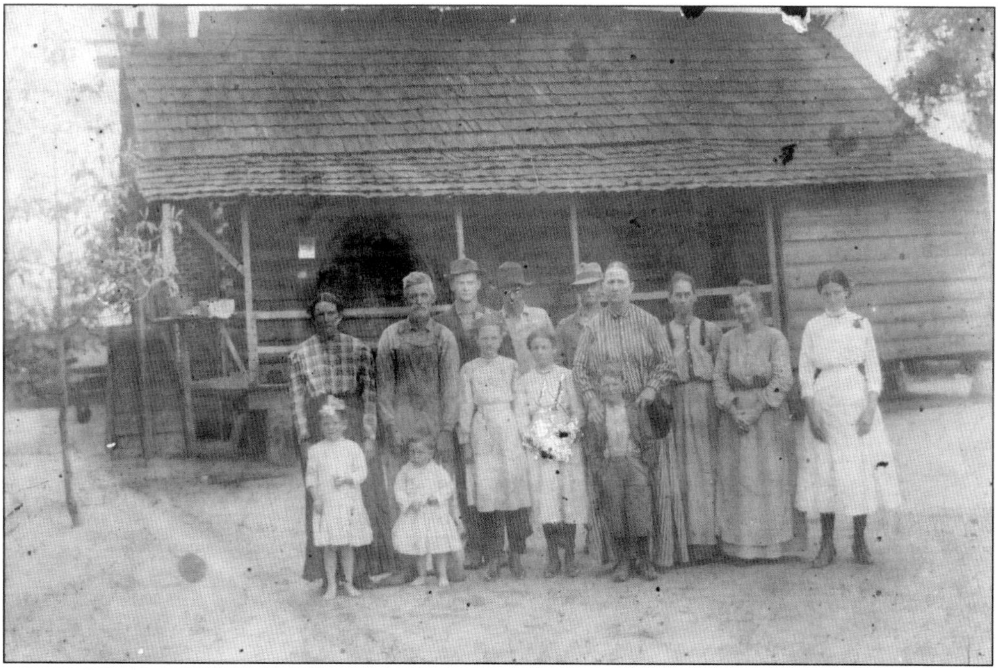

Pictured is the Lewis Hutcheson family in front of their old log home around 1880. John Lewis Hutcheson (1824–1899), a son of Thomas E. Hutcheson and his first wife (unidentified), married Penina Jane "Penny" Miller (1837–1888), daughter of Thomas "Gopher Back" Miller and Nancy Vick, in 1855. Note the well and washstand at the end of the front porch. (Courtesy of Norris Hutcheson.)

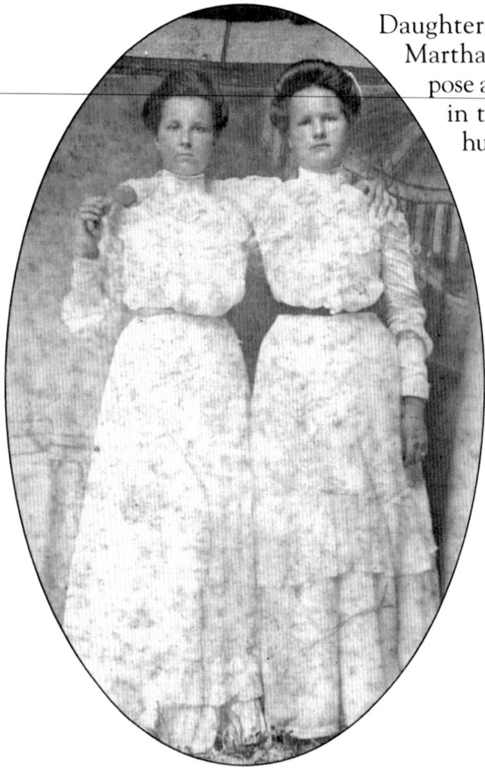

Daughters of Hiram and Matilda Williamson Kirby, Martha P. "Mattie" (left) and Mary O. "Mollie" Kirby pose arm in arm in this c. 1905 picture. Mollie is buried in the Boiling Springs Church cemetery beside her husband, Meada E. Phillips.

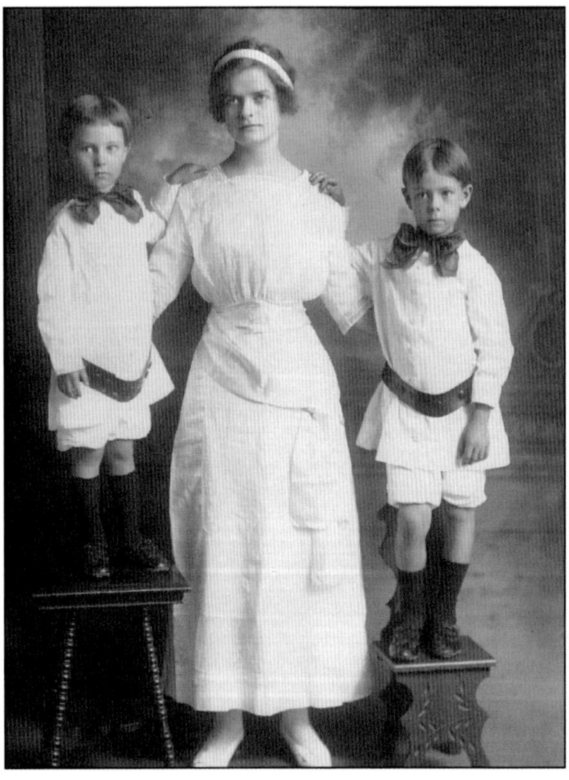

Preston Brooks "Peddy" Moring (1909–1982), left, and his brother, Joel Josephus "Doey" Moring Jr. (1907–1990), are shown posing with their aunt, Mamie Rabun Denson, in Soperton around 1912. (Courtesy of Lena Moring Wiley.)

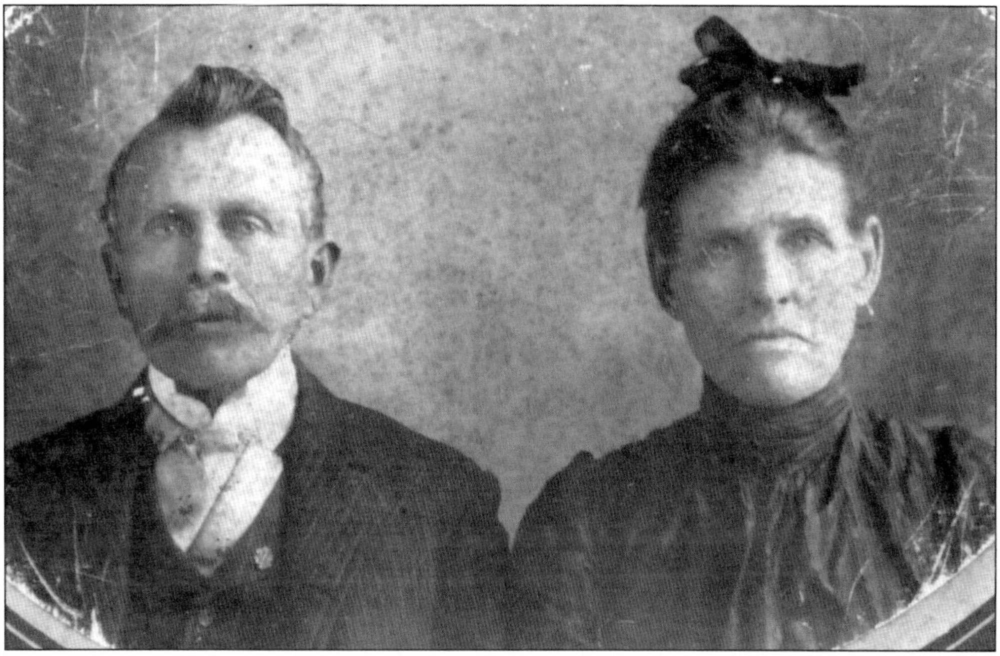

Andrew Jackson Williamson II (1844–1910) and his wife, the former Lecy Ann Phillips (1848–1917), are pictured here in their Sunday best. Andrew was a son of William J. and Jane (née Flowers) Phillips Williamson; Lecy Ann was a daughter of Drewry (née Taylor) and Sarah Moore Phillips. (Courtesy of Marie Braddy Sumner.)

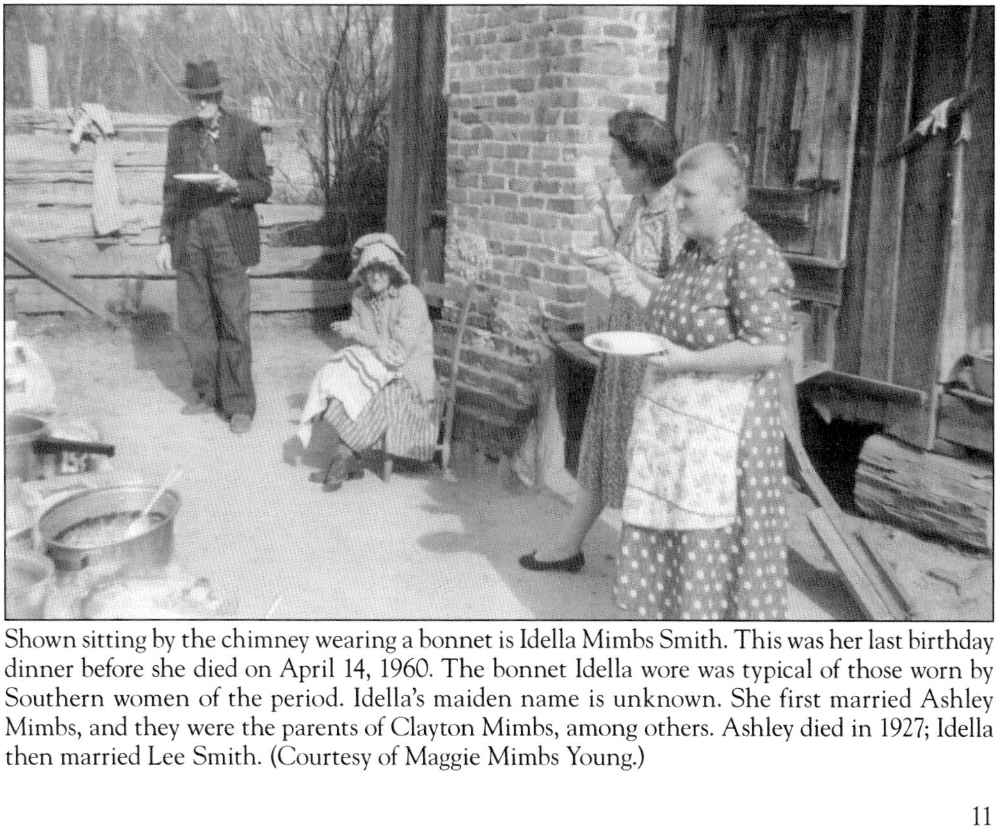

Shown sitting by the chimney wearing a bonnet is Idella Mimbs Smith. This was her last birthday dinner before she died on April 14, 1960. The bonnet Idella wore was typical of those worn by Southern women of the period. Idella's maiden name is unknown. She first married Ashley Mimbs, and they were the parents of Clayton Mimbs, among others. Ashley died in 1927; Idella then married Lee Smith. (Courtesy of Maggie Mimbs Young.)

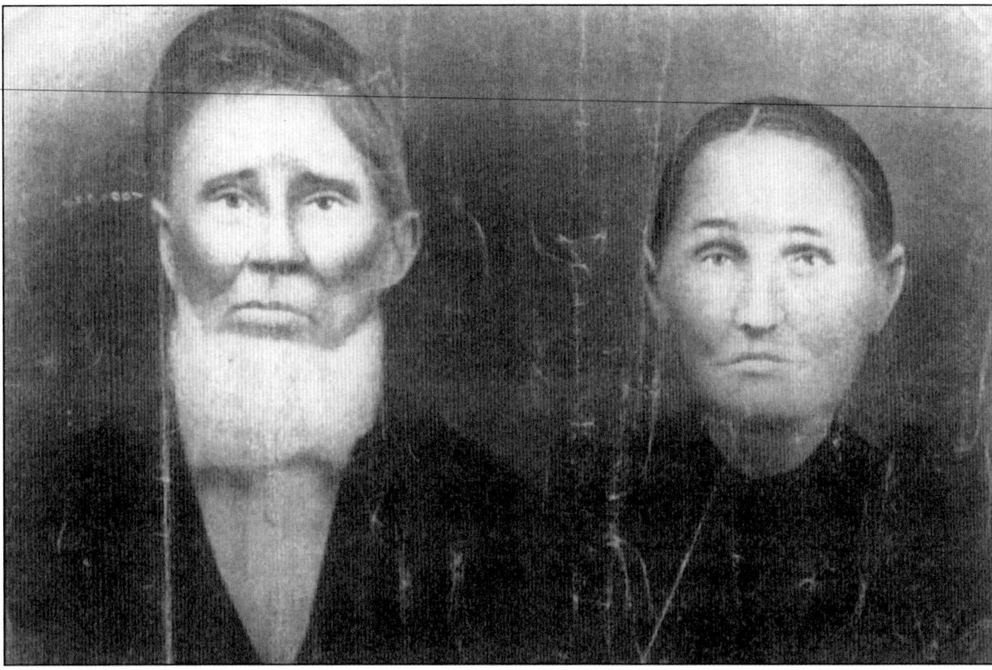

Shown in this old photograph are Warren W. Ricks (1829–1910) and his wife, Lecy Anne Barwick (1830–1918). They reared a large family in the portion of Emanuel County that later became Treutlen County. (Courtesy of Tracy Manning Gillikin.)

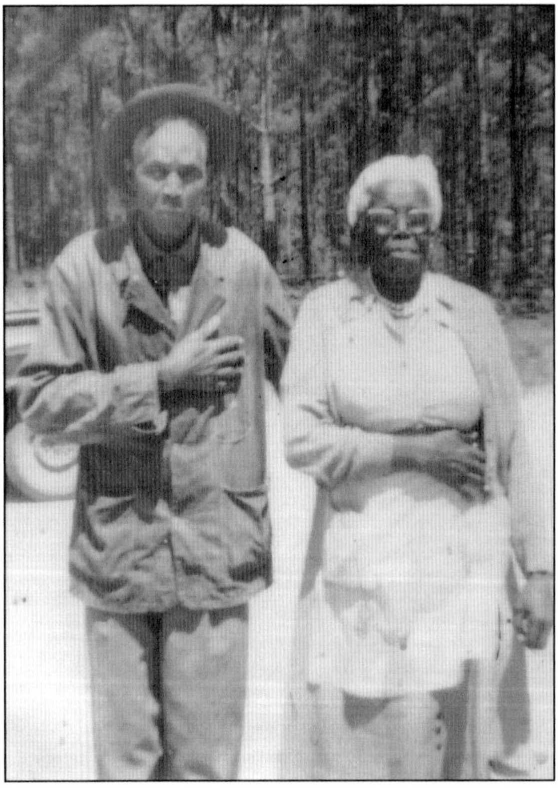

Pictured here are Rollie and Ada Renfroe Wicker. This couple moved from Washington County, Georgia, to Soperton in the early 1900s. Among their children are Emmitt, Rollie Jr. "Junior," Robert, Marie, and Corene. (Courtesy of Corene Wicker McLeod.)

Murdoch B. Gillis (1861–1939) was a son of John Gillis and Mary Ann Gillis. Three of his grandparents were immigrants from Scotland to North Carolina and then to Montgomery County, Georgia. (Courtesy of Hal Jones.)

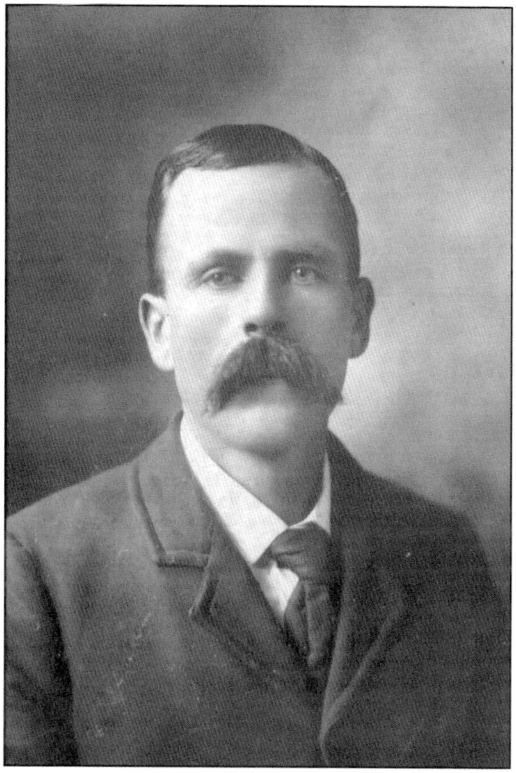

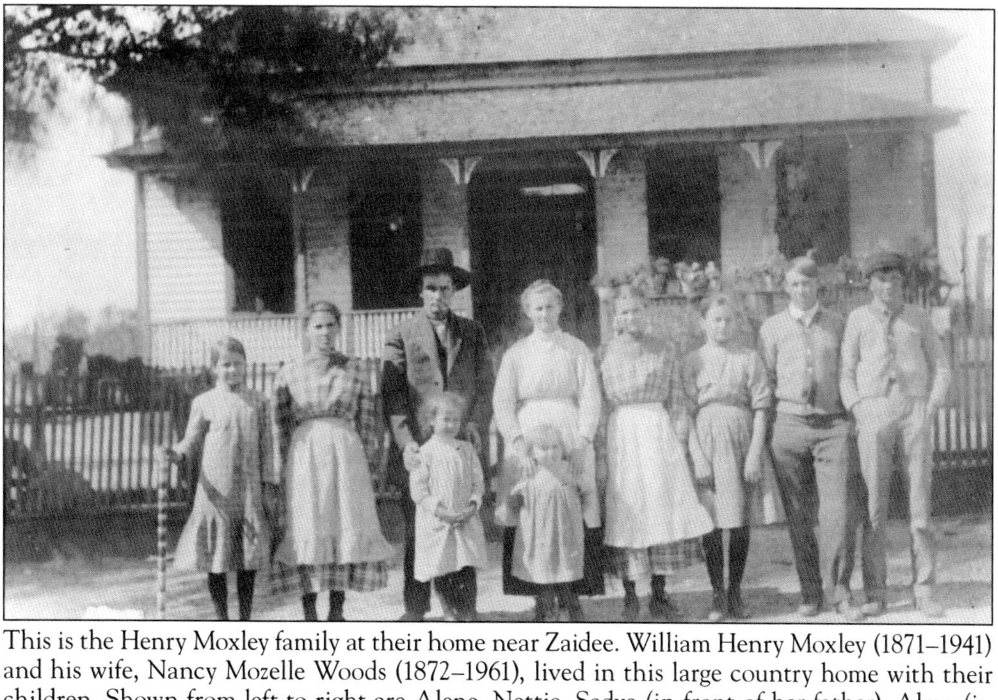

This is the Henry Moxley family at their home near Zaidee. William Henry Moxley (1871–1941) and his wife, Nancy Mozelle Woods (1872–1961), lived in this large country home with their children. Shown from left to right are Alene, Nettie, Sadye (in front of her father), Alma (in front of her mother), Mettie, Mattie, Chess Flanders (a cousin), and Newton. (Courtesy of Juanita Lindsey Youmans.)

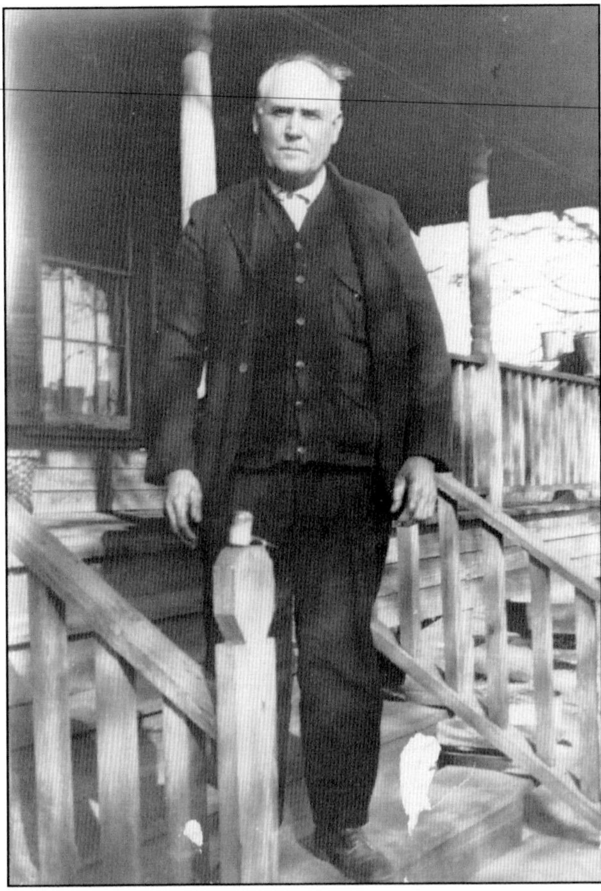

Shown standing on the front doorstep of his lovely Victorian home is James Daniel Simons Jr. (1875–1938). A son of James Daniel Simons and Mary McGahee, he married Maggie Eliza Calhoun (1878–1950), daughter of James Irving Calhoun II and Nancy Clarissa Connell. (Courtesy of Loyce Poole Simons.)

Posing for this formal picture below are William Norris Hutcheson (1868–1944) and his wife, Emma Love (1872–1939). This picture was probably made in 1892 when they were married. (Courtesy of Norris Hutcheson.)

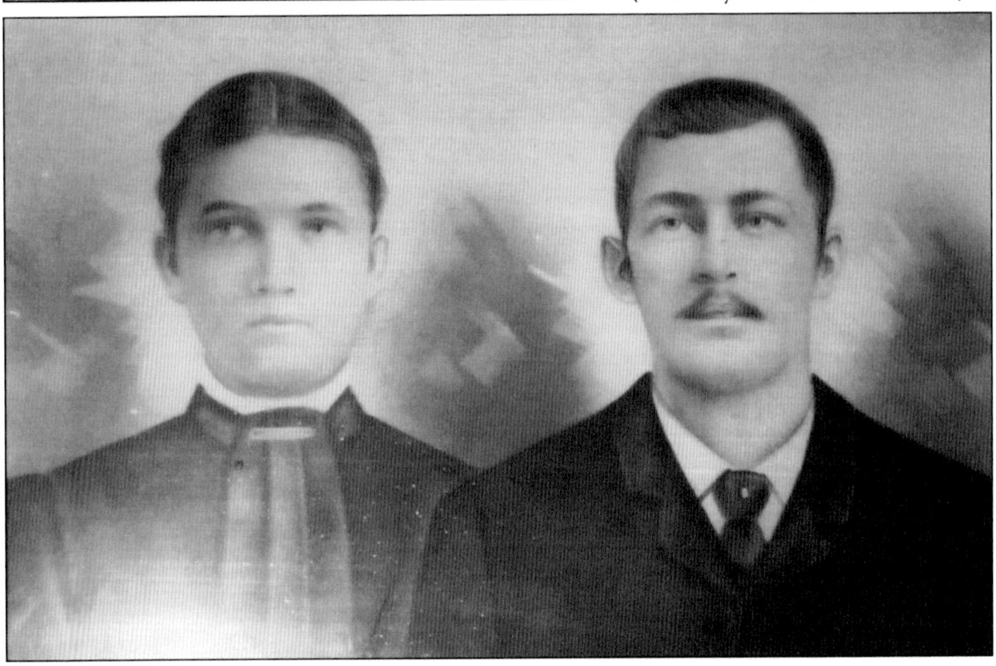

Benjamin Franklin Soper (1856–1907), for whom Soperton was named, was a railroad construction engineer with the Macon, Dublin, and Savannah Railroad and the owner of B. F. Soper and Company of Nashville, Tennessee.

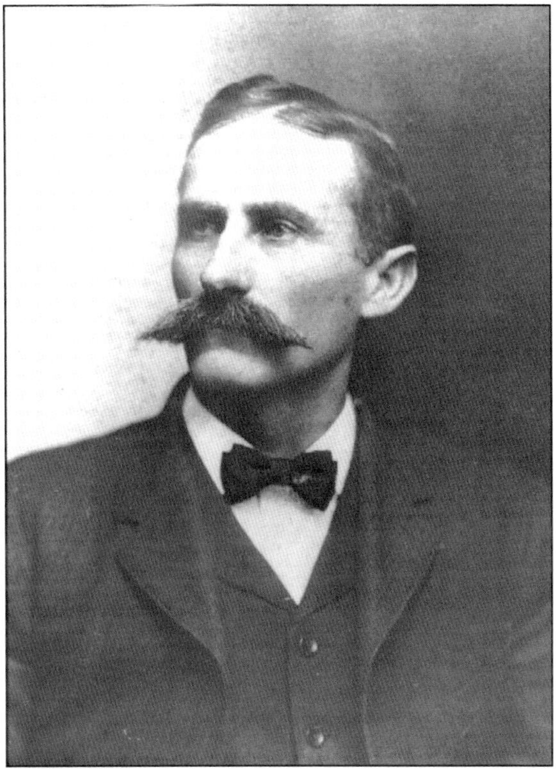

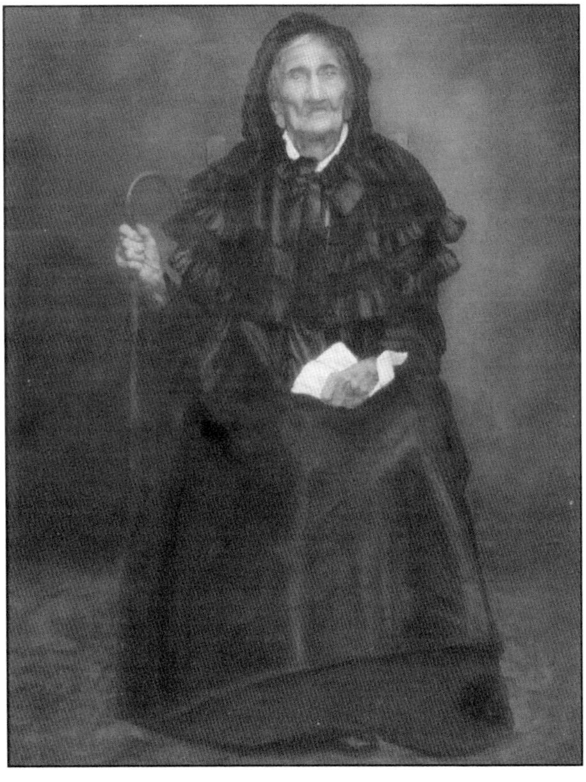

Eliza Ann Collins Adams (1804–1905) is pictured here on her 100th birthday. Eliza was born in Tattnall County to Josiah Collins Jr. and Susannah Summerlin. In 1820, she married Matthias Adams (1800–1855), son of Penelope Adams, and they reared 11 children whose descendants have spread out across Treutlen and adjoining counties.

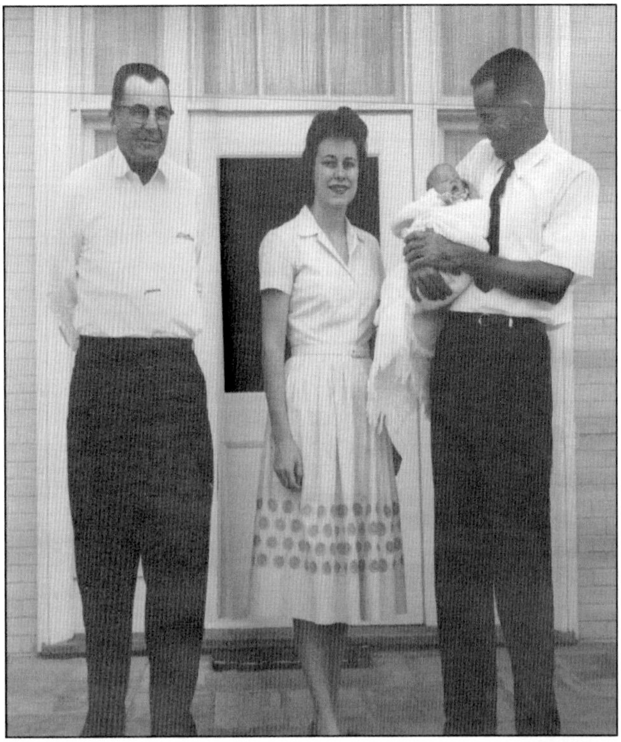

Standing on the front porch of the Jim L. Gillis house, located east of Soperton, are James Lester "Jim L." Gillis Sr. (1892–1975), Marianne Gillis Persons, and her father, James Lester Gillis Jr., holding his grandson, Ogden Persons III. This four-generations photograph was made in the summer of 1960. (Courtesy of James Lester Gillis Jr.)

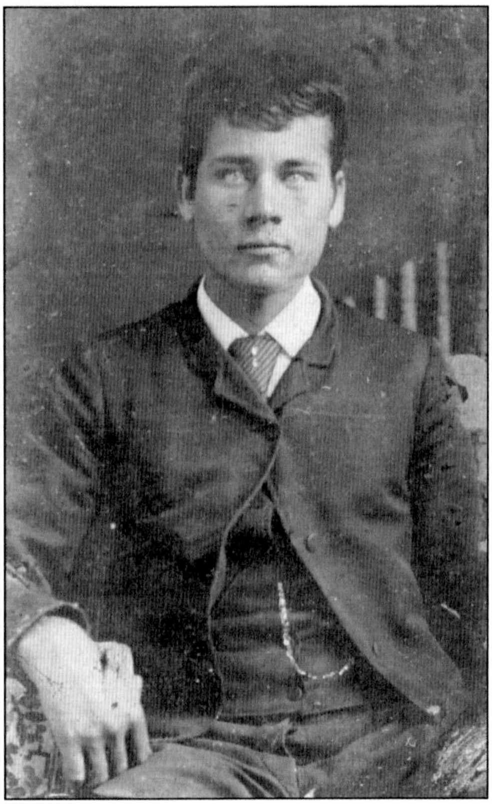

Anthony Lindsey Adams (1870–1929) was a son of William Riley Adams and Mary "Polly" Hamilton. In 1895, he married Ruth Elizabeth Williamson (1871–1953), daughter of Andrew Jackson Williamson II and Lecy Ann Phillips. They reared their children in the Kibbee community. (Courtesy of Marie Braddy Sumner.)

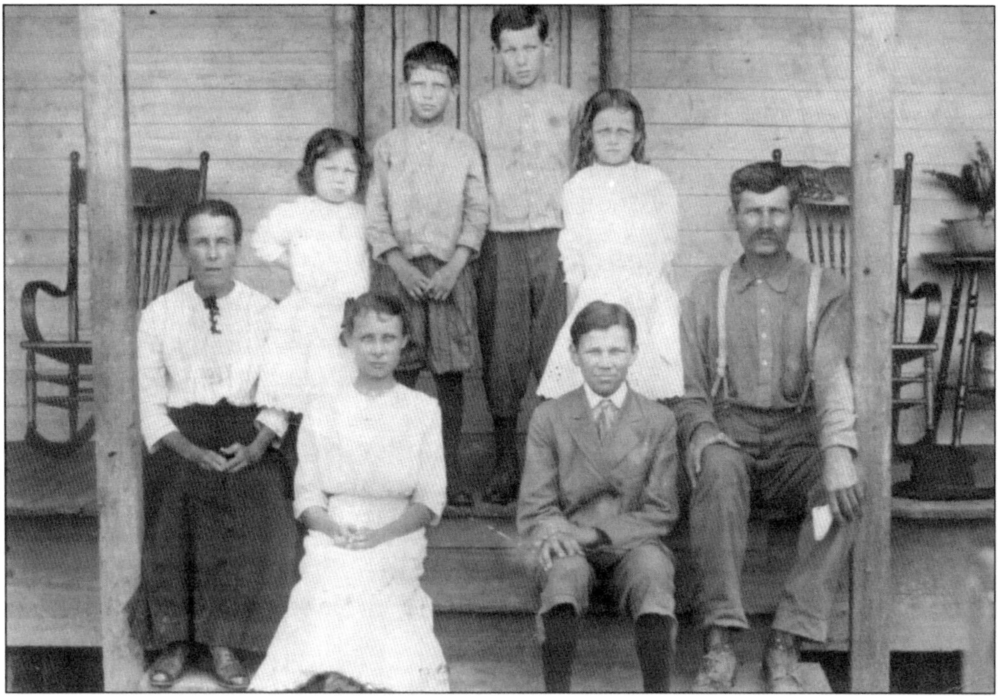

The Anthony Lindsey Adams family gathered on their front porch for this picture (above) made about 1910. Most of this family is buried in the Jack Williamson Cemetery near Kibbee in Montgomery County. (Courtesy of Marie Braddy Sumner.)

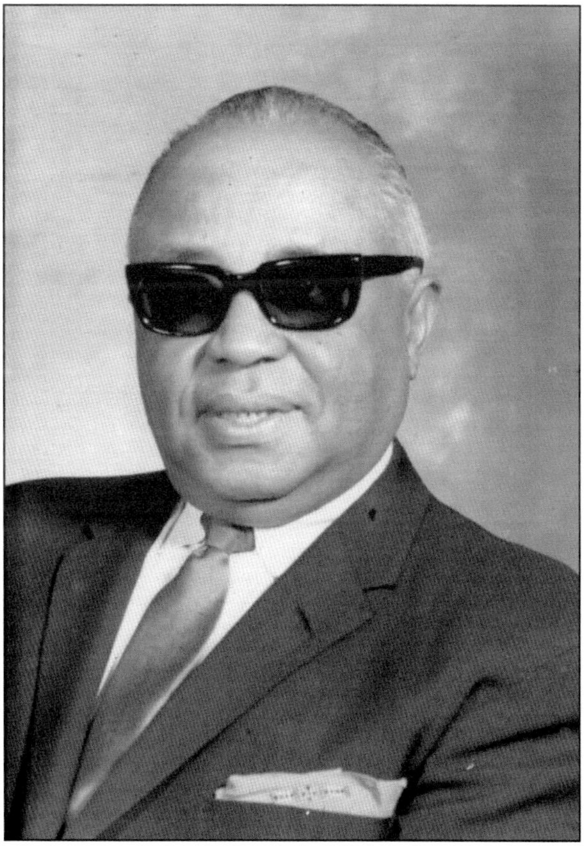

Pictured here is Augustus McArthur, who taught for many years at the old Treutlen County Training School near Soperton. He was a leader in the education of black children in the area.

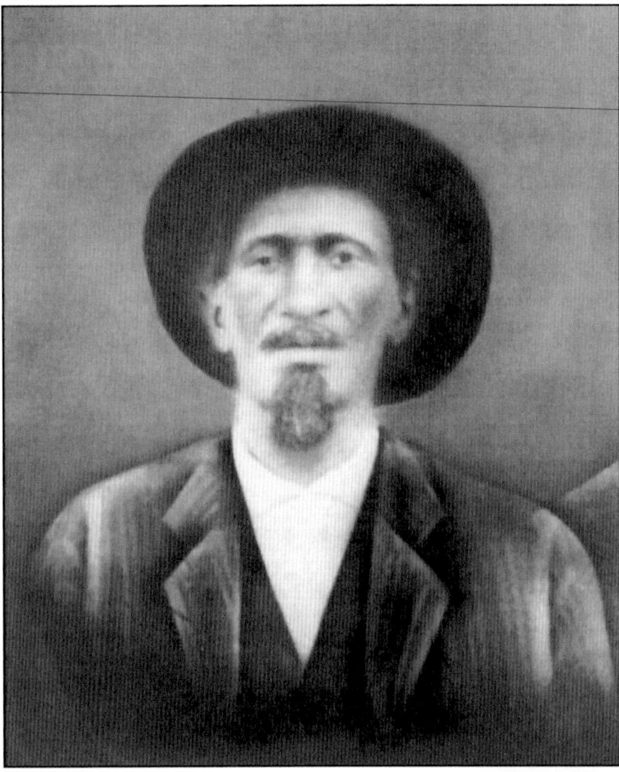

John Love and his wife, Augusta Cook, came to Montgomery County, Georgia, in 1869 from Richmond, Virginia, with their children: George Cook, Eddie, Armstead, Bertha, Charlotte, Laura, Susan, and Ellen Love. John purchased 500 acres of land near present-day Highway 221. This area came to be known as the Love Quarters. In 1884, John Love was nominated to represent Montgomery County in the Georgia House of Legislature. (Courtesy of the Love family.)

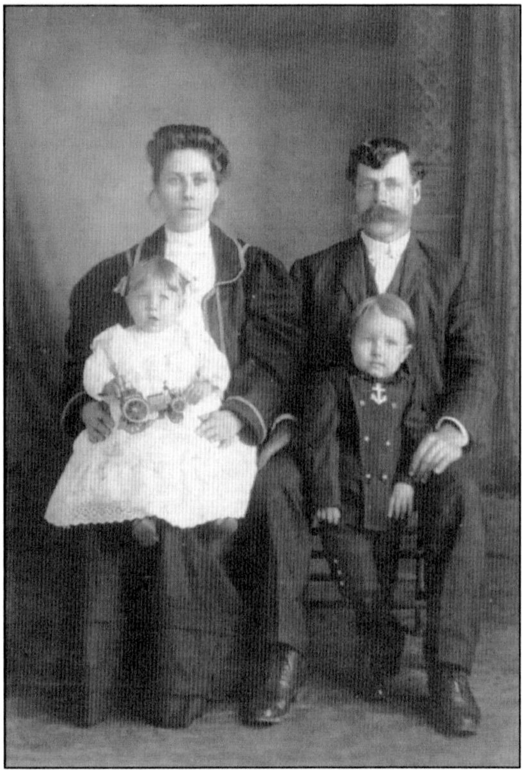

John Bell Ricks (1869–1921) is pictured in this 1900 photograph with his wife, Harvie Frances Youngblood, and their children, Morris and Minnie. John B. Ricks served on the first board of education from 1919 until his death. This family lived at Blackville, moving to Soperton in about 1914.

John Gillis (1807–1891) and Mary Ann Gillis (1827–1897) are shown in this painting, created from an old tintype made in their later years. They were married in Montgomery County in 1853 and were the parents of eight known children. Many of their descendants currently live in Treutlen County. (Courtesy of Hal Jones.)

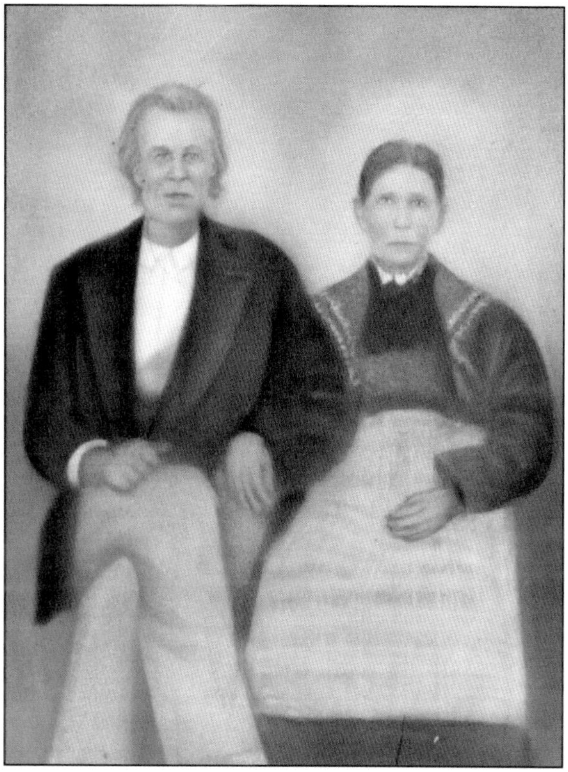

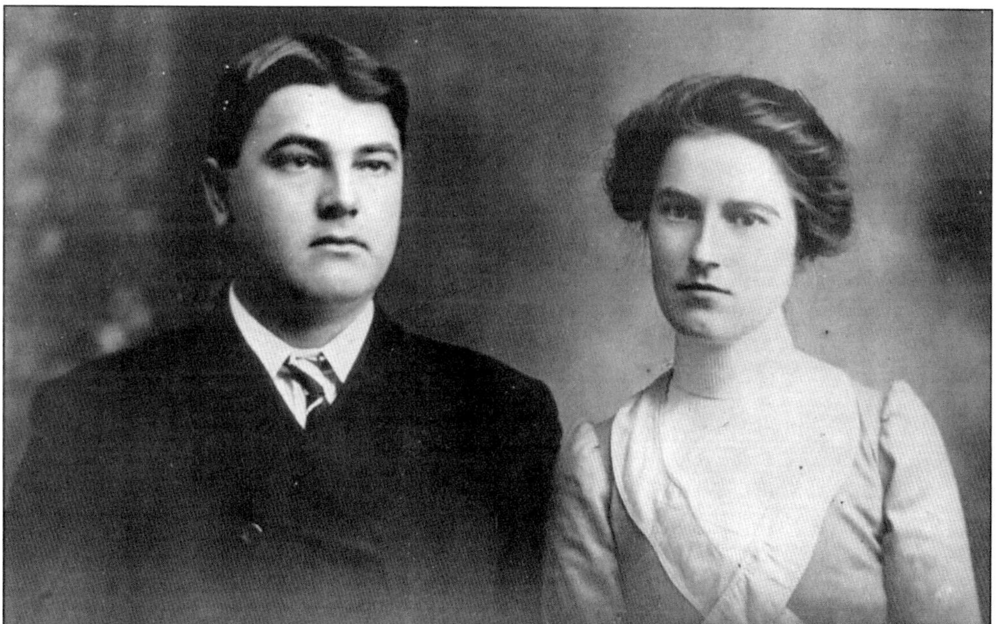

Joel Josephus Moring (1878–1926) was born in Swainsboro, Georgia, to Preston Brooks Moring and Mary Elizabeth "Mollie" Camp. He practiced law in Swainsboro until about 1904, when he moved to Soperton. He married Lena Corine Rabun (1881–1966) in 1902, a daughter of Rev. Isaac Cicero Gibson Rabun, a noted Methodist minister. (Courtesy of Lena Moring Wiley.)

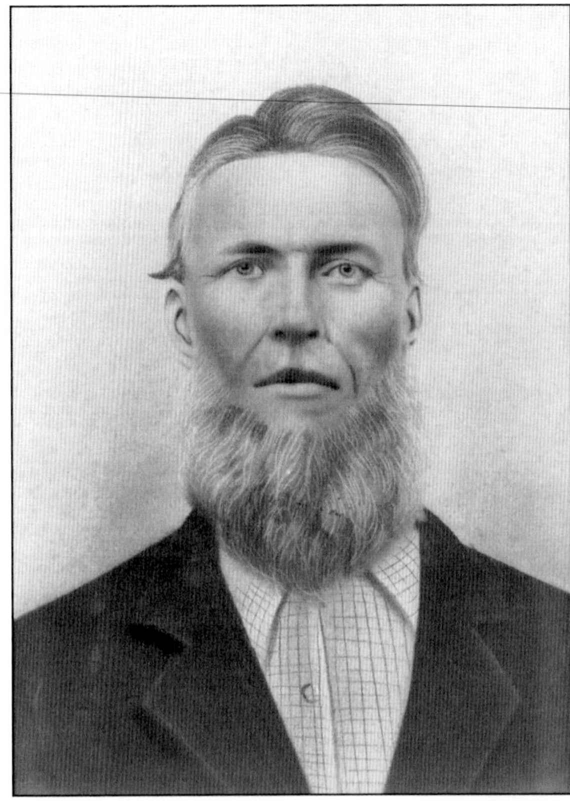

John Miller Jr. (1818–1904) was a son of John Miller and Isabella Hall and was married to Laura Ann McCrimmon, daughter of George W. McCrimmon and Catherine Ann McLeod. He was the founder of Miller's Institute and Miller's Mill in the Lothair community.

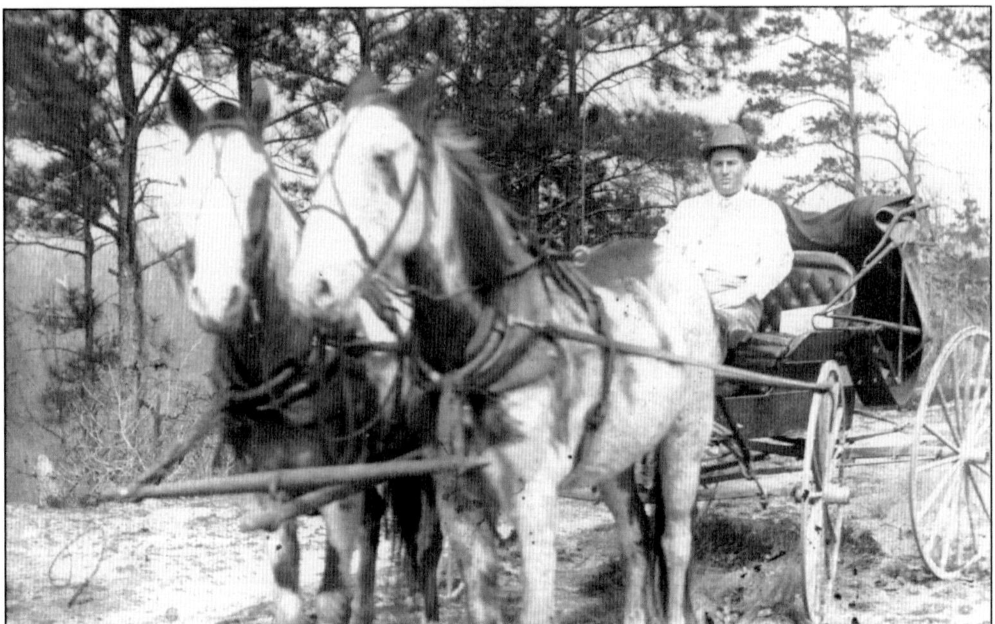

Pictured *c.* 1915 is John Newton Evans (1895–1937) driving a surrey drawn by two fine horses. John was a son of William Elisha Evans and Mary Ella Rogers and married Eva Bragg. This couple had no children.

Pictured here around 1923 is the John William Wickstrom family of the Mount Shady Church community. John (1884–1963) was married to Missouri Wilkes (1888–1948). Shown here from left to right are (first row) Annie Lee (on John's lap), Milledge (between his parents), and John C. (on Missouri's lap); (second row) Katie, N. L., Essie Mae, and Charlie. (Courtesy of Kay Wickstrom.)

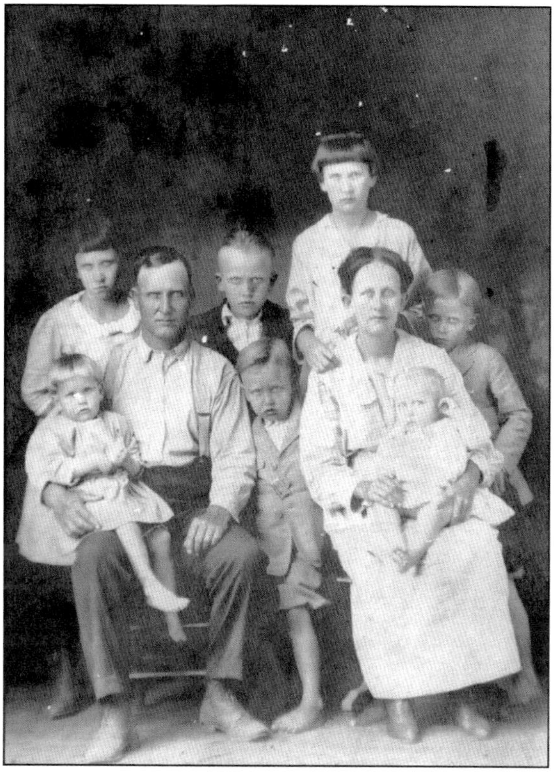

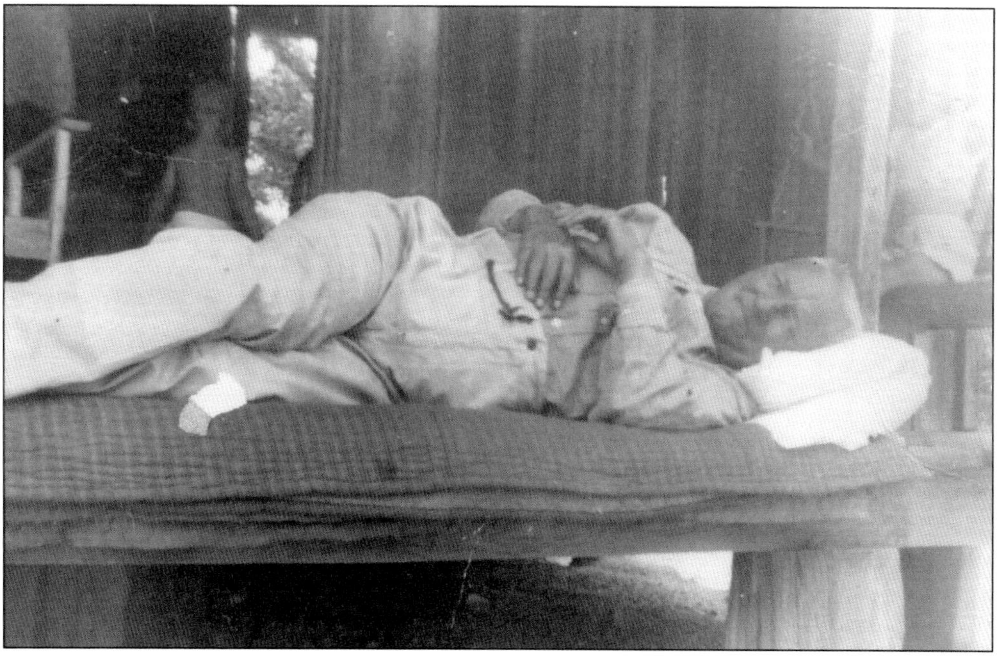

John W. Wickstrom is shown lounging on the front porch, resting after his noon meal before returning to the field. The uses of porches in the 1800s and early 1900s in the South were many. John was a son of Charles William Wickstrom, an immigrant from Finland who arrived in Emanuel County in 1873. (Courtesy of Kay Wickstrom.)

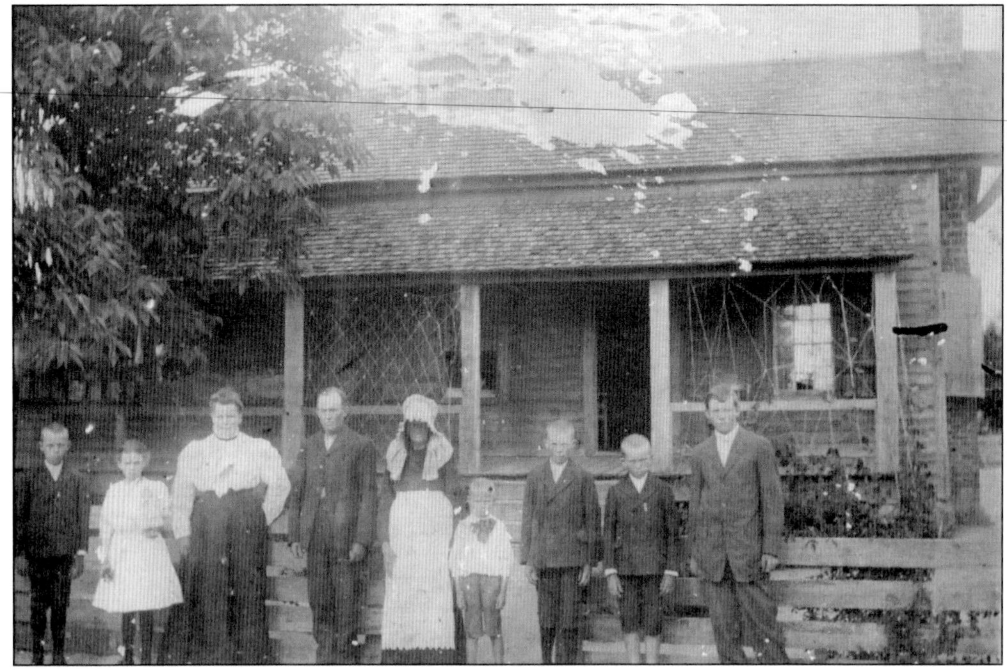

The John Washington Meeks family posed in this 1907 picture in front of their home near Soperton. From left to right are Erie, Elizabeth Jane, Mary Elizabeth "Missy" Bussell Meeks, John Washington Meeks, Didania Melissa Jane Brown Meeks (mother of John W. Meeks), Noah, Solomon, Uel, and Matthew.

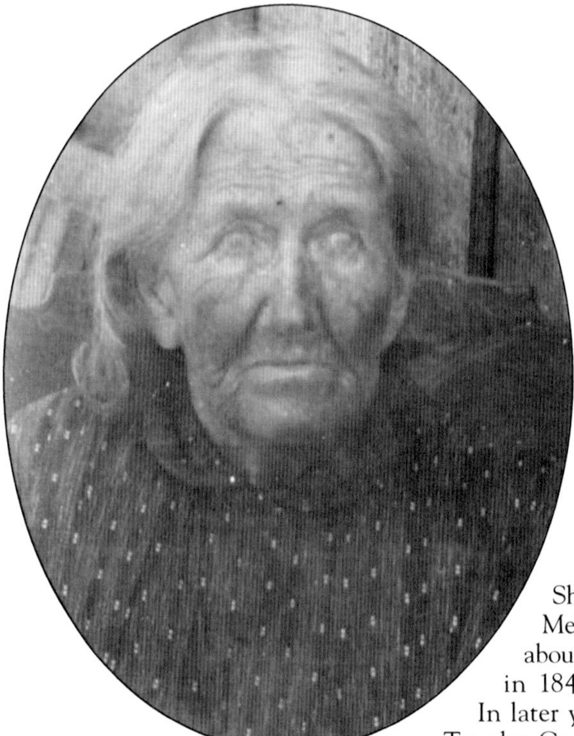

Shown in this 1900 photograph is Didania Melissa Jane Brown Meeks, who was born about 1830. She married Washington Meeks in 1847 in Washington County, Georgia. In later years, she moved with her children to Treutlen County.

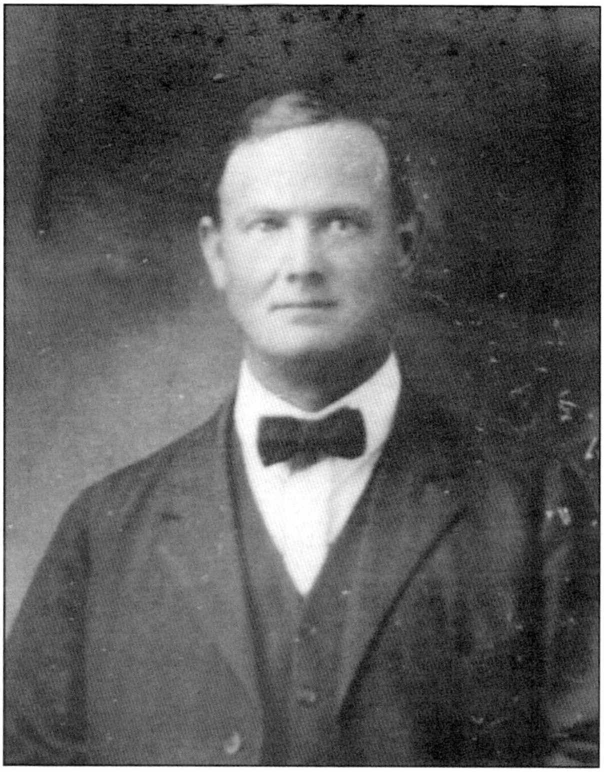

Lamar Holmes (1878–1926) was a prominent businessman in Soperton. His home was located on Railroad Avenue. Active in many civic projects in Soperton, he served as mayor in 1913 and was a member of the school board.

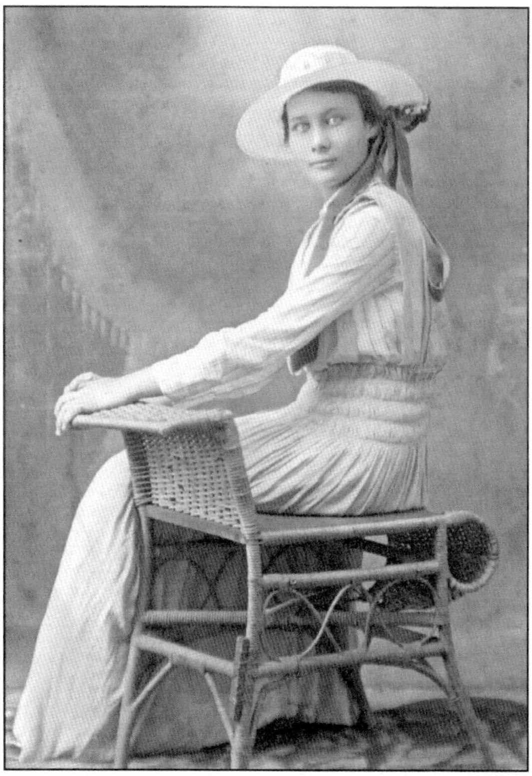

Shown in a beautiful outfit of the period, Mary Adams Lowman (1901–1960) posed for this studio picture about 1918. She was a daughter of Anthony Lindsey Adams and Ruth Elizabeth Williamson and married Thomas M. Lowman, son of George W. and Loretta Catherine Lowman. (Courtesy of Marie Braddy Sumner.)

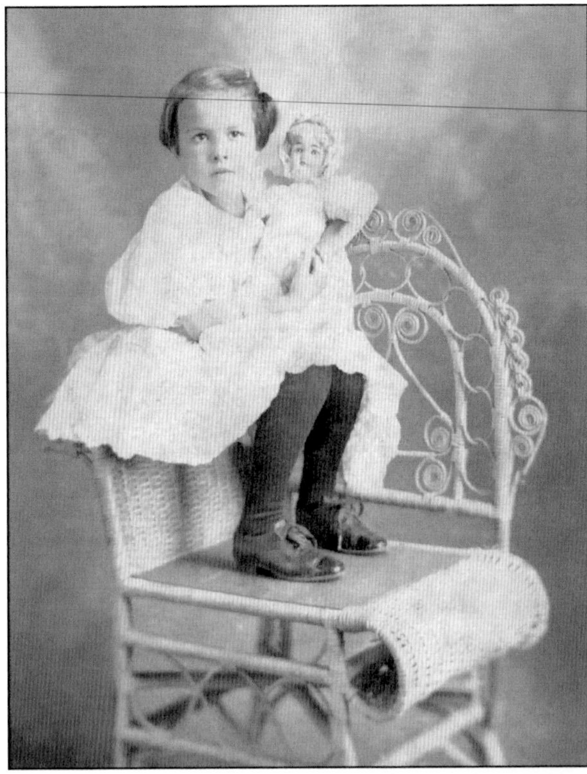

Mary Delilah "Lila" Williamson (1901–1987) posed in this studio picture around 1905. She was a daughter of Millard Milton Williamson and Mary Ann Delilah Adams and married Virgil Henry Burns.

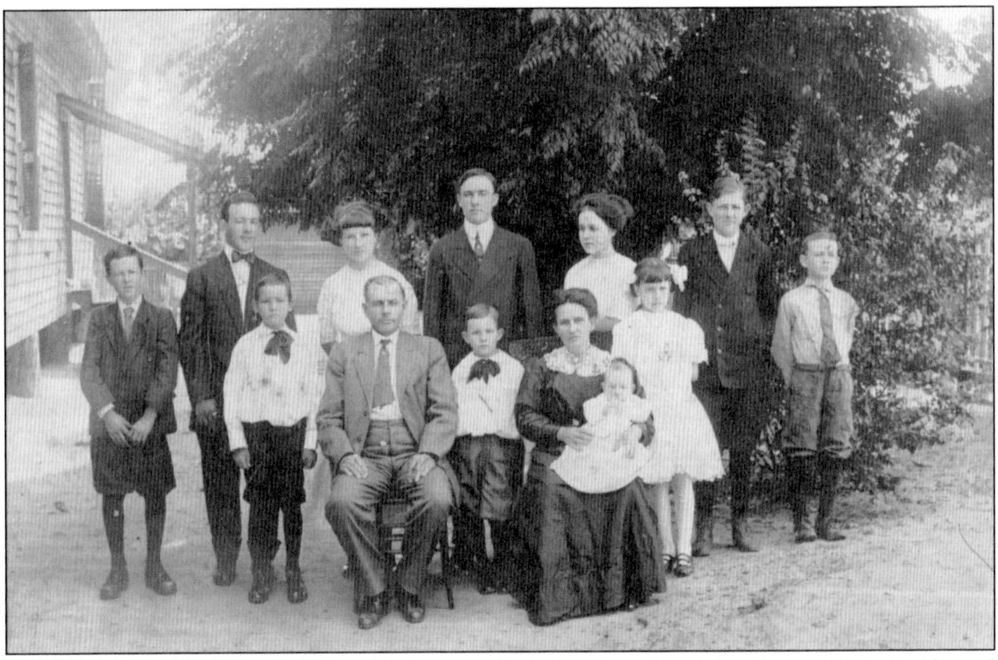

Millard Milton Williamson (1862–1939), his wife, Mary Ann Delilah Adams (1872–1939), and their children pose in 1911 beside their home. Milton was a son of Andrew Jackson Williamson and Lecy Ann Moore, and Mary was the daughter of William Thomas Ezekiel "W. T. E." Adams and Delilah Browning. This family had a large farm on present-day Highway 297.

Millard Milton Williamson is pictured here about 1900. He was successful in farming, raising livestock, harvesting timber, and working with his older brother, Drewry Steeley Williamson, in the sales of a stump-pulling apparatus, which Drewry had invented in the late 1800s. Drewry was the great-grandfather of Jody Powell, press secretary to former U.S. president Jimmy Carter.

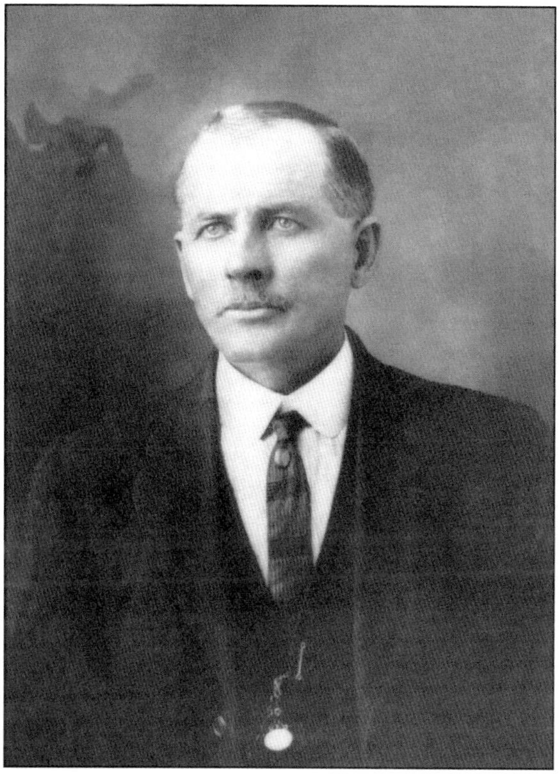

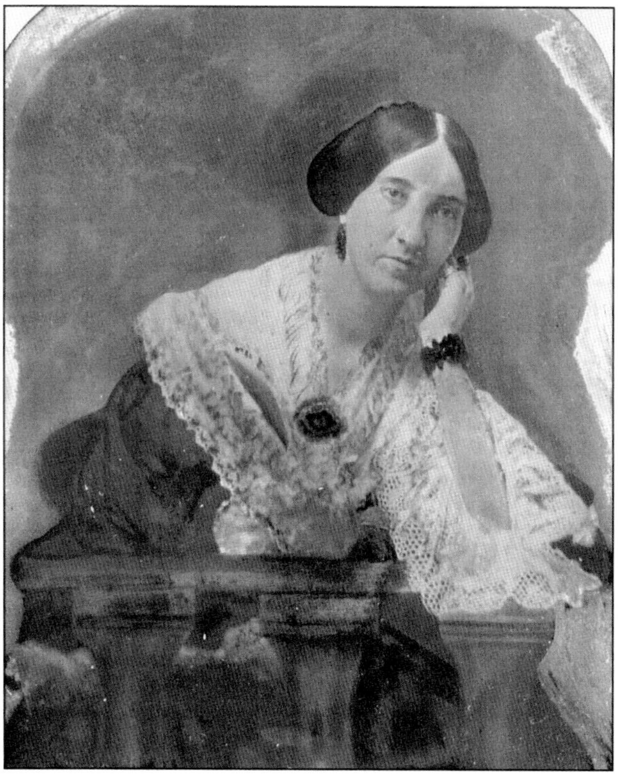

This is a rare (because of its large size) old tintype of Caroline M. Campbell, born in 1828 in South Carolina, a daughter of Alexander W. Campbell. She married Thomas Flournoy Williams of Cedar Grove, a plantation located just outside present-day Soperton. Thomas was a son of Charles Dixon Williams and Sara Ann Flournoy. (Courtesy of Buck Crumpler.)

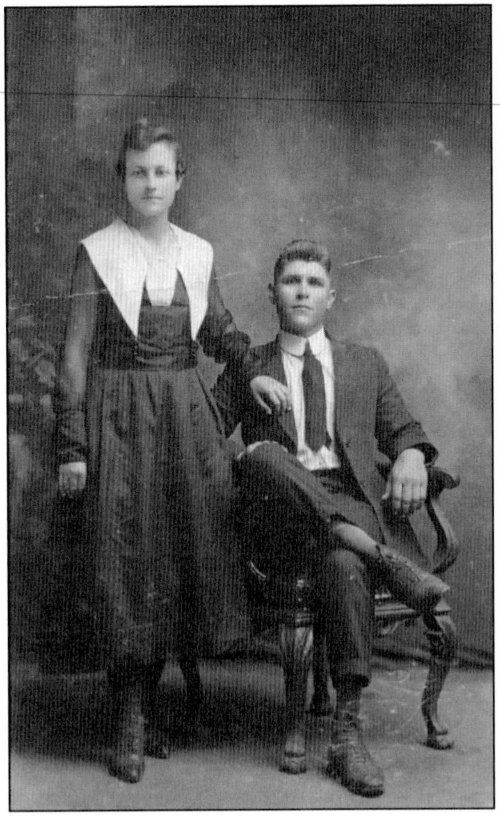

John Lee Burns (1892–1960) is shown here with his wife, Nettie C. Phillips (1899–1985). This photograph was probably made about 1918 when they married. John Lee was a son of Robert Lee Burns and Martha Jane Ellis, and Nettie was a daughter of Clement A. Phillips and Sidney Lightfoot. This family lived on their farm on Highway 297.

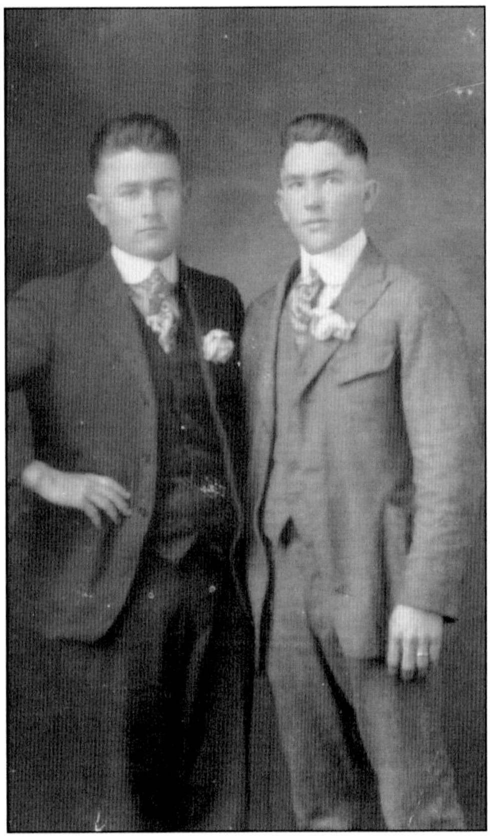

Virgil Henry Burns (1898–1977), son of Robert Lee Burns and Martha Jane Ellis, is shown on the right in this c. 1920. The other gentleman is unidentified. They appear to have attended a wedding since they are both wearing boutonnieres.

Shown in this photograph made about 1942 are Jack D. Burns (1921–1969) and his sister, Reba Burns Braddy. They were the eldest children of Virgil Henry Burns and Mary Delilah "Lila" Williamson. Jack married Relia Mock, and Reba married M. A. Braddy. (Courtesy of Reba Burns Braddy.)

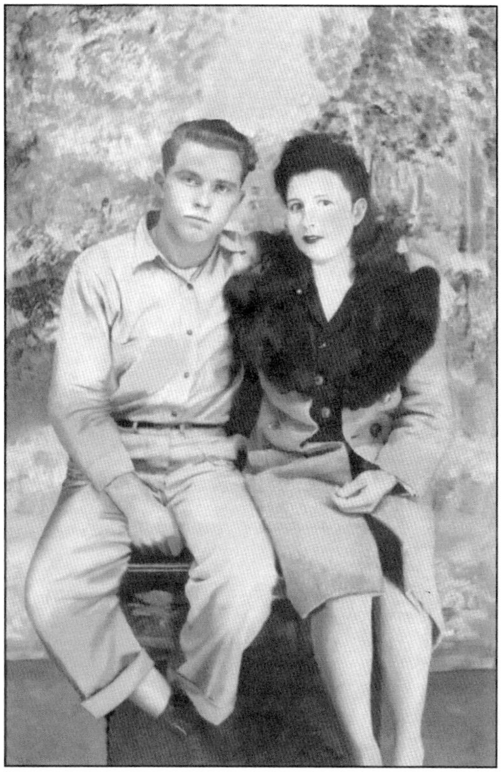

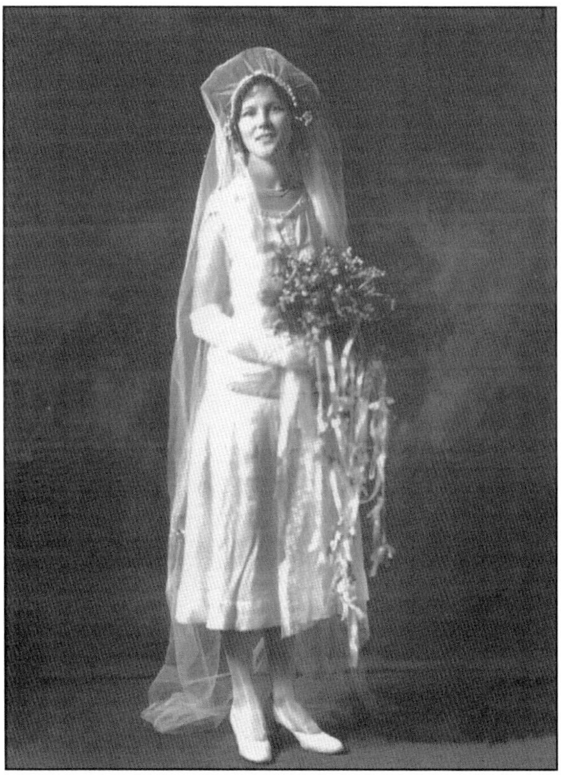

This is a lovely wedding picture of Clara Beatrice Corbin Mumby (1901–1990). The eldest child of Neal Corbin and Dora Kirby, she married Frank Welford Mumby Jr. in Savannah in 1925. They were the parents of two sons, Frank Welford Mumby III and Dr. Robert Corbin Mumby.

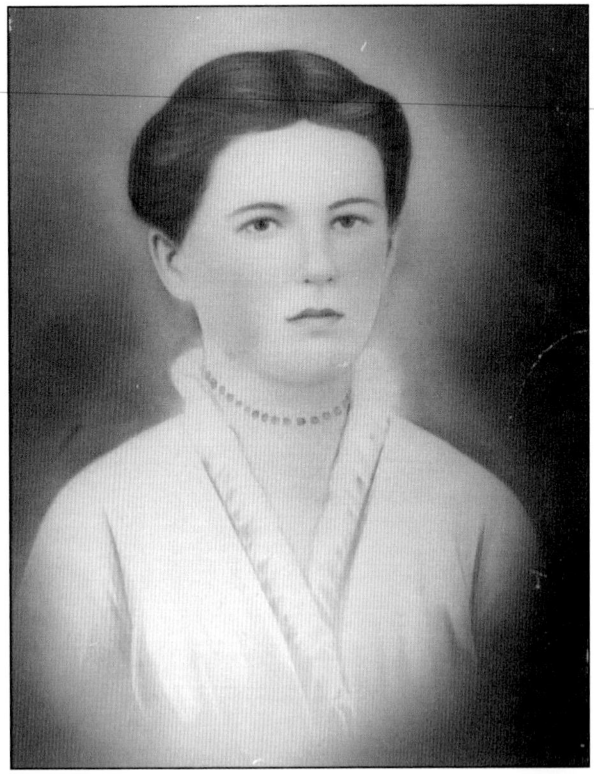

Dora Kirby (1881–1951) is pictured here at the age of 16. A daughter of Hiram Kirby Jr. and Matilda Williamson, in 1900, she married Neal E. Corbin (1878–1928), son of Nelson W. Corbin and Nancy Williamson. Neal and Dora are buried in the Corbin Family Cemetery in Emanuel County just over the Treutlen County line.

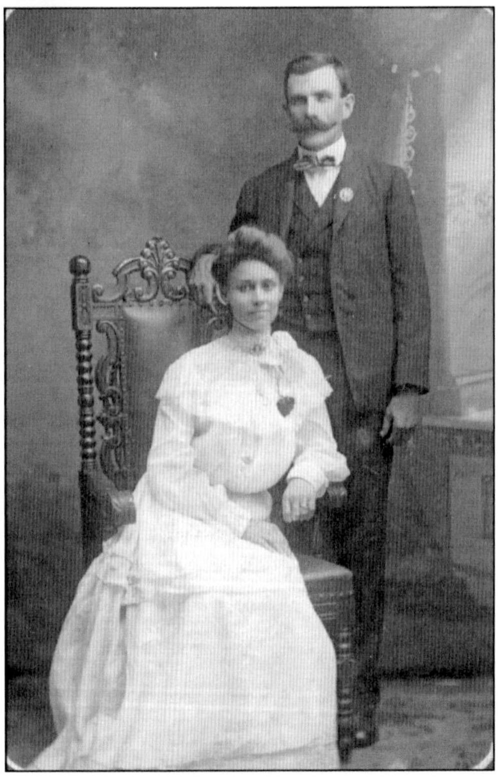

Shown in this c. 1905 studio picture are Roderick Lonzo Gillis (1867–1926) and his wife, the former Georgann Elizabeth "Lizzie" Thompson (1882–1977). They were married in 1905 and had three children: Odessa, Rubye Ocilla, and Roderick Lonzo Jr. (Courtesy of Hal Jones.)

Roderick Lonzo Gillis is shown here picking a banjo. He apparently married into a family that was musically inclined, as there are several pictures of the Thompson brothers with instruments in their hands. This picture was probably made prior to his 1905 marriage to Georgann. (Courtesy of Hal Jones.)

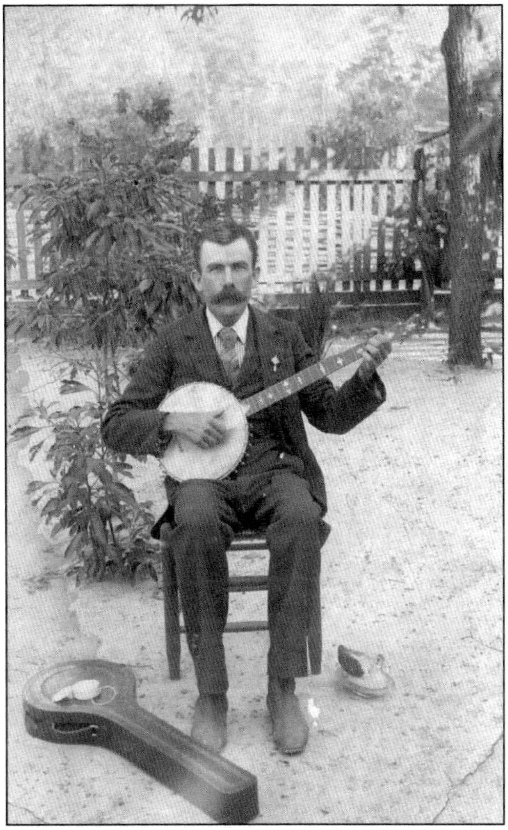

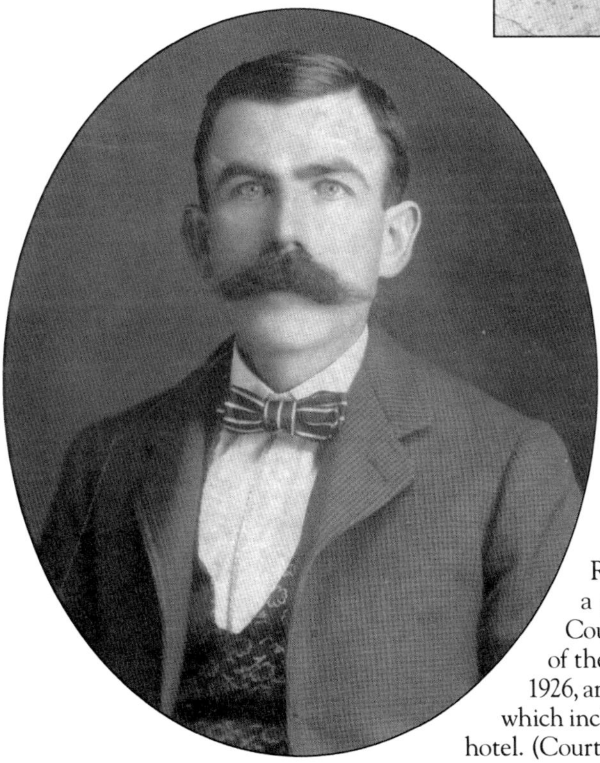

Roderick Lonzo Gillis (1867–1926) was a prominent businessman in Treutlen County, an extensive landowner, a member of the first board of education from 1919 to 1926, and a founder of Gillis Springs community, which included a recreational facility, school, and hotel. (Courtesy of Hal Jones.)

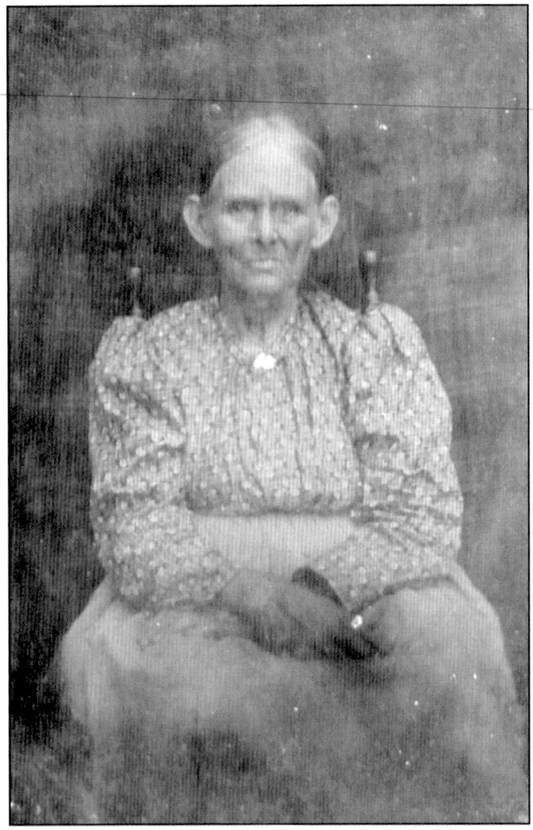

Mary Miller Gillis (1830–1904) was a daughter of Samuel Miller and Pharaba Pate. She married Archibald Gillis (1822–1892) in 1848, and they were the parents of 13 children. They are buried in the Gillis Cemetery in Treutlen County. (Courtesy of Patsy Gillis Ware.)

Below is a *c.* 1888 picture of William Thomas "W. T." Dickens (1864–1937) and his wife, Elizabeth "Betty" Calhoun (1864–1949), who lived near Tarrytown. W. T. was a son of Elijah Dickens and Temperance Downs, and Betty was a daughter of Samuel Hargroves Calhoun and Lucinda Hamilton. (Courtesy of Curtis Dickens.)

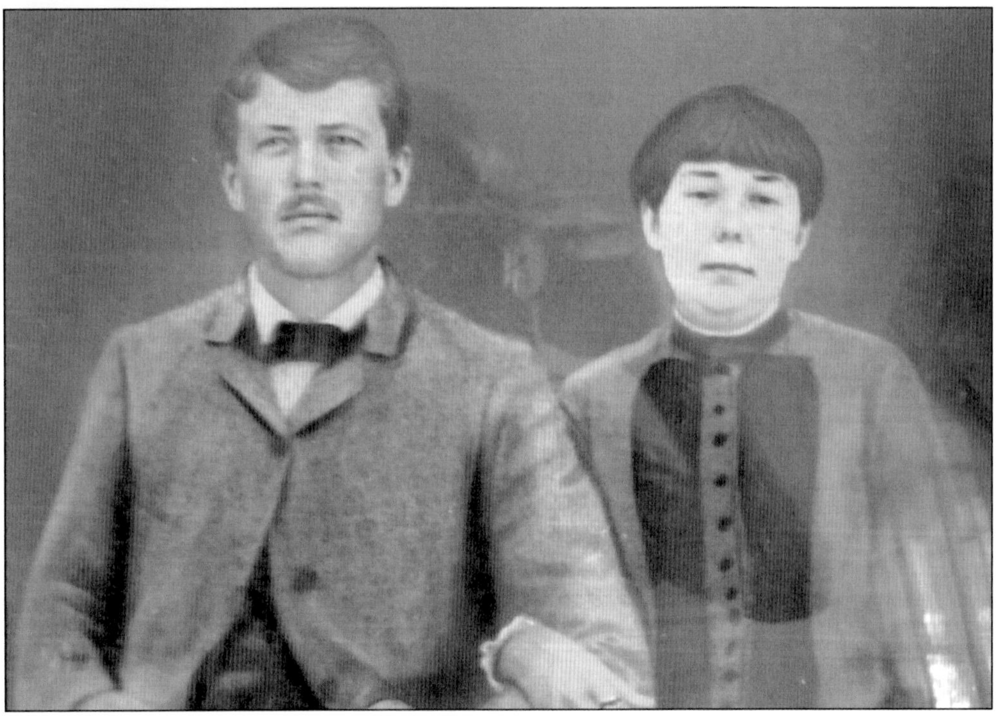

This picture of Rufus and Mary Alice Kight was made about 1900. They were the children of James Alvie Kight and Alice Williamson, who are buried in the Westview Cemetery in Soperton. (Courtesy of Leatrice Brinson Kight.)

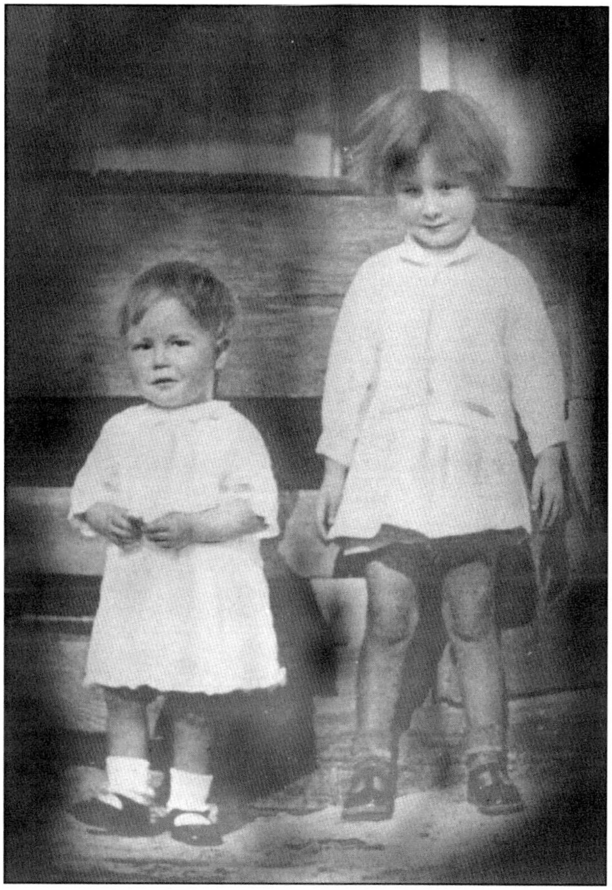

Born 1824 in Barnwell County, South Carolina, Samuel Hargroves Calhoun (below, left) moved with his family to Montgomery County, Georgia, in 1837. He married Lucinda Hamilton (1826–1899), center, daughter of Josiah Hamilton and Mary Poole. Samuel served in the War between the States and died in 1899. Their old home, built in 1847 shortly after their marriage, is still standing in Tarrytown. On the right is their unmarried daughter, Martha Calhoun.

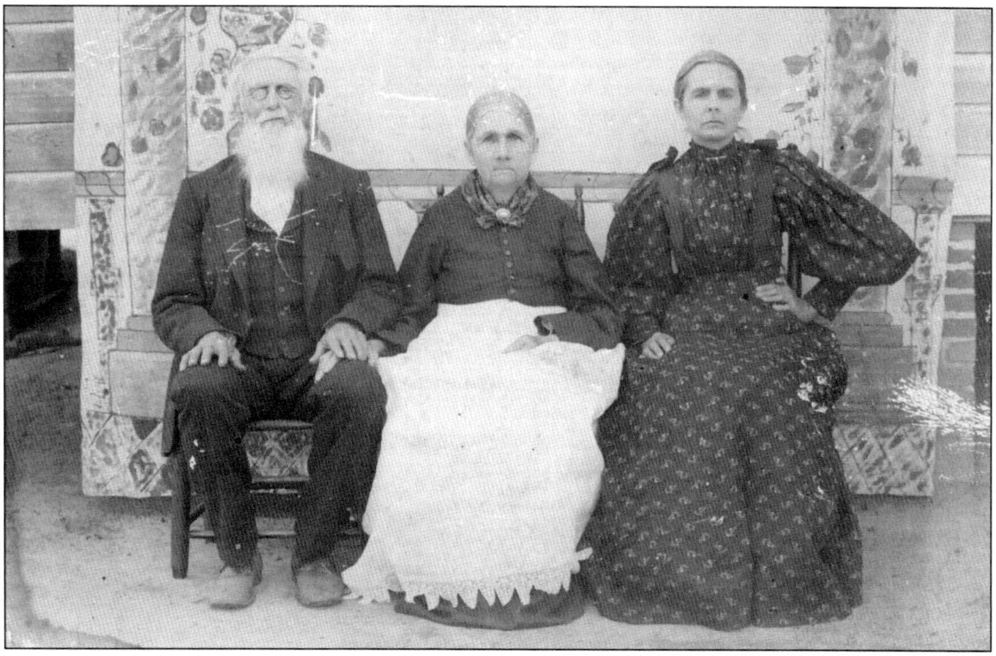

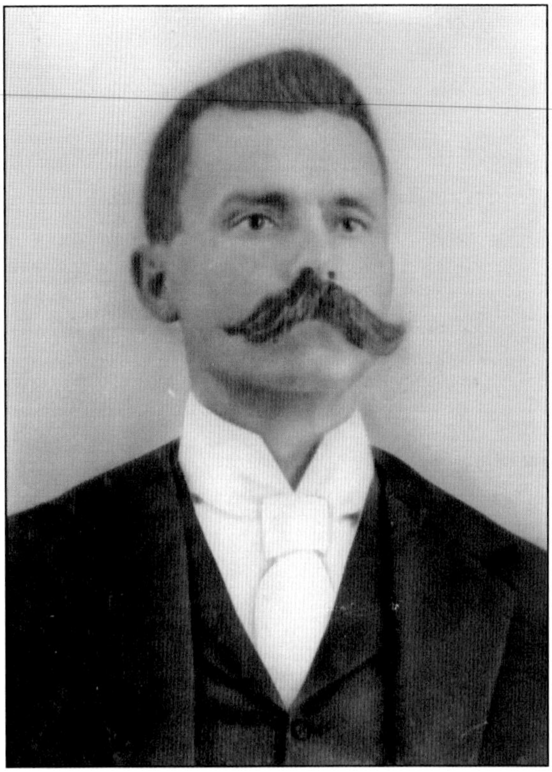

This is a c. 1900 photograph of Benjamin Stewart "Benny" Calhoun (1861–1951), who was born in Montgomery County to Samuel Hargroves Calhoun and Lucinda Hamilton. He was a banker in Glenwood and instrumental in the founding of the Brewton-Parker Institute. In 1892, he married Mary Susan Frances Kent (1872–1900), daughter of William James Washington Kent and Martha Ann Beckworth.

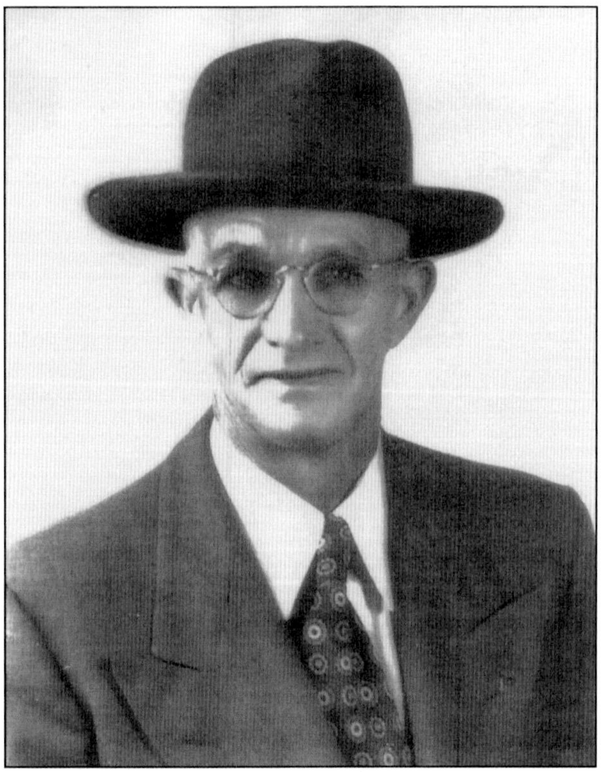

William Thomas "Tom" Kitchens (1894–1964) was a son of William Alfred Kitchens and Leila Boyd. Born in Washington County, he grew up in Soperton and is buried at the Harmony Baptist Church. He married Eva Sammons (1904–1981), and they were the parents of five children. (Courtesy of Yvonne Scott.)

Remembered as the "Father of Treutlen County," Neil Lee Gillis (1864–1933) was a local bank director and a large landowner who campaigned successfully for the creation of the county. A native of Emanuel County, he was married to Lougenia Youmans (1867–1922). Their home is still standing east of Soperton and is currently used as a bed-and-breakfast.

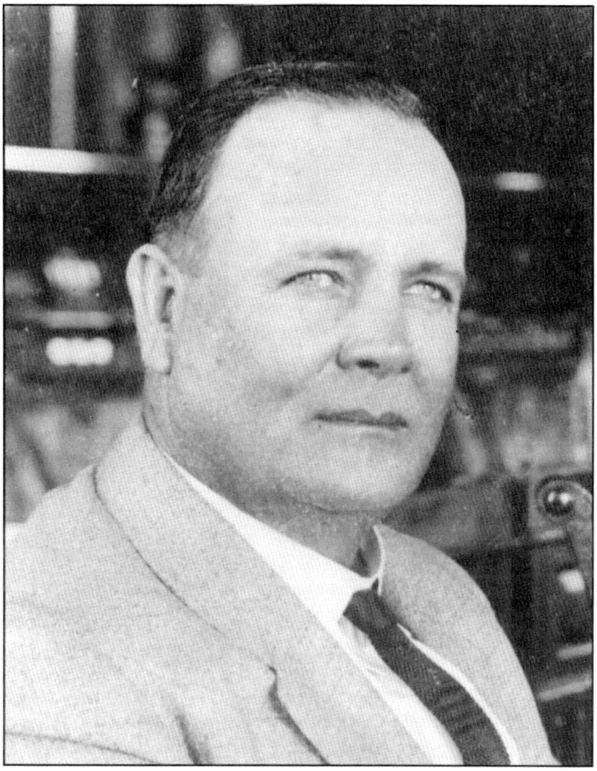

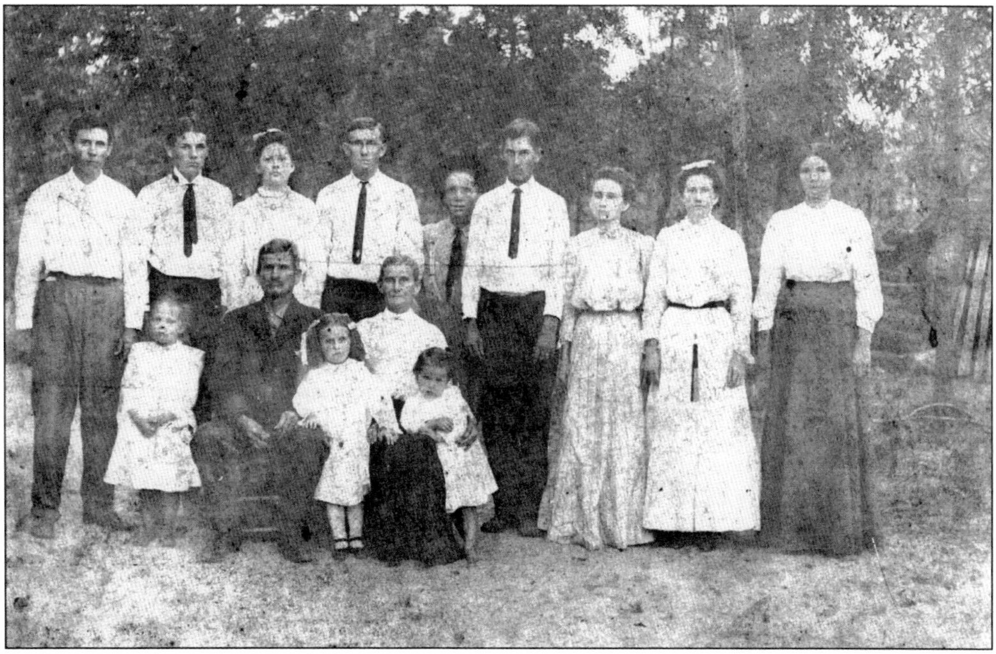

William Herndon (1852–1920), shown sitting by his wife, Catherine Jane Blount (1858–1925), was a son of Henry Herndon and Samantha Miller, and Catherine was a daughter of William Blount and Catherine "Katie" O'Slattery. This family moved to Calhoun County, Florida, in 1903, and it is said they drove their cattle all the way. (Courtesy of John Herndon.)

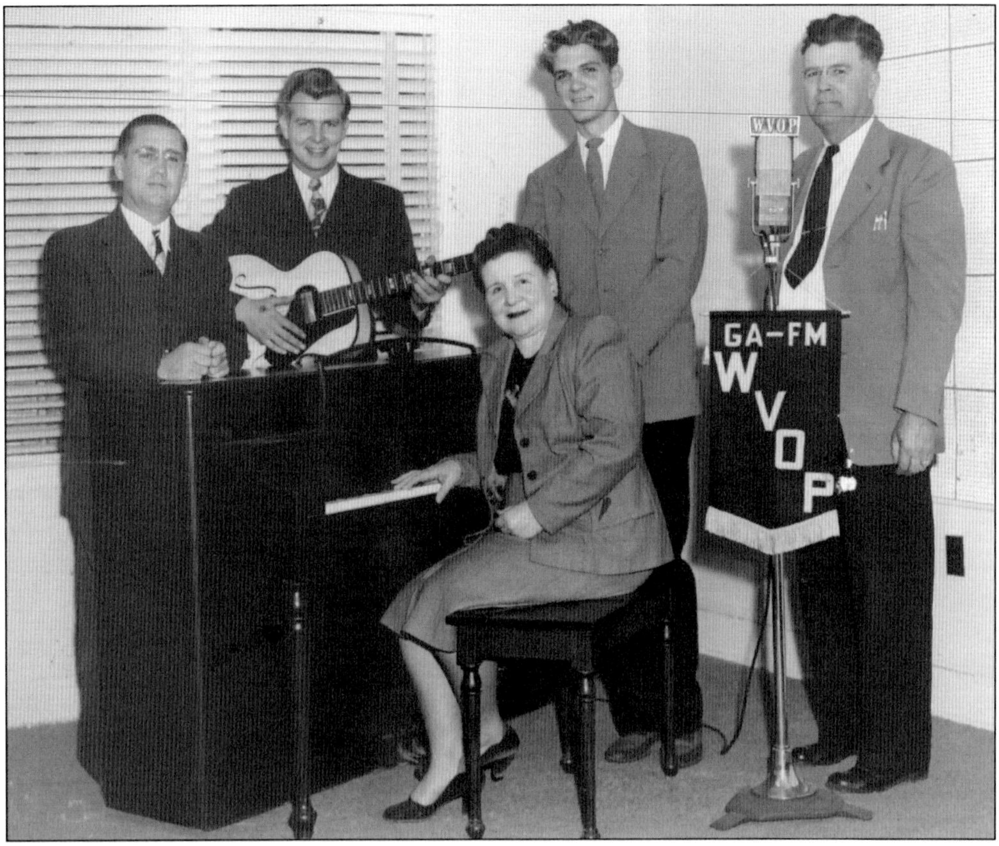

The Gillis-Henry Quartet is pictured above in the 1940s. Standing from left to right are Dennis Davis, Pope Henry, Charles Gillis, and Charlie Gillis, with Rubye Gillis Henry sitting at the piano. Rubye was a renowned pianist, and this group performed for years at events throughout the area. (Courtesy of the Gillis family.)

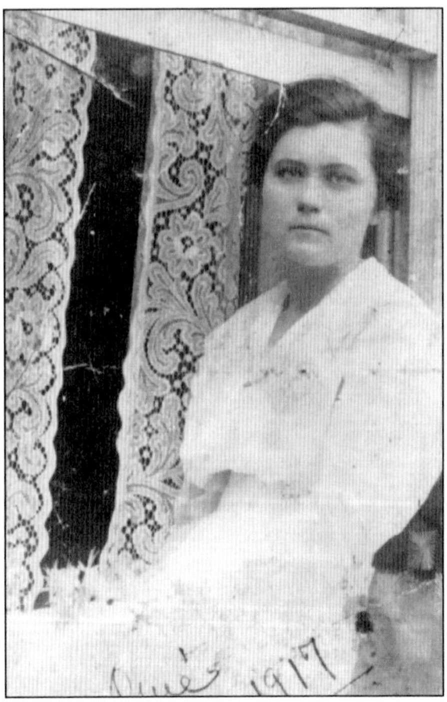

This 1917 photograph of Onie Calhoun Williamson (1895–1984) was probably made when she was at Tift College. Onie was the daughter of Benjamin Stewart Calhoun and Mary Susan Frances Kent. She first married Frederick William Kea in 1912. She divorced him and married her cousin Gaston Williamson in 1917, and they were the parents of 10 children.

Many children died during the 1800s and early 1900s. This is a rare photograph of the corpse of a baby, and beside her is the grieving mother. It is presumed that the sad scene was taken outside so there would be enough light to make a picture. The people are unidentified but are said to be members of the Thompson family. (Courtesy of Hal Jones.)

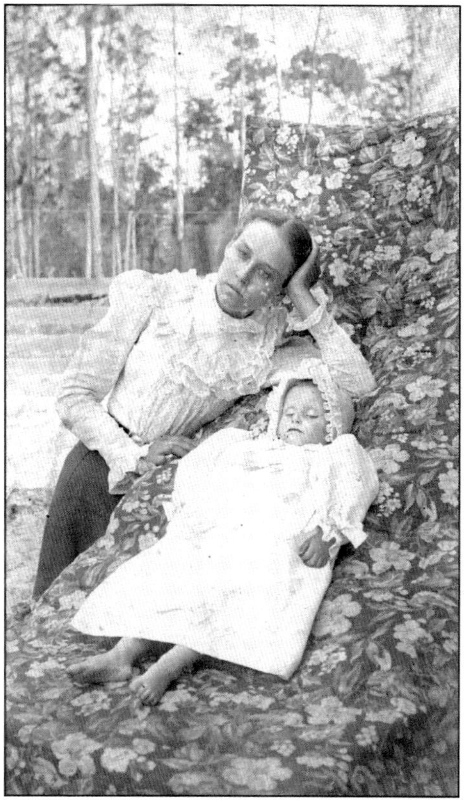

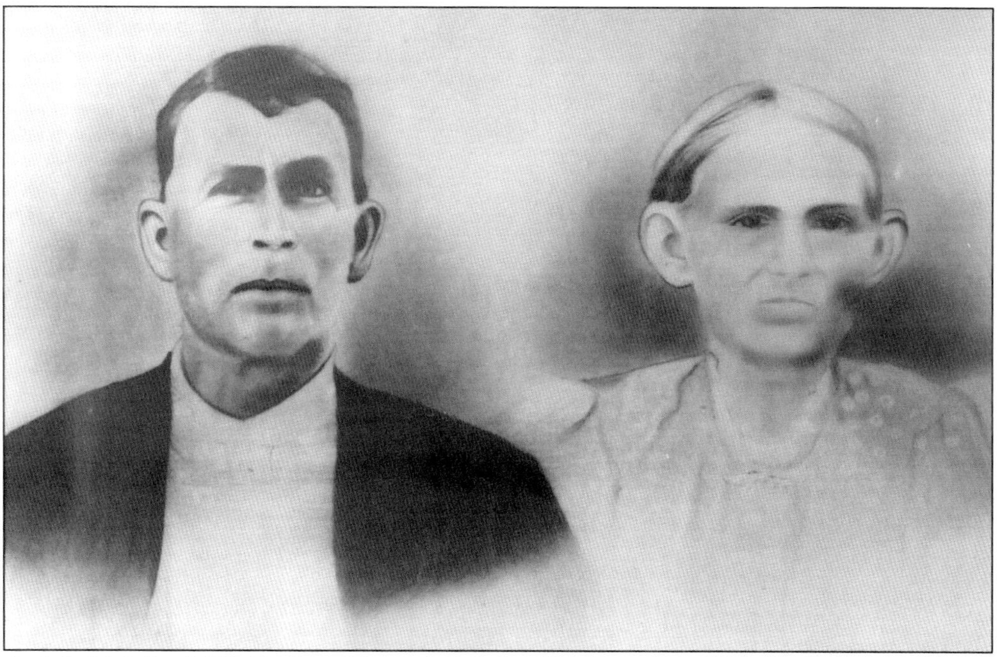

Archibald Gillis (1822–1892) and his wife, Mary Miller (1830–1904), are shown in this *c.* 1870 picture, which seems to have been enhanced with crayon by the photographer, as many were during that period. Archibald was a son of John C. "Hickory John" Gillis and Mary Ann MacAlpine.

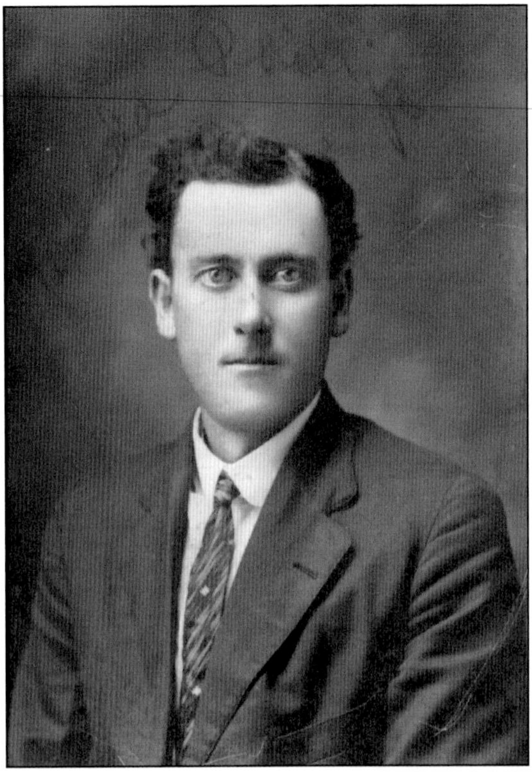

This is a studio picture made around 1905 of Meada E. Phillips (1883–1924), son of William Con (née Sullivan) Phillips and Elizabeth "Betty" Williamson. Meada married Mollie Kirby, and their family lived on the Ohoopee River.

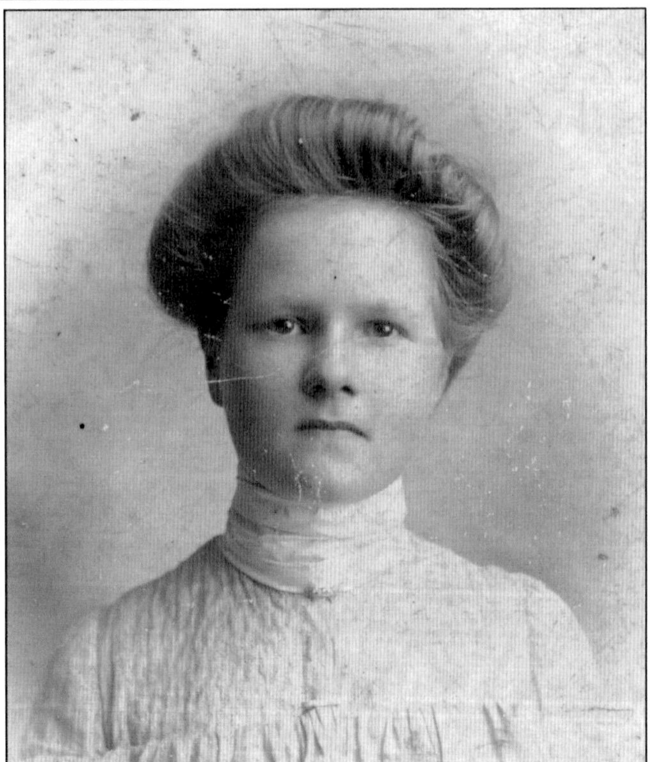

This picture of Mary O. "Mollie" Kirby (1889–1970) was made in about 1905. A daughter of Hiram Kirby Jr. and Matilda Williamson, she married Meada Phillips in 1907. Mollie is remembered for her delicious cakes and pies, as well as her remarkable wit.

This is a c. 1919 photograph of the children of Meada and Mollie Phillips. From left to right are Theron, Ruth (McVey), Ethes, Alton, Vernon, and Floyd. Their last child, Reba, was born after this picture was made.

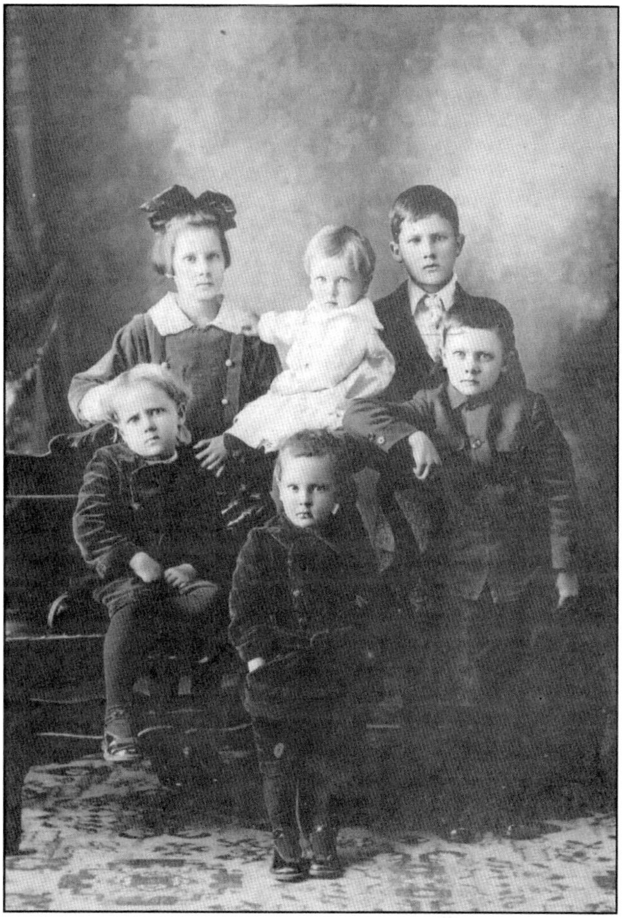

The family of Moses Algerine "M. A." Braddy (1847–1918) and his wife, Florence Herndon (1857–1942), are pictured below in about 1891. M. A. Braddy was born in North Carolina and came with his parents, Oliver B. and Sarah Braddy, to Washington County, Georgia, shortly before 1850. Florence was a daughter of Henry Herndon and Samantha Miller.

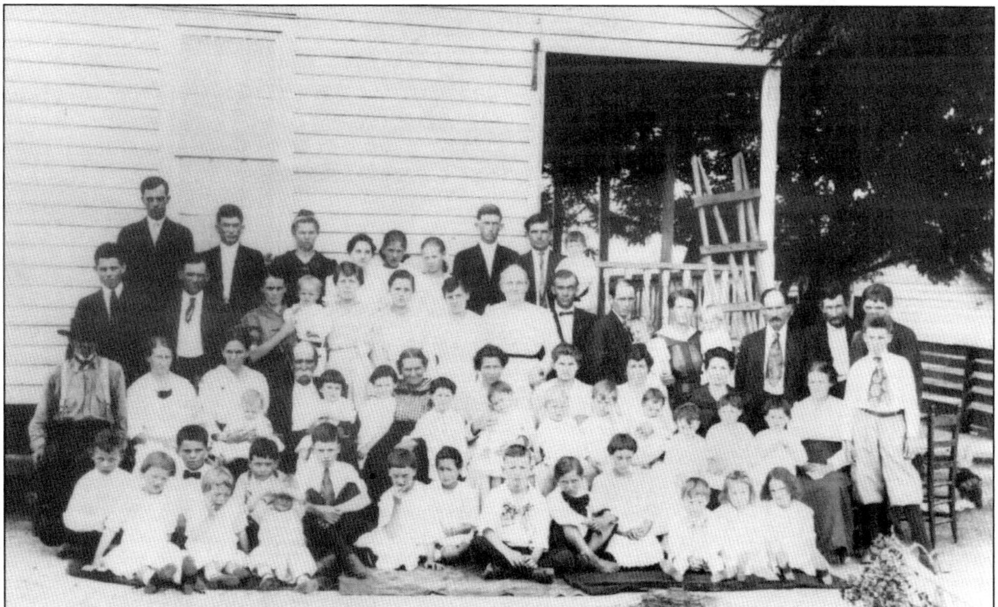

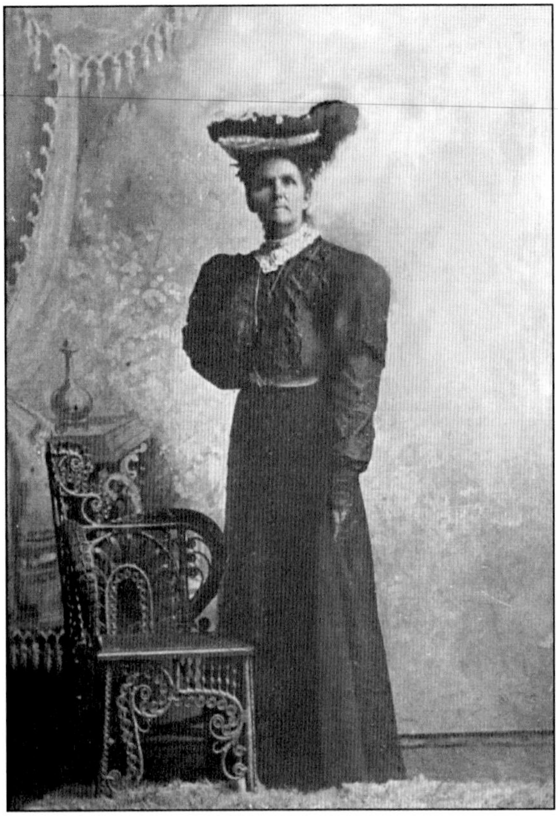

Clarissa Calhoun Williamson (1858–1950) posed for this photograph in approximately 1902 in Brown's Studio in Swainsboro. She was about 45 years of age. Clarissa was a daughter of Samuel Hargroves Calhoun and Lucinda Hamilton. She married Solomon Williamson (1823–1901), son of John Williamson and Elizabeth Sullivan, of Emanuel County in 1878 when he was 55 and she was 20.

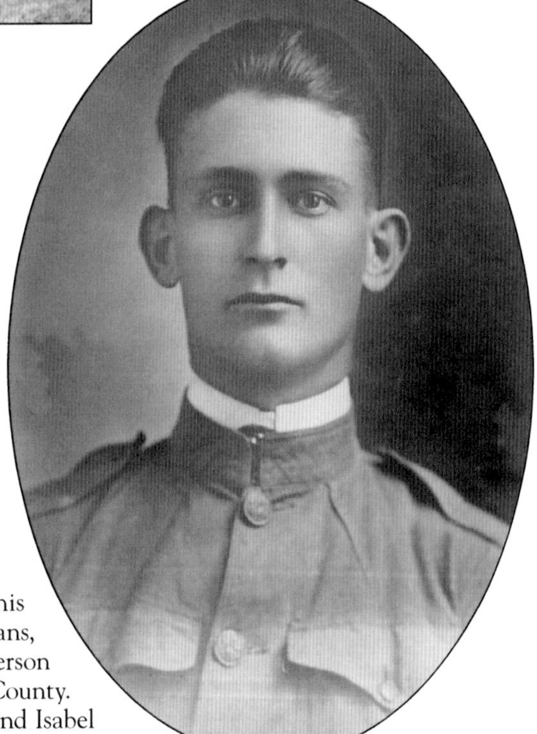

Frank Fowler (1895–1918) is pictured here in his army uniform. He was killed in action in Le Mans, France, in World War I and was the first person buried in the Fowler Cemetery in Treutlen County. He was a son of William Herschel Fowler and Isabel Catherine Miller. (Courtesy of Billy Wade Jr.)

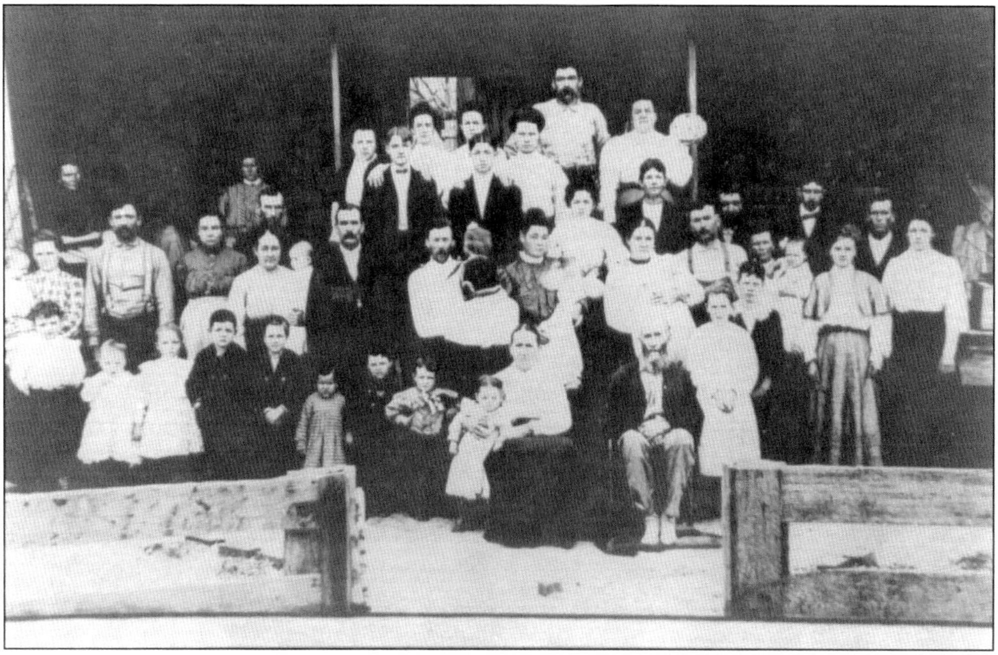

Shown here around 1898 is a reunion of the Bill Love family probably at the home of George Travis Gillis and Armaretta Della Love. William Norris "Bill" Love (1840–1912), a son of Lemuel Love and Mary Tyson, first married Elizabeth Grant (1850–1887), and after her death, he married Susan Woods (1859–1901).

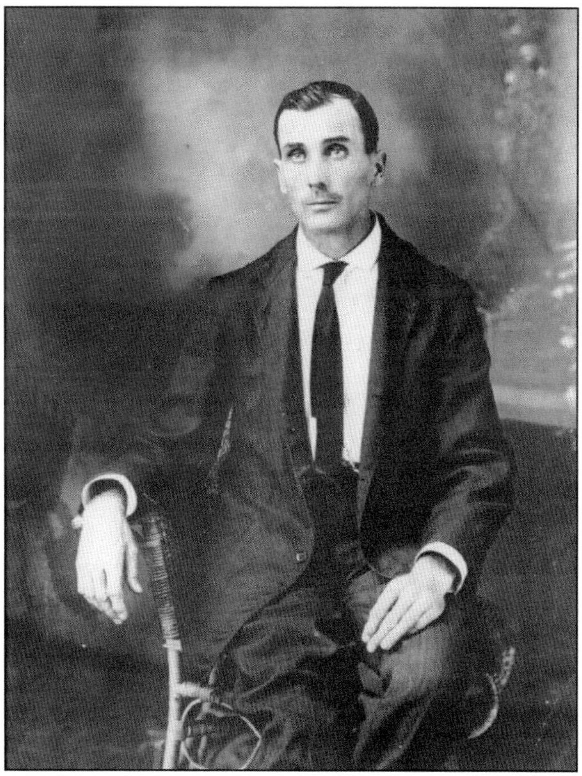

Morris L. O'Brien (1870–1937) was a prominent farmer in Treutlen County. His father was born in Ireland; fought for the North during the War between the States, and moved from Connecticut to Montgomery County, Georgia, shortly thereafter. Morris was a member of the first board of education from 1919 to 1937, holding the office of chairman at the time of his death.

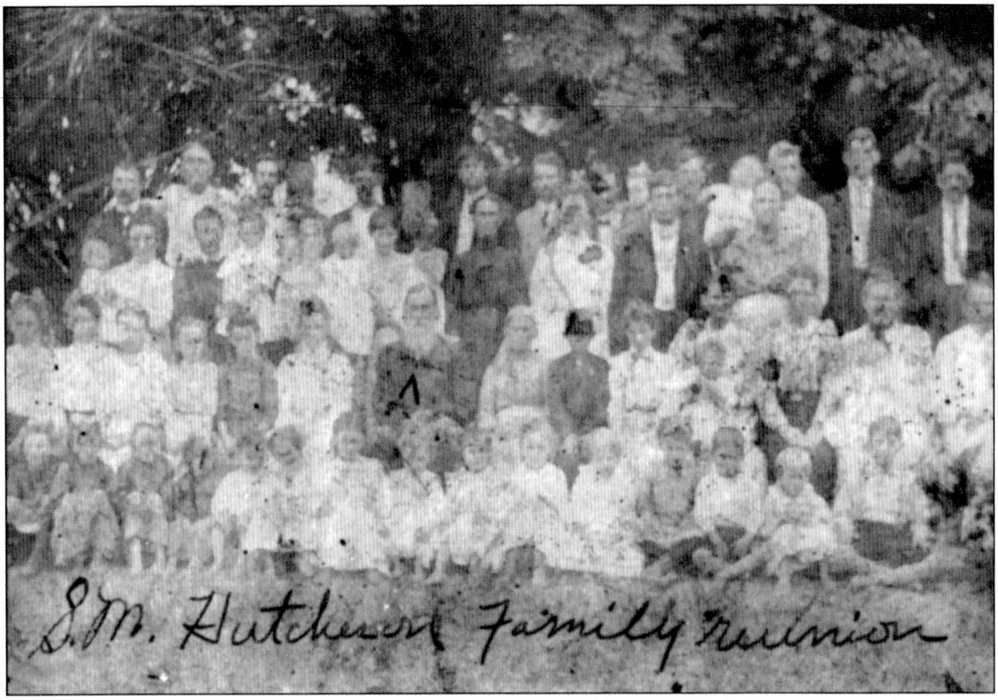

Posing together at a family reunion held in the late 1800s are members of the Stephen Mills Hutcheson family. Family reunions have always been an important part of Southern culture. (Courtesy of Norris Hutcheson.)

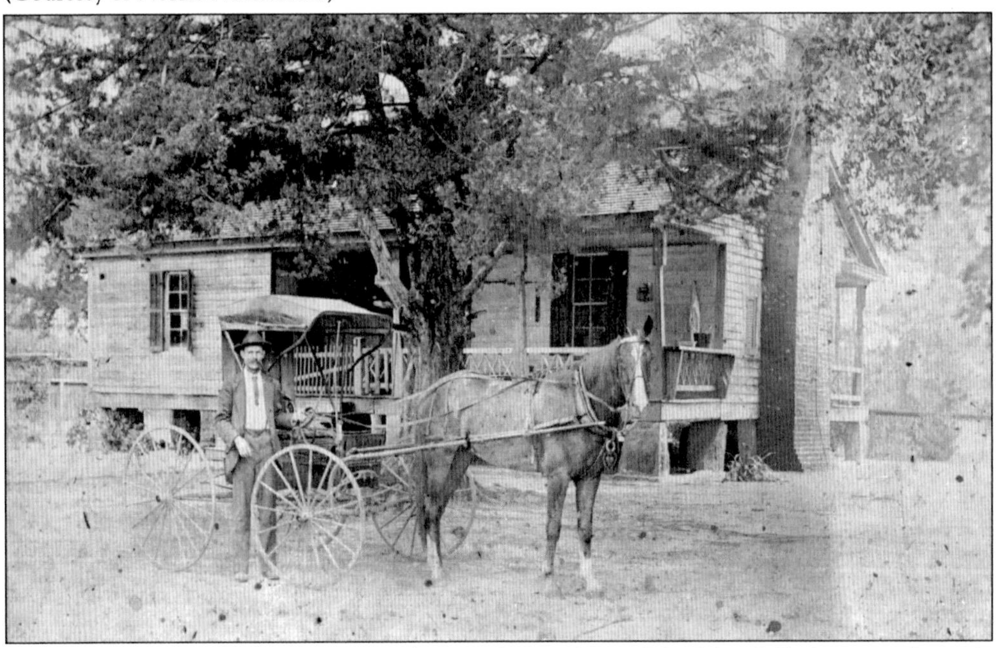

Marion Marvin "Bay" Gillis (1868–1946) is standing in front of the John Gillis house in the early 1900s. The house still stands on present-day Highway 86, near the Neil Lee Gillis Sr. home place and the Gillis Family Cemetery. Bay was a son of John Gillis and Mary Ann Gillis. (Courtesy of Hal Jones.)

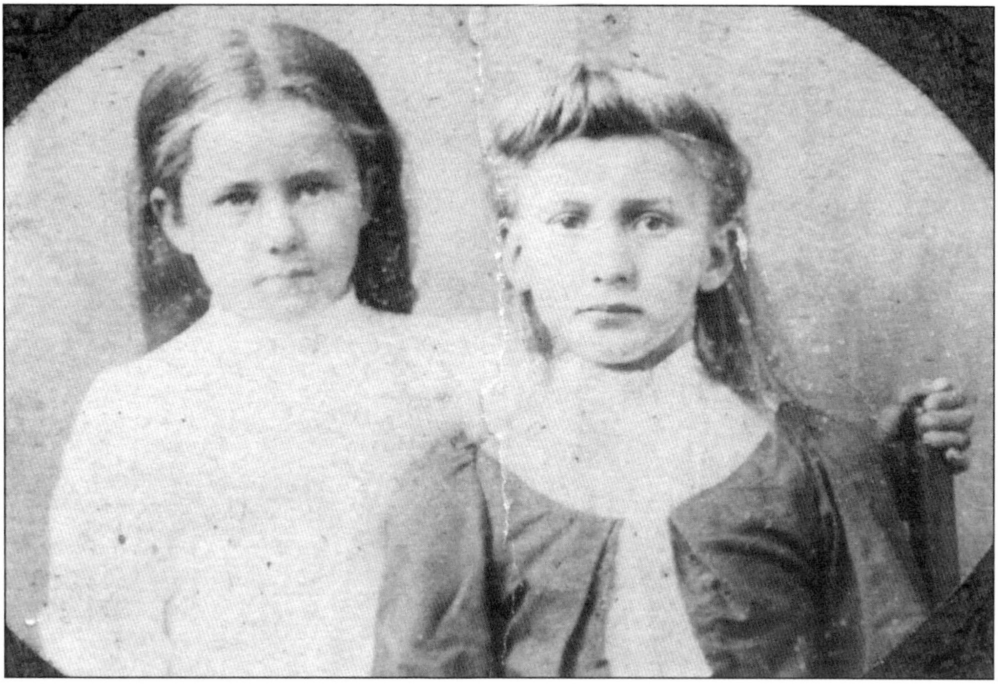

Alice Williamson Kight (1897–1986), left, and Sarah Williamson Collins (1890–1955) were the daughters of Benjamin D. Williamson and Eliza Collins. Alice and her husband, James Alvie Kight, are buried in the Westview Cemetery in Soperton. (Courtesy of Leatrice Brinson Kight.)

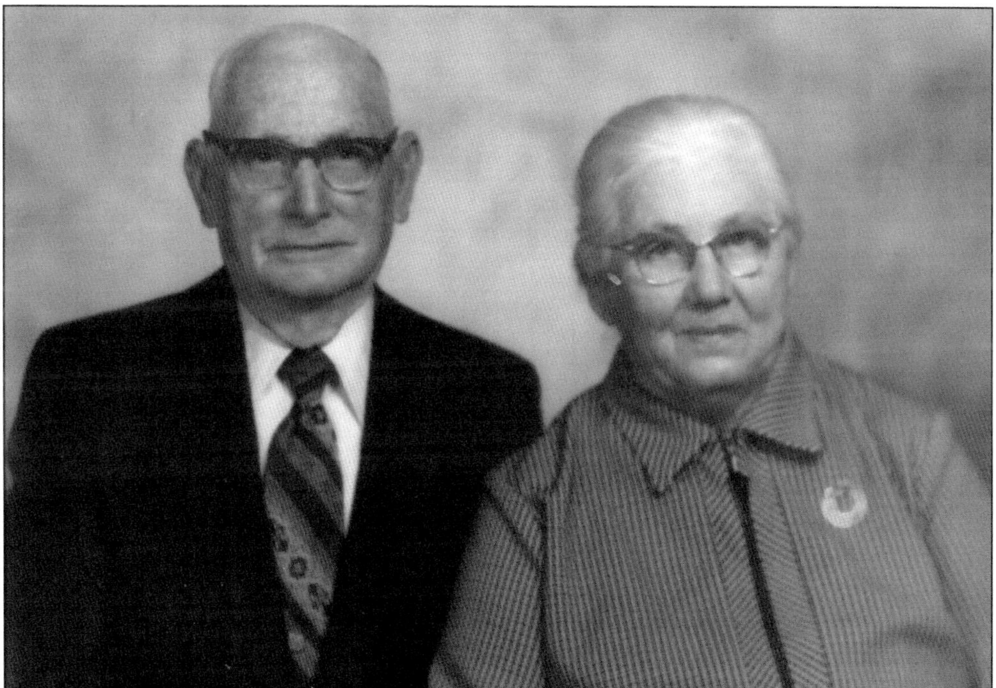

James Alvie Kight (1895–1988) is posing here with his wife, the former Alice Williamson. James was a son of John Wesley "Tone" Kight and Amanda Price. (Courtesy of Leatrice Brinson Kight.)

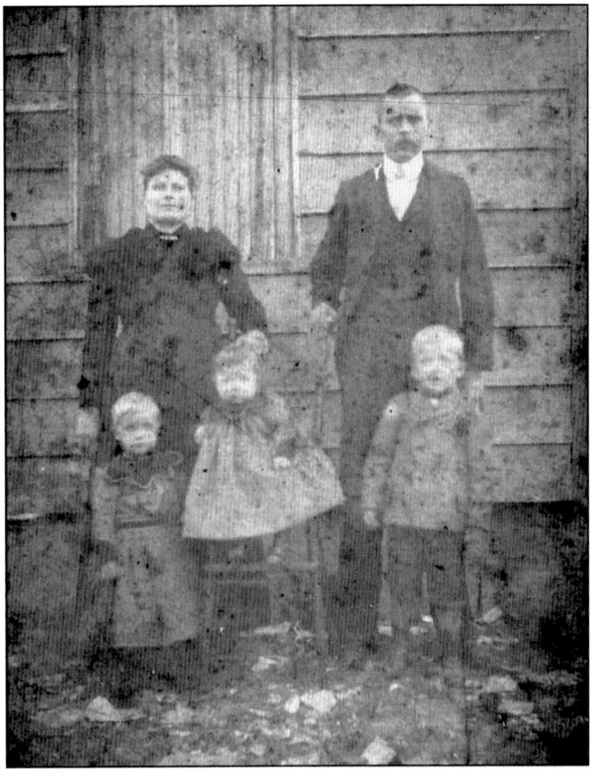

Daniel Tilton "Babe" Ricks (1878–1953) and his wife, Arrilla Youngblood (1878–1905), are pictured together in this *c.* 1901 photograph. Babe Ricks was a son of Warren W. Ricks and Lecy Ann Barwick, and Arrilla was a daughter of William Franklin Youngblood and Laura Martin. From left to right, the children are Lena Mae, Laura, and Osborne. (Courtesy of Tracy Manning Gillikin.)

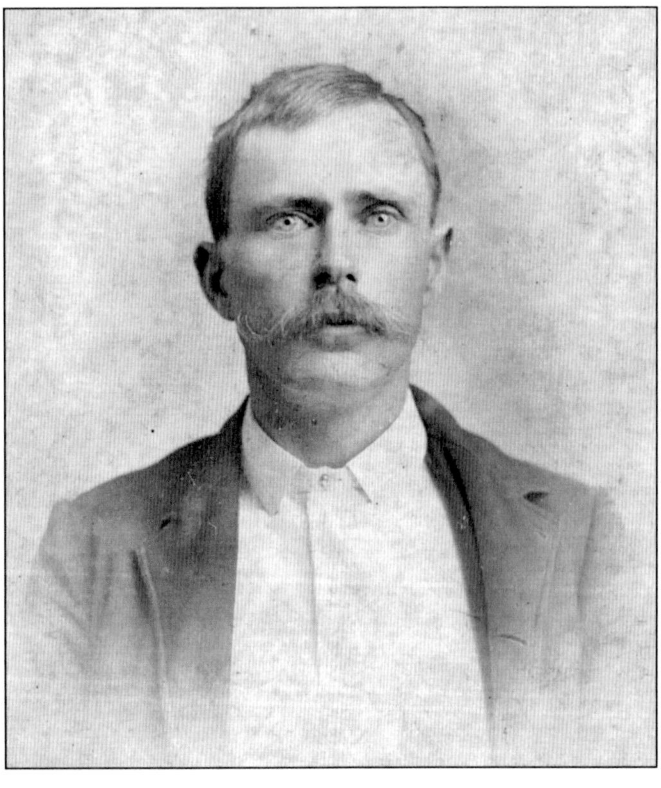

This studio picture of Daniel Tilton "Babe" Ricks was made around 1900. The Ricks family lived in the vicinity of Blackville. Still standing is the old log cabin where Babe's parents reared their children. (Courtesy of Tracy Manning Gillikin.)

Shown at the podium in the state senate around 1980 is Sen. Hugh Marion Gillis of Soperton, who served in the Georgia State Senate for more than 50 years, longer than any other legislator in the nation. He was a son of James Lester "Jim L." Gillis and Annie Lois Walker. (Courtesy of Hugh Gillis.)

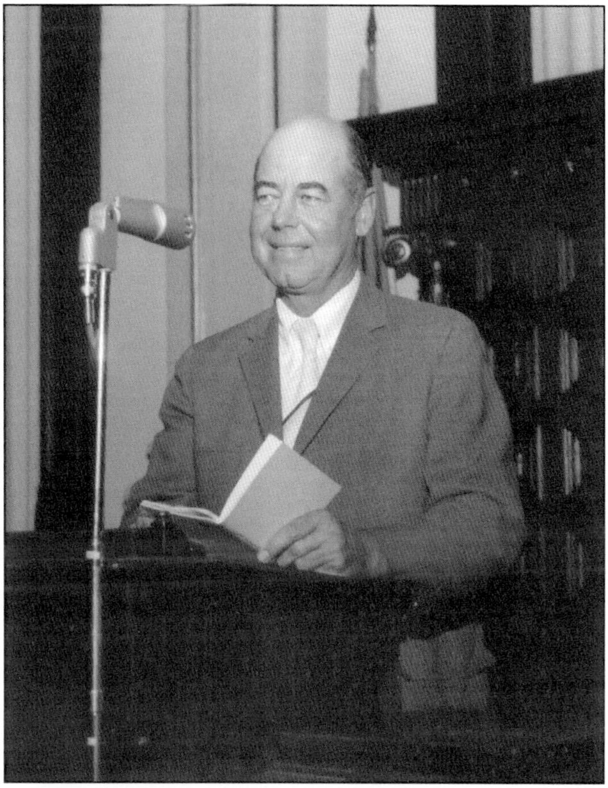

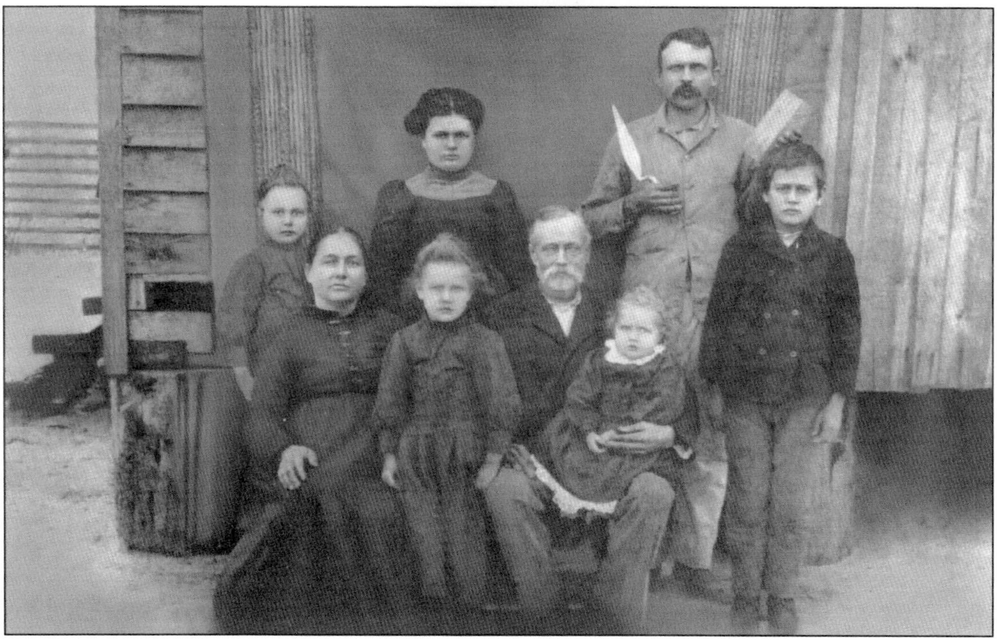

The George Washington Stewart family posed for this *c.* 1905 picture at their home in present-day northeastern Treutlen County. Shown with George (1846–1922) and his third wife, Mollie, are some of his children. Hattie Lee (Holton) and James (holding trowel and brick) are standing in the back. The others are unidentified. (Courtesy of Susie Holton.)

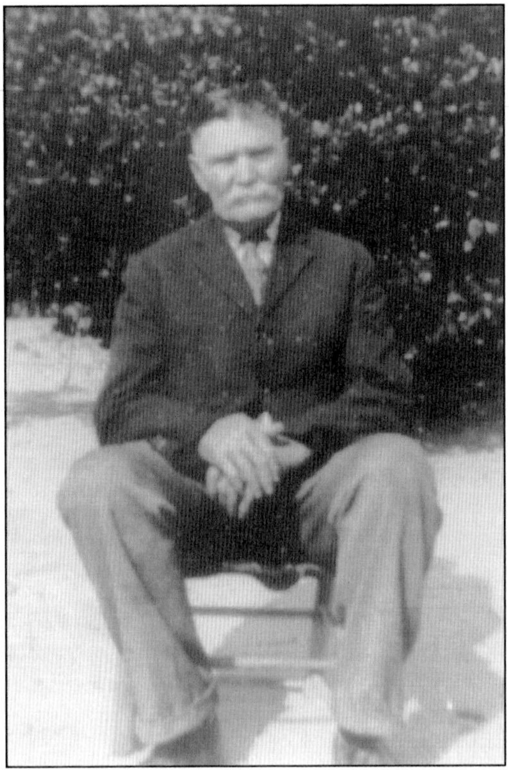

George L. Calhoun (1859–1935) was the sixth child of James Irvin Calhoun II and Nancy Clarissa Connell. He first married Anna Arrena Cauley (1866–1915), a daughter of James William Cauley and Rachel Herndon. George and Rena moved to Florida, and after eight children, they divorced. He then married Emma Victoria Bennett.

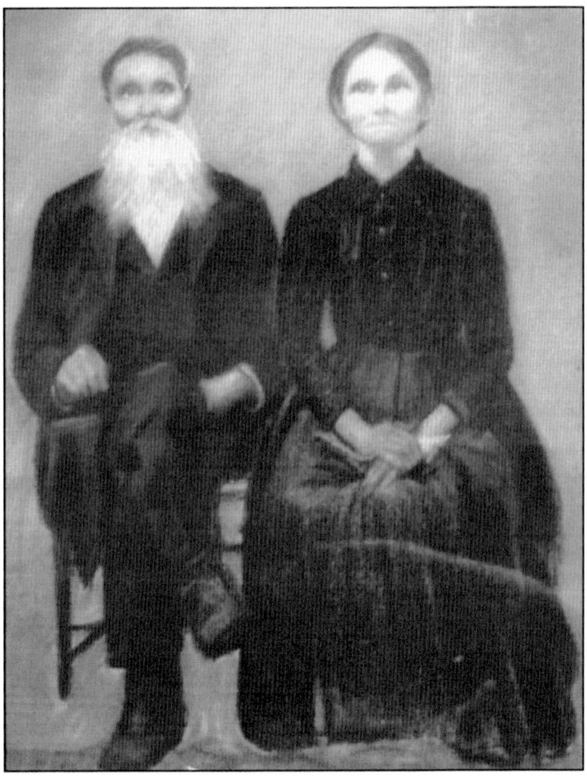

James Irving Calhoun II (1827–1911) and Nancy Clarissa Connell (1833–1909) were married in Montgomery County in 1850, and they were the parents of 16 children. James was a son of Burrell Rogers Calhoun and Mary Darley, and Nancy was a daughter of John Connell, a Revolutionary soldier, and his wife, Clarissa Hamilton.

Bessie White Fowler (1890–1931), a native of Lebanon, Tennessee, poses in this photograph with her husband, James C. "Jim" Fowler. Bessie held the office of superintendent of the Treutlen County Schools from 1929 until her death and was the first woman in the state of Georgia to hold this title.

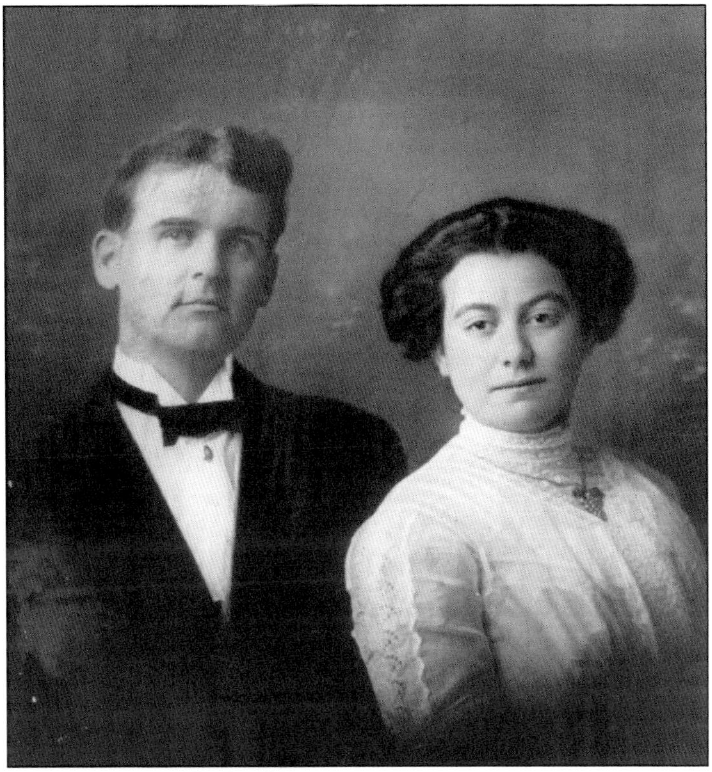

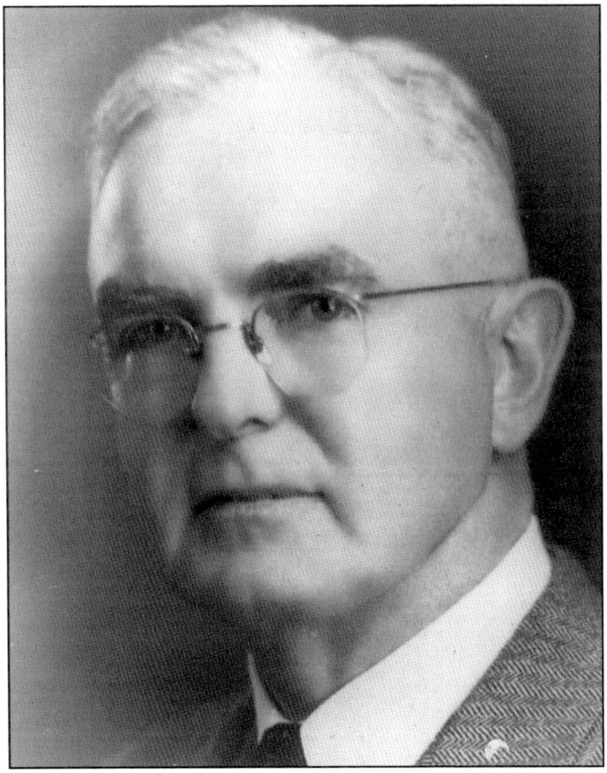

James "Jim" Peterson (1893–1967) served as Soperton's mayor from 1942 to 1949. He was a son of William James Peterson and Catherine Joannah Calhoun of Montgomery County. He married Laura Katherine Gillis (1897–1991), daughter of Neil Lee Gillis and Lougenia Youmans.

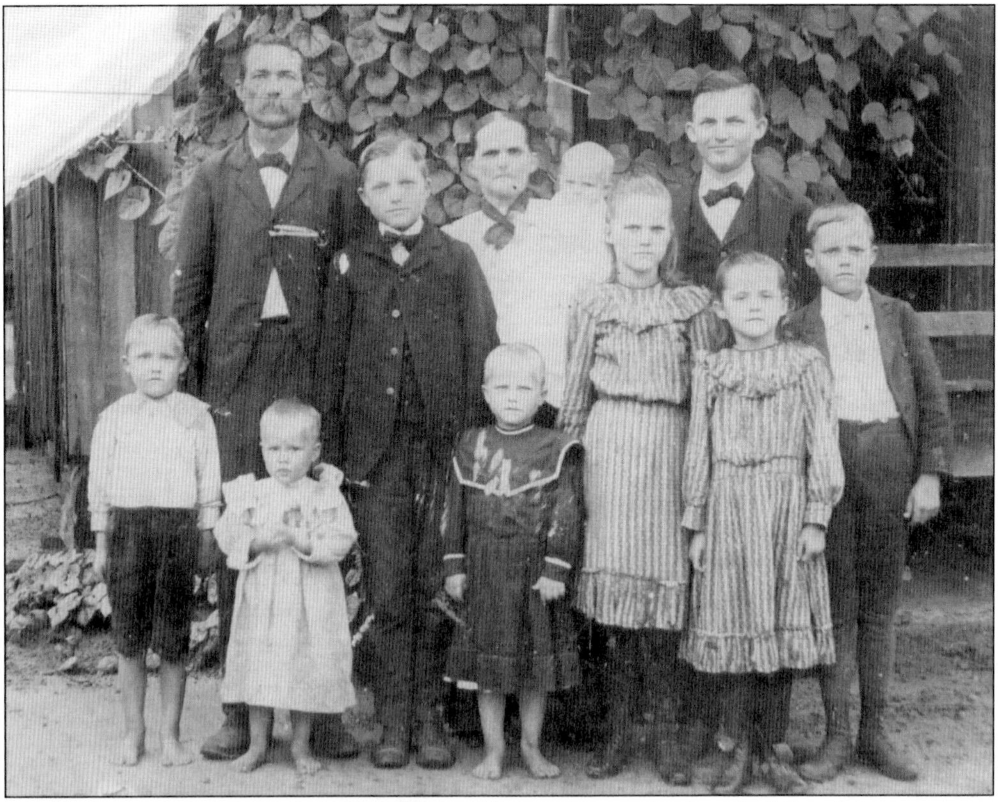

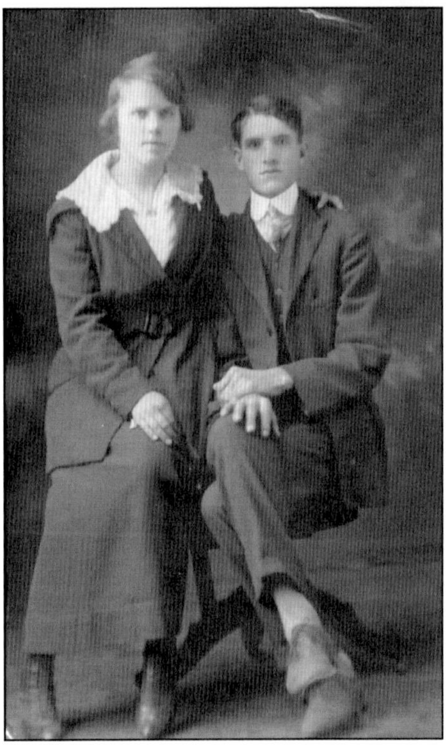

Shown above is the Joseph Allen Atkins family around 1904. Joseph (1856–1924) was a son of David Atkins and Frances R. Allen. He married Mary Eugenia Claxton (1867–1936), daughter of Zachariah J. Claxton and Temperance Powell, and they reared 13 children. (Courtesy of Dean McKenzie Morris.)

Pictured on their wedding day in 1919 are Vollie Lee McKenzie (1900–1986) and Mary Tempie Atkins (1899–1976). Vollie and Mary lived in Treutlen County their entire married life and reared seven children. The family farmed and raised livestock. (Courtesy of Dean McKenzie Morris.)

Shown at right are Willis W. Wade (1879–1944), his wife, the former Louvenia Tapley (1891–1980), and their son, Willis W. Wade Jr. (1921–1943).

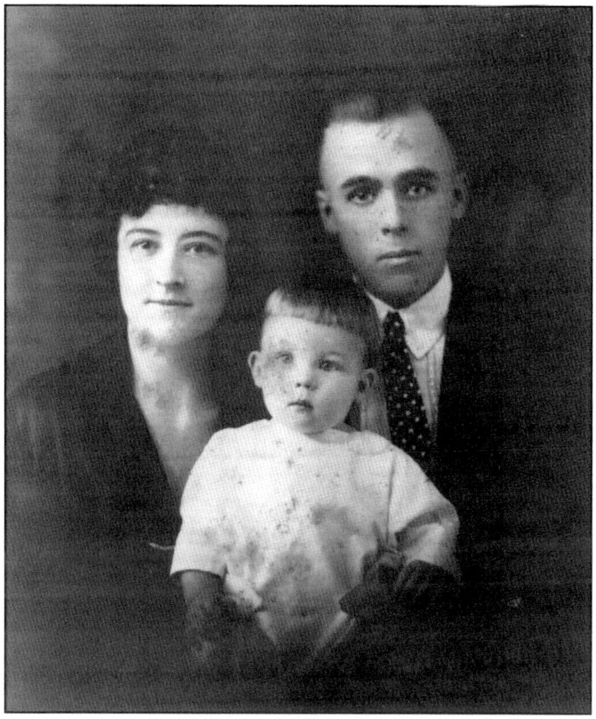

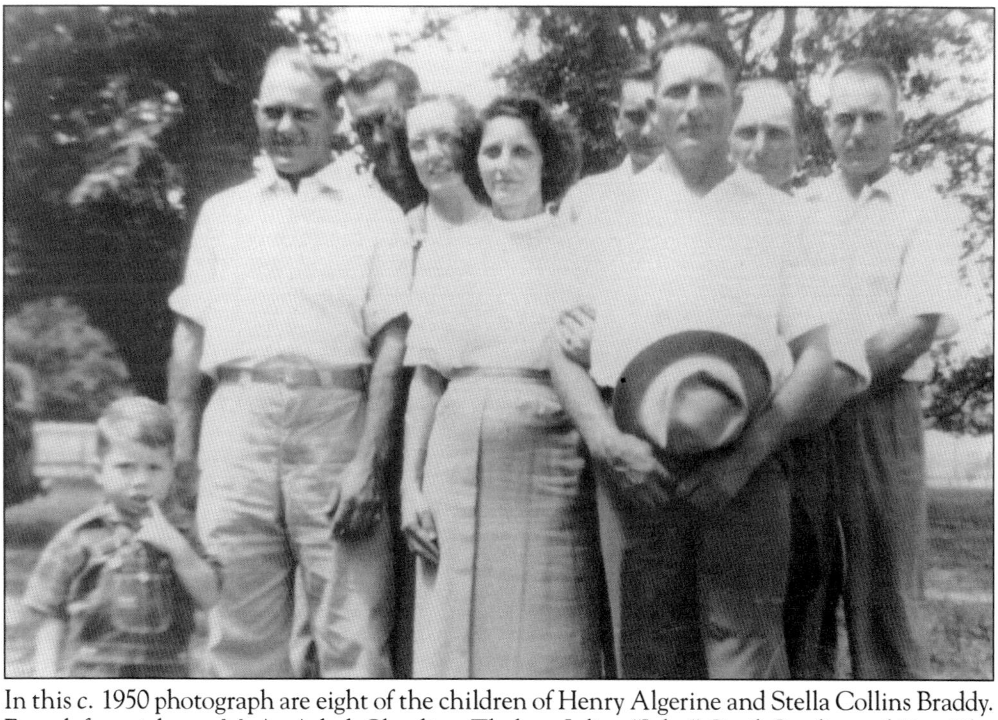

In this *c.* 1950 photograph are eight of the children of Henry Algerine and Stella Collins Braddy. From left to right are M. A., Athel, Claudine, Thelma, Julian "Juke," Cecil, Steelie, and Van. The little boy standing at the far left is Larry Braddy, the eldest child of M. A. The picture was made at a family reunion of the descendants of Moses Algerine and Florence Herndon Braddy, held at the Calhoun-Warnock Pond near Tarrytown.

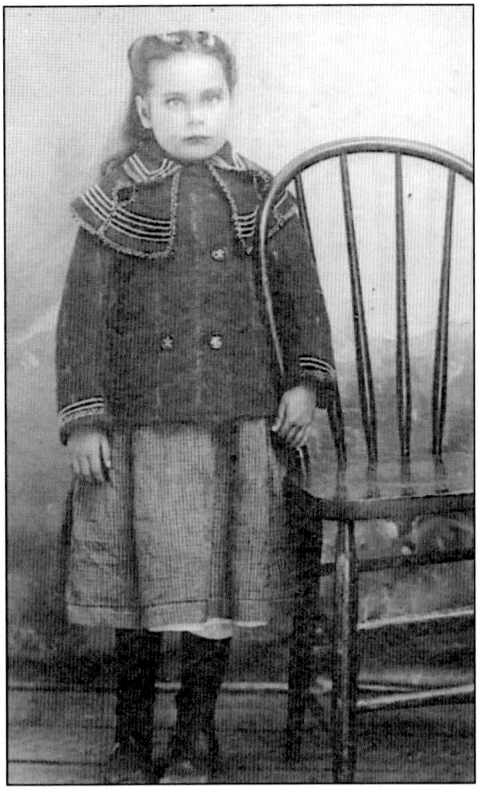

Matilda Alice Spivey (1902–1997) is shown here posing in a photographer's studio about 1909. She was a daughter of Thomas A. Spivey and Matilda Alice Darley. She married Leslie Rogers Meeks, and they are buried at the Red Bluff Cemetery. (Courtesy of Shawn Spivey Arnold.)

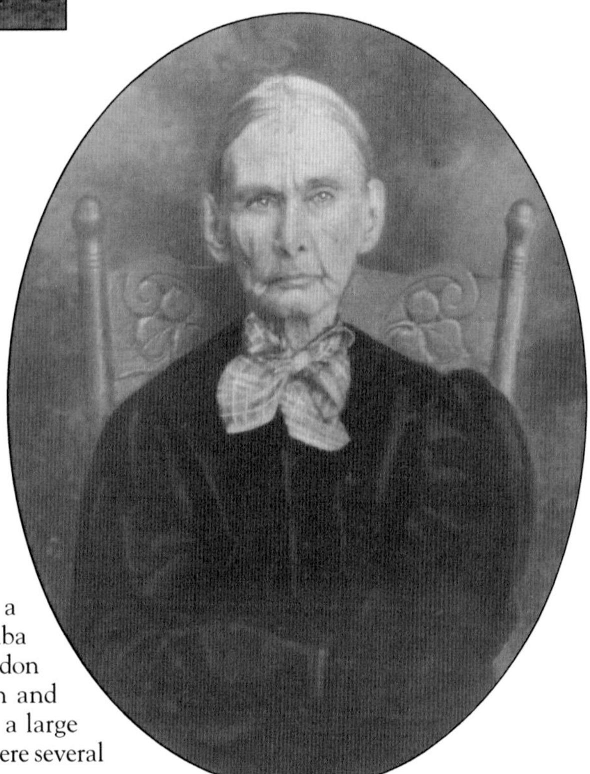

Samantha Miller (1830–1914) was a daughter of Samuel Miller and Pharaba Pate. In 1848, she married Henry Herndon (1821–1885), son of George Herndon and Rachel Branch. This family lived on a large farm about a mile south of Soperton, where several of their descendants live today.

Mamie Carrington Spikes (1891–1970), daughter of Gus and Katie Carrington of Montgomery County, and her husband, Oda Spikes, were very active in the Mount Zion Church in Soperton as well as other community affairs. (Courtesy of Lillian E. Spikes Smith.)

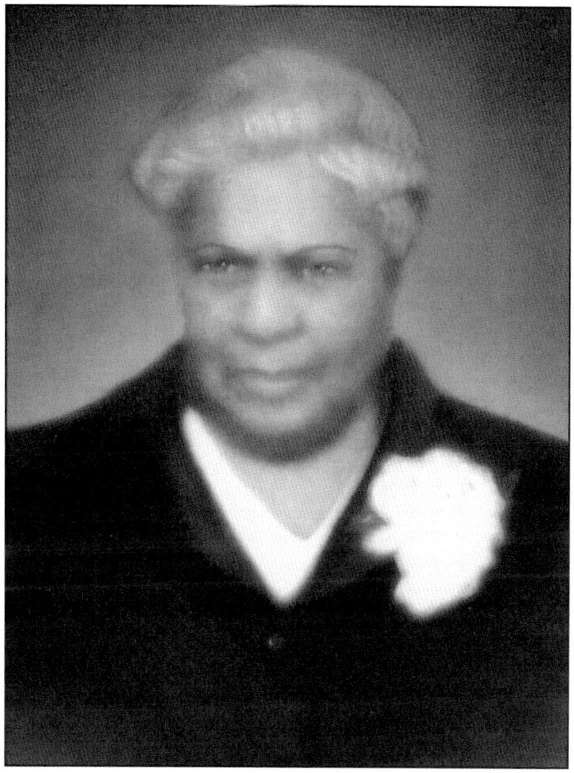

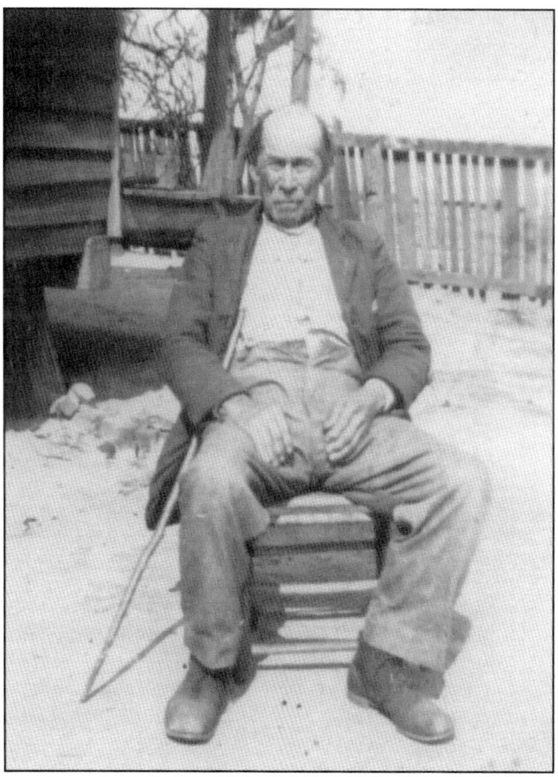

Hiram "Hi" Gillis (1849–1931) is shown here in his later years relaxing in the yard. His hands appear to be crippled with arthritis. Hiram was the eldest child of Archibald Gillis and Mary Miller. In 1870, he married Lavinia Herndon, daughter of William Herndon and Mary Jane Gainus. After her death, he married Theodosia Ellen Ware. (Courtesy of Patsy Gillis Ware.)

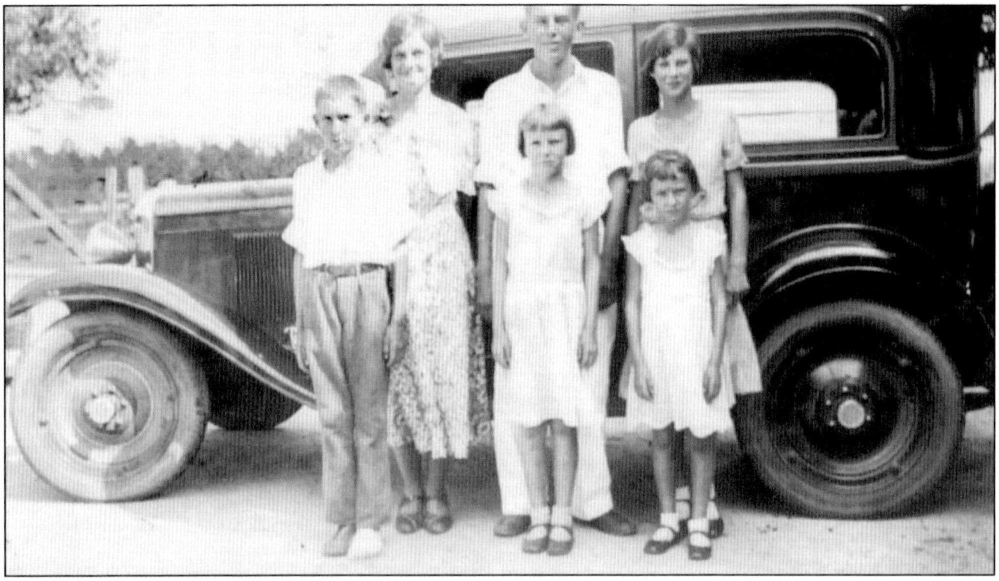

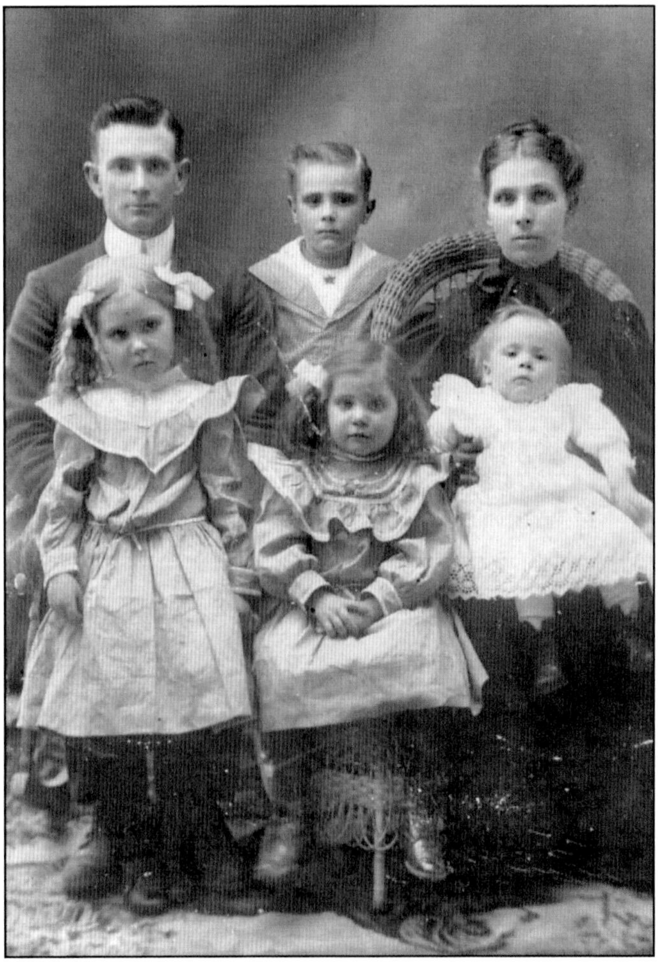

Pictured above by their Ford Model A in this *c.* 1940 photograph are, from left to right, (first row) John Allen Page Jr., Juanita Page Williams, and Helen Page Kelly; (second row) Irene Page Spivey, Elmer Page, and Lucille Page Rogers. (Courtesy of the Page family.)

In this studio photograph of the Willie Gay family, Lewis Gay stands in the middle between his parents, Willie and Julia Elizabeth Sammons Gay. In front, from left to right, are Ida Mae, Nannie Lou, and Otis on his mother's lap. Willie (1876–1936) was a son of Calvin Gay and Ann Elizabeth Anderson.

Gladys Phillips Corbin (1908–1990) is shown here about 1910. The daughter of Thomas Hilton Phillips and Maggie Phillips, she married Leo Corbin in 1924. Leo (1904–1994) was a son of Lucian Corbin and Mamie Barwick. This family lived on the O'Hoopee River. (Courtesy of Grayson Phillips.)

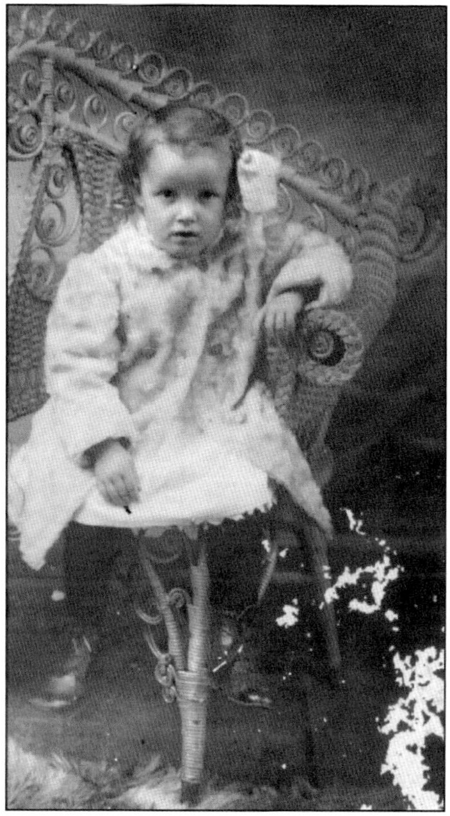

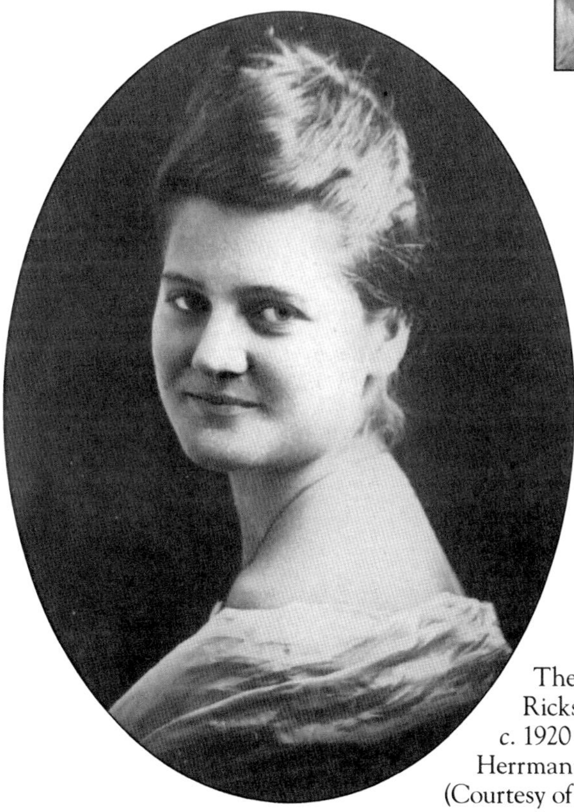

Thelma Ricks, a daughter of Daniel Tilton Ricks and Arrilla Youngblood, is shown in this c. 1920 formal pose. She married William Emory Herrmann, and they lived in the Blackville area. (Courtesy of Tracy Manning Gillikin.)

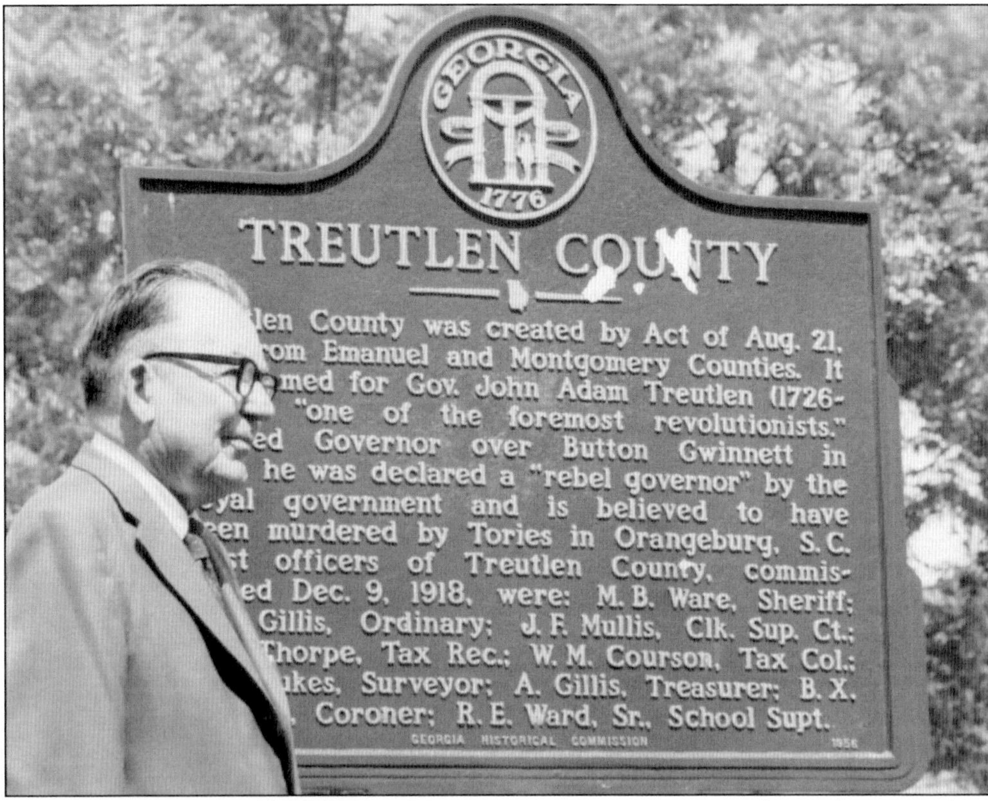

James Lester "Jim L." Gillis Sr. (1892–1975), shown above in about 1972, was the man who brought Georgia from mud roads to a system of superhighways. He served as Georgia's highway director for 18 years—longer than any other man. Probably his greatest achievement in the area is Interstate Highway 16, which has been named for him.

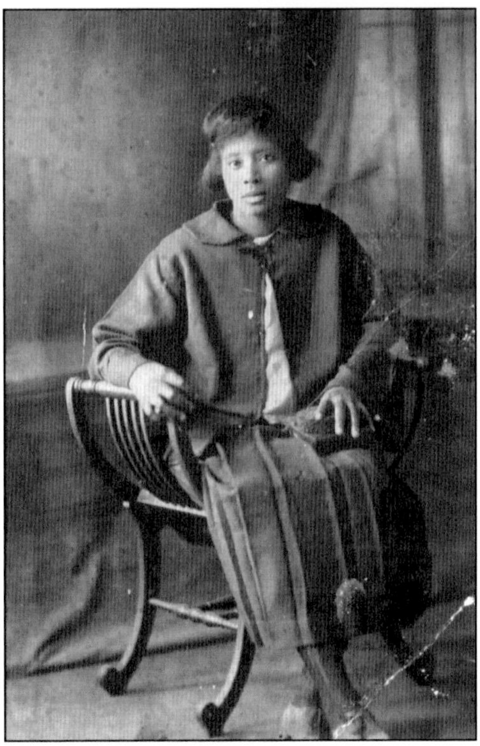

Beatrice Baker Hodges, pictured here c. 1930, was a daughter of Aaron Baker and Bertha Love. She married Jimmy Hodges, and they were the parents of Louise, Nellie, Woodrow, Mamie, Curtis, Braiford, Ernest, Jimmy Jr., and Dr. Dean R. Hodges. (Courtesy of Vivian Baker Bullock.)

Thomas Jefferson Morris (1819–1874) was a son of Jesse Morris and Ann "Nancy" Blackman of Screven County. He married Margaret Williamson (1818–1897), daughter of John Williamson and Elizabeth Sullivan. Family tradition states that he helped build the Boiling Springs Baptist Church, where he and two of his sons, Andy and Mandel, are buried. (Courtesy of Keith Lawson.)

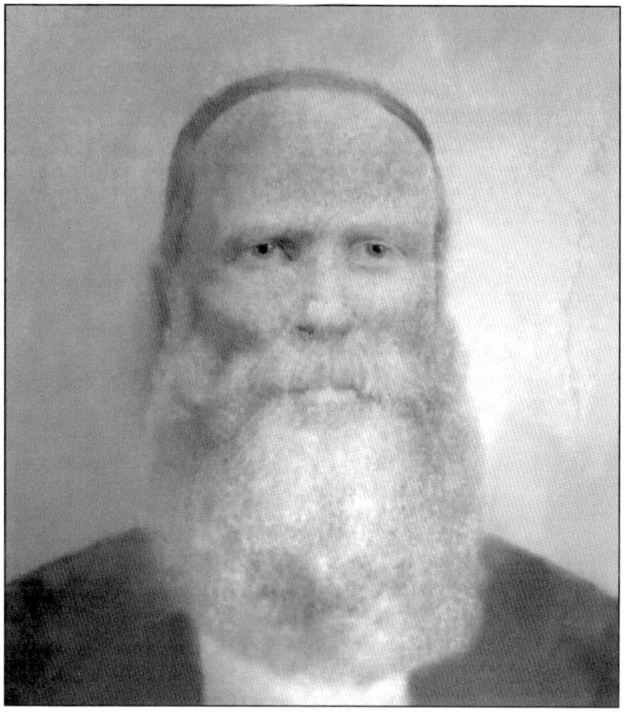

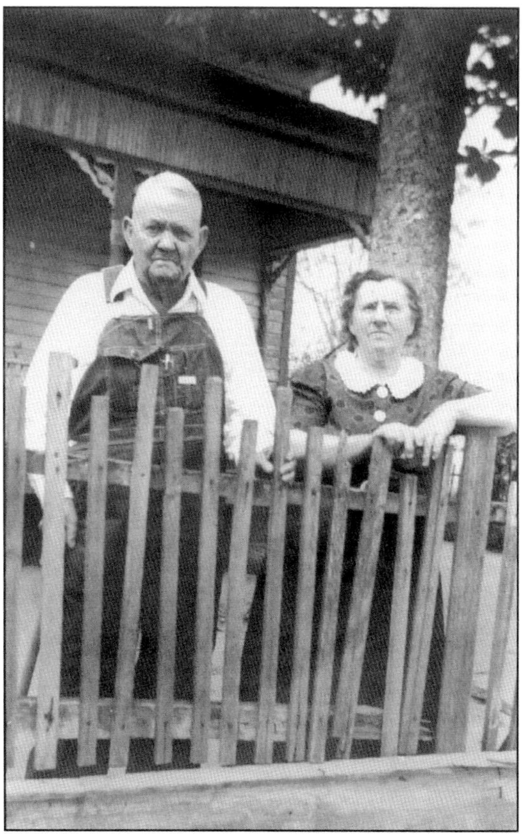

Joseph Thomas Moxley and his second wife, Sallie Penelope Woods, are pictured here about 1910 standing at the gate of their home near Zaidee. Joseph and Sallie worked their farm and raised livestock. (Courtesy of Bill Phillips.)

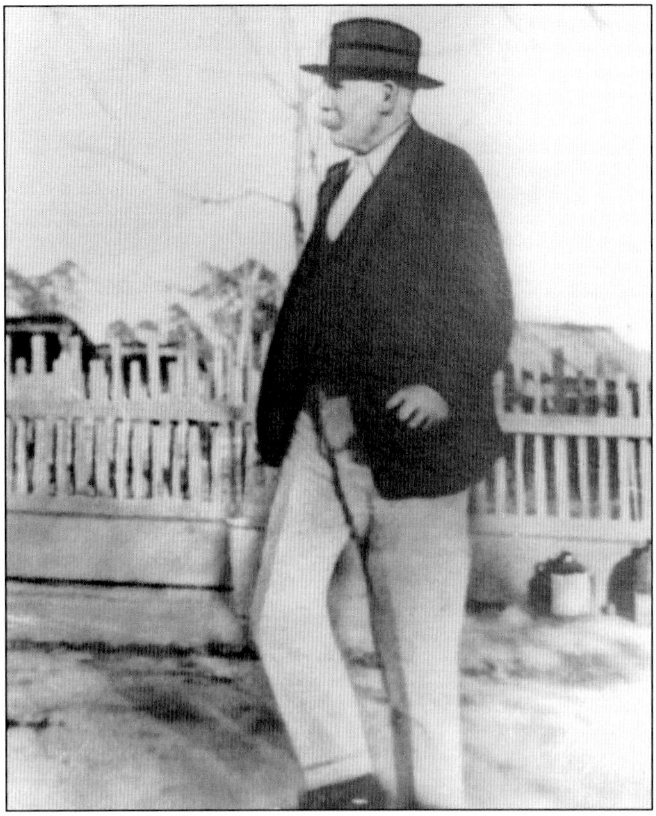

Walter Hart Duke (1858–1928) is taking a stroll in this photograph from about 1920. In 1880, he married Margaret Louise Webster (1859–1924). He was the father of Louella Duke McCrimmon. (Courtesy of Suella McCrimmon.)

The Jim Oatts family is posing together for the photograph below. Among those pictured are Freeman Miller, John H. Oatts, Jim Oatts, Carrie Eason, and Pat Oatts.

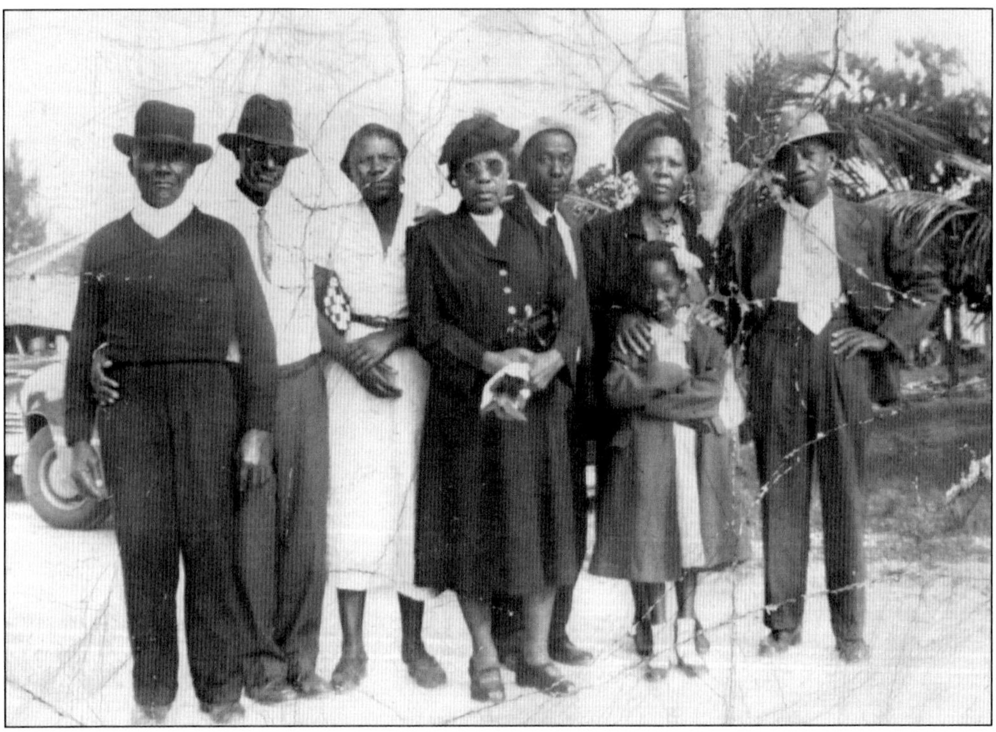

Robert Morgan Sparks (1885–1967) and his wife, Anna Hughes Sparks (1887–1970), are pictured here in 1959 in front of the Sparks Memorial Library, which they gave in memory of their son, Robert Hughes Sparks. They also donated the Treutlen County Health Center in 1951.

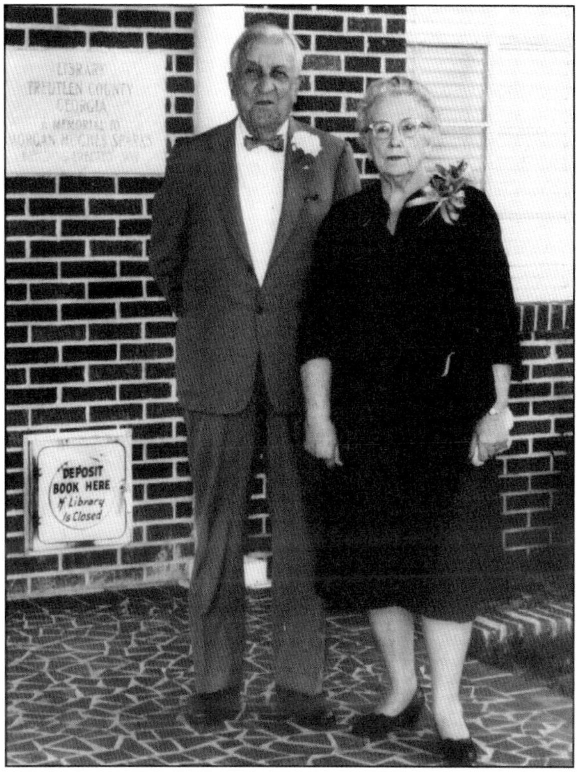

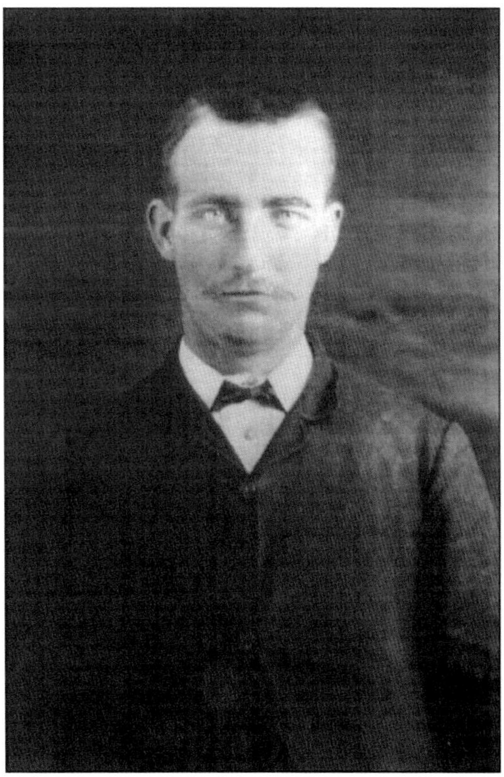

Thomas A. Spivey (1860–1910) posed around 1880 for this picture. He was a son of James Irwin Spivey and Bethany Davis and married Matilda Alice Darley, daughter of Penelope Darley. (Courtesy of Shawn Spivey Arnold.)

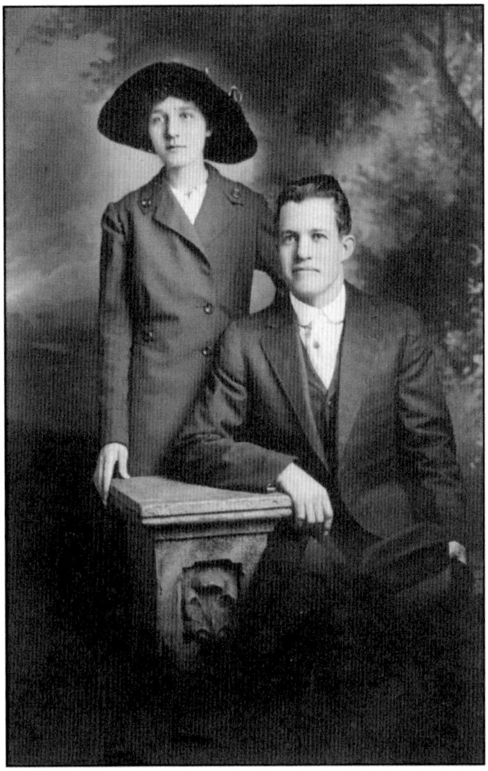

James Thomas Waller and his wife, Annie Sue Pipkin, are shown in this *c.* 1920 photograph. They were active in many community affairs. James served as the mayor of Soperton from 1950 to 1951. He held extensive farming interests and was the owner of Waller's Gin and Warehouse. (Courtesy of James T. Waller.)

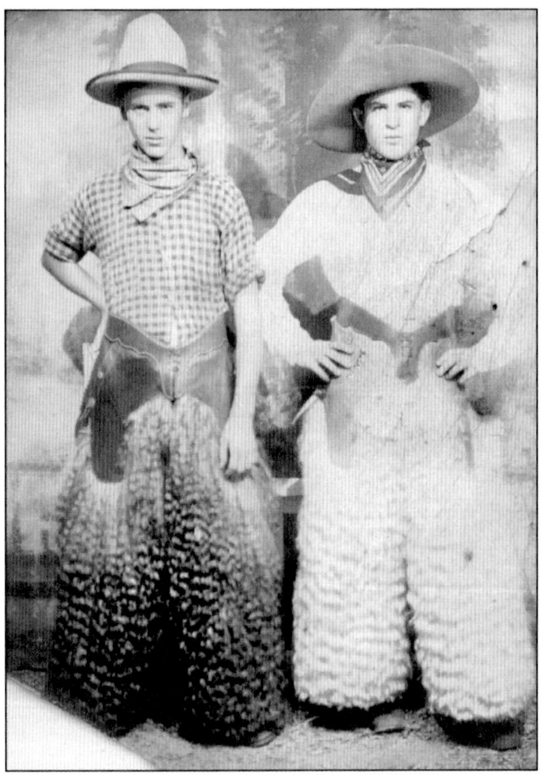

Enjoying an outing at the county fair are Ernest "Buck" Corbin (left) and Lemuel Williamson, who later became brothers-in-law. They donned this western attire in the photographer's booth. This picture was made about 1925, probably in Swainsboro. Buck and his wife, Lena, later moved to Louisiana Avenue in Soperton.

Pictured here around 1910 is Collington Pharo Phillips (1879–1941), the oldest child of Sherrod "Doc" Phillips and Ellen Cornelia Youngblood. He was born and reared in southern Treutlen County and married Arley Mosley (1885–1966), daughter of Andrew Jackson Mosley and Rosena Williamson.

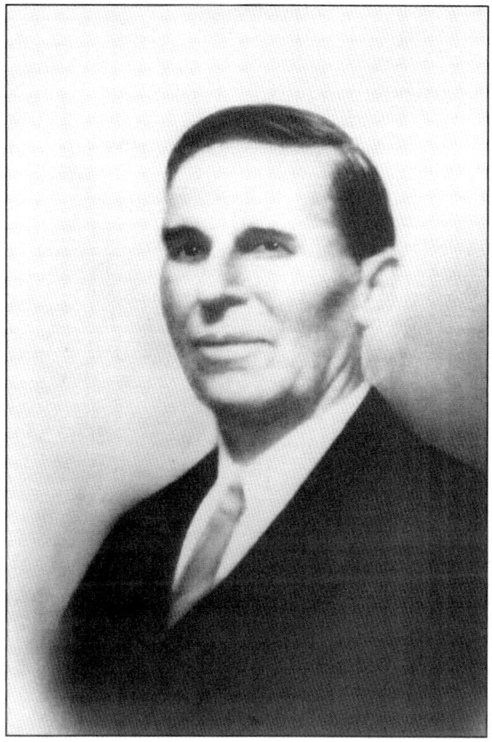

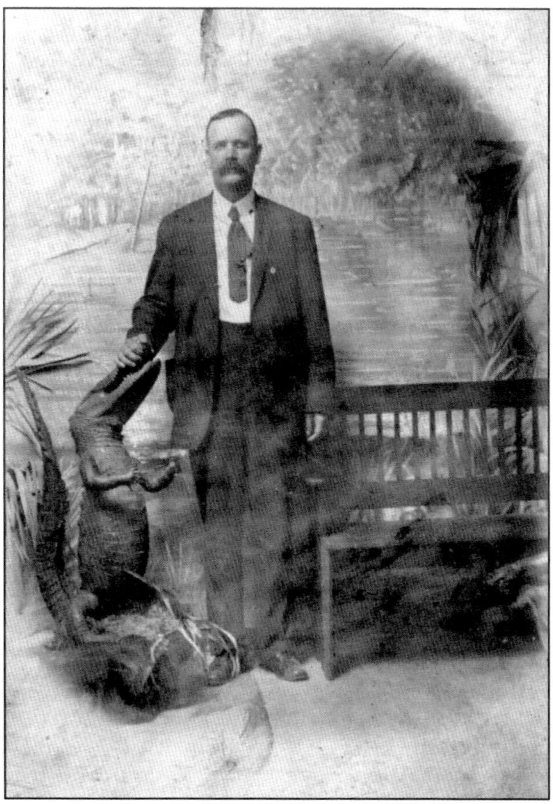

Neil Lee Gillis posed with a stuffed alligator as a prop on one of his trips to Florida in the 1890s. He sent a card home to his brother, Roderick, stating the shrimping was very good and more and more people were locating to the area. (Courtesy of Hal Jones.)

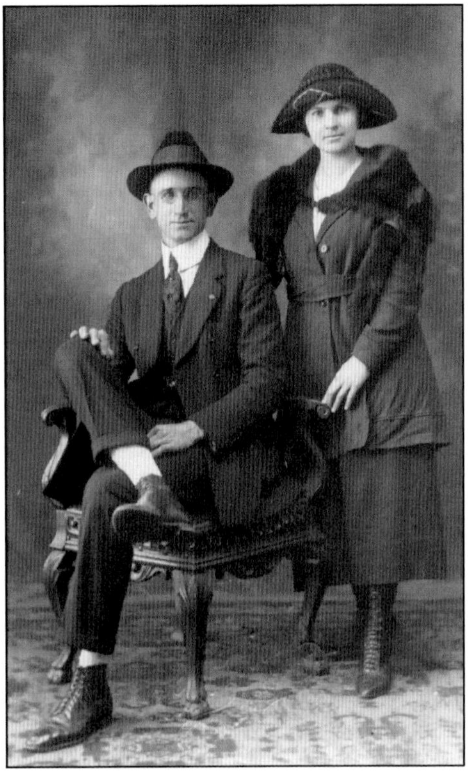

Shown about 1930 are Arthur Clayton Lindsey, son of Lawson and Elizabeth Lindsey of Washington County, and his wife, Nettie Ree Moxley, daughter of William Henry Moxley and Nancy Mozelle Woods. (Courtesy of Juanita Lindsey Youmans.)

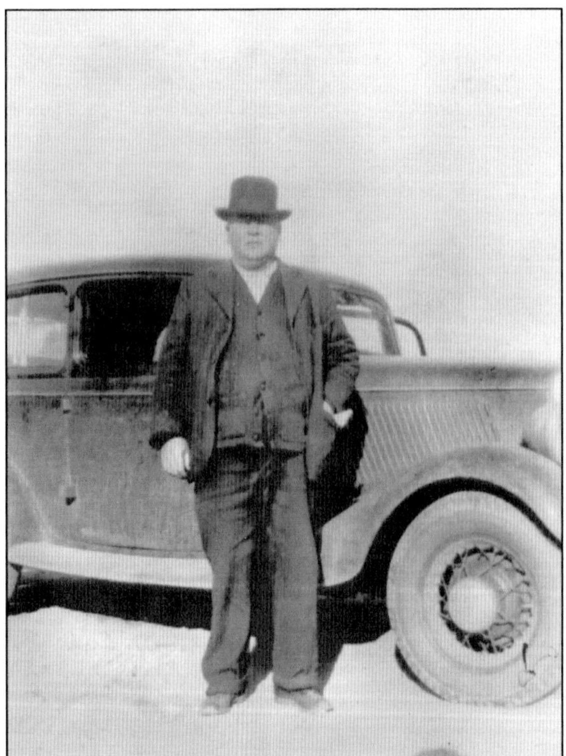

Morris H. "Happ" Newsome (1870–1942) was born in Washington County to Lorenzo Dow and Sarah O. Newsome. He married Florence Valerie Miller (1877–1966), daughter of John Miller Jr. and Laura Ann McCrimmon. Morris owned extensive farm operations as well as two turpentine stills.

A son of John Lee Brinson and Mary Catherine Phillips, Arnett Lawson Brinson (1876–1938) posed for this c. 1910 picture with his wife, Mattie Holton (1881–1939), and three of their children, (from left to right) Gabriel, Eulas, and Tyrus. (Courtesy of the Binson family.)

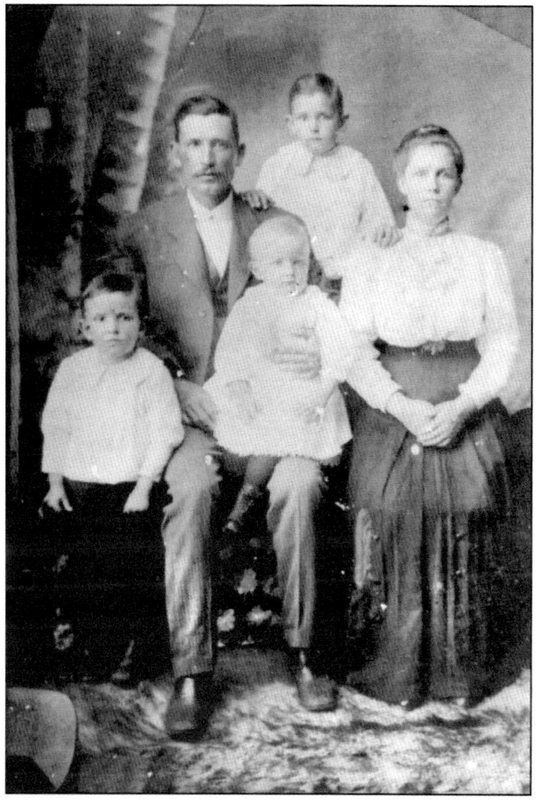

Below is an early-1900s picture at the Calvin Ace Beasley home. The event was to honor Delilah Hutcheson Durden (1828–1918) on her birthday. She is in the center of the group, wearing black. Delilah was the mother of Catherine Delilah Durden, who married Calvin Ace Beasley in 1882. (Courtesy of the Beasley family.)

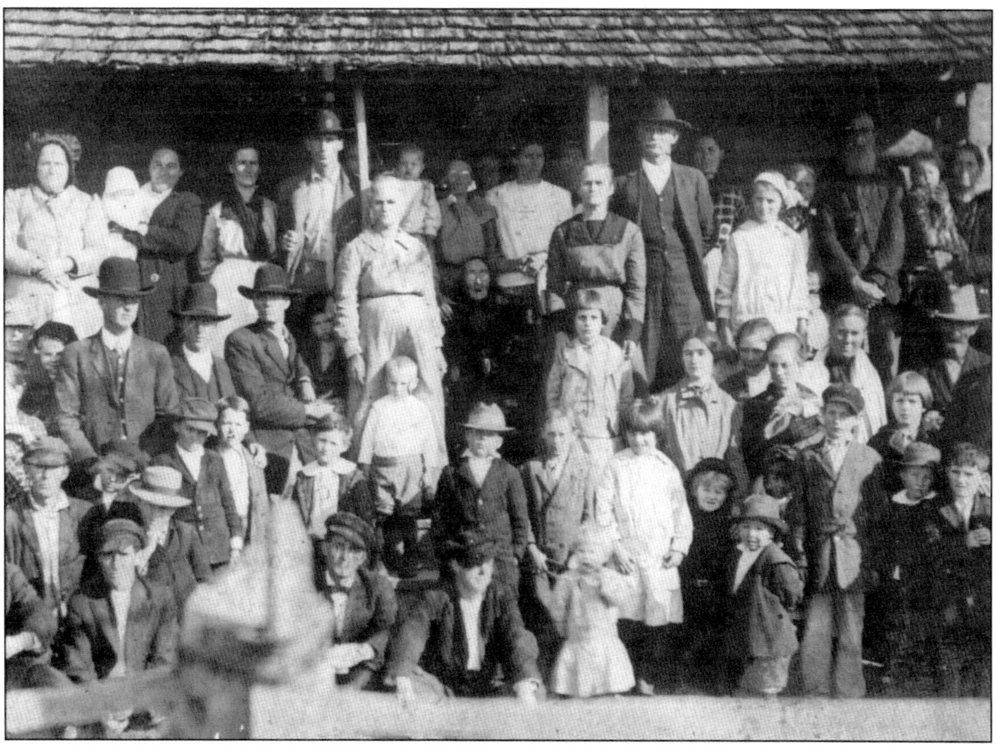

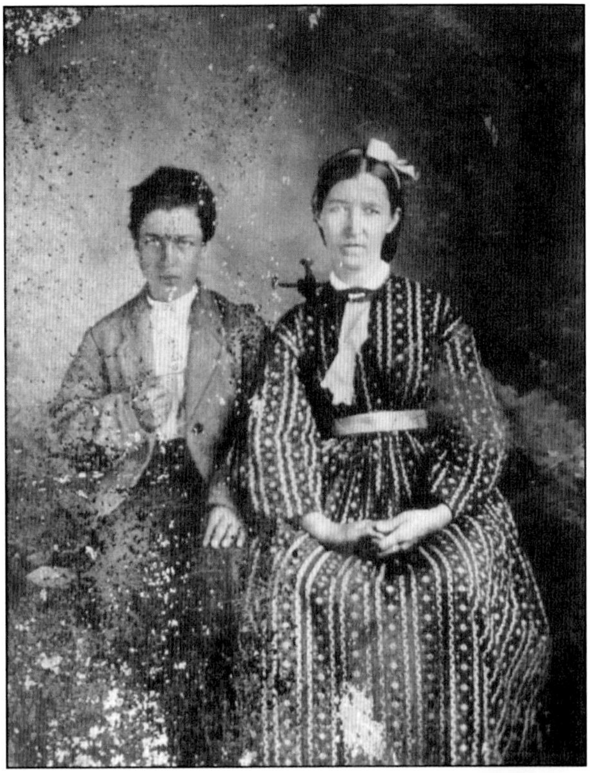

Calvin Ace Beasley (1858–1942) posed for this *c.* 1860 picture with his mother, Pharaba Beasley (1837–1902). Pharaba was the 11th of 14 children born to Daniel Elijah Beasley and Rebekah Barnes of Emanuel County. (Courtesy of the Beasley family.)

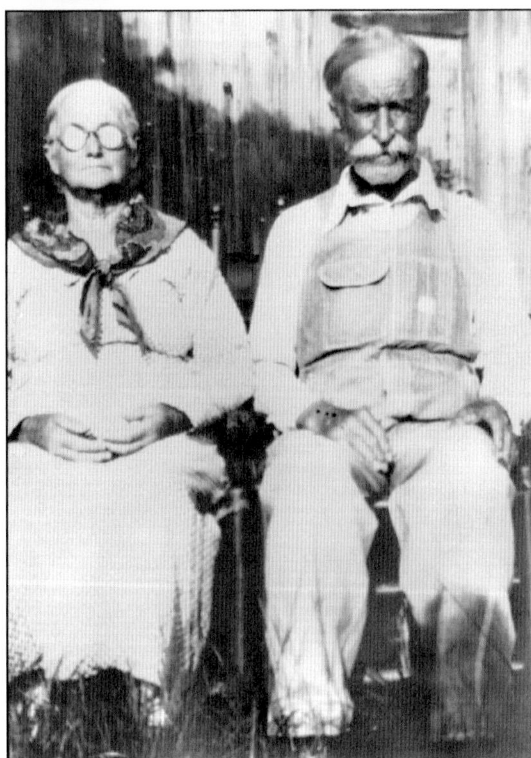

In this *c.* 1930 picture, Calvin Ace Beasley is shown with his wife, Catherine Delilah Durden (1867–1937), daughter of William Nathan Durden and Delilah Hutcheson. (Courtesy of the Beasley family.)

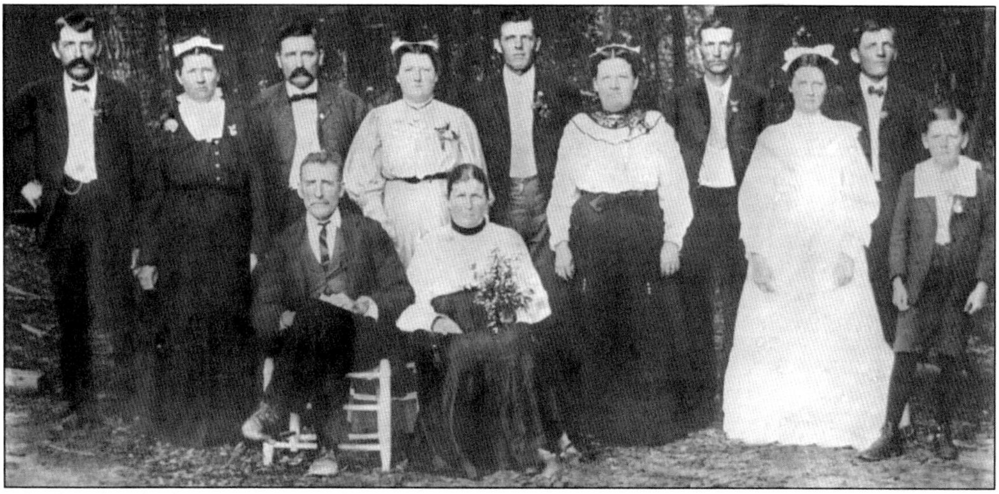

The family of John Lee Brinson (1848–1914) and his wife, Mary Catherine Phillips (1851–1928), are pictured here (seated) at a family reunion, held in 1897 at the Brinson home place. John Lee was a son of Jane "Jincy" Turner, and Mary Catherine was a daughter of Martha Phillips. (Courtesy of the Brinson family.)

Charlotte "Lottie" Herndon Morris (1842–1910) was the eldest child of Henry Herndon and Genna Davis. Lottie married Thomas Riley Morris (1850–1930), son of Thomas Jefferson Morris and Margaret Williamson, and they were the parents of Lenora, Benjamin Millard, George Mandell, Emma, and Maggie. (Courtesy of Keith Lawson.)

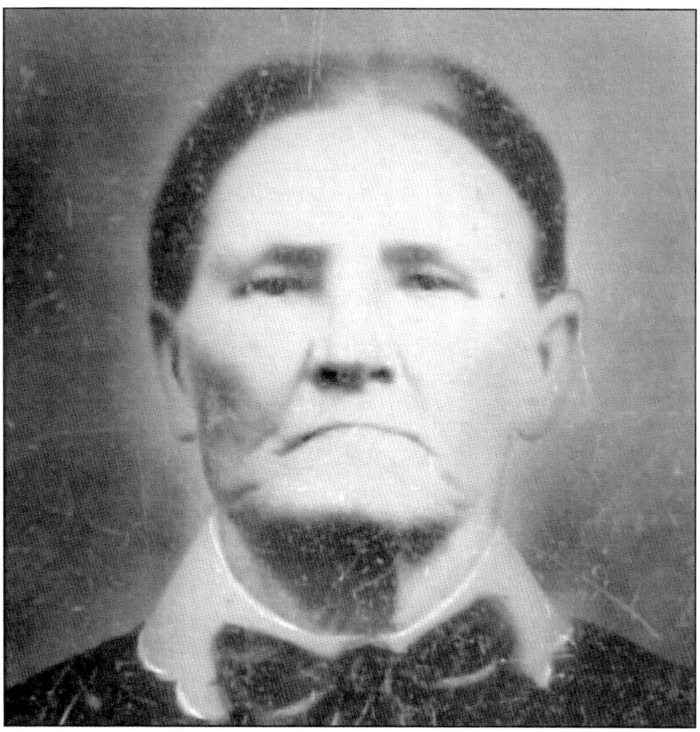

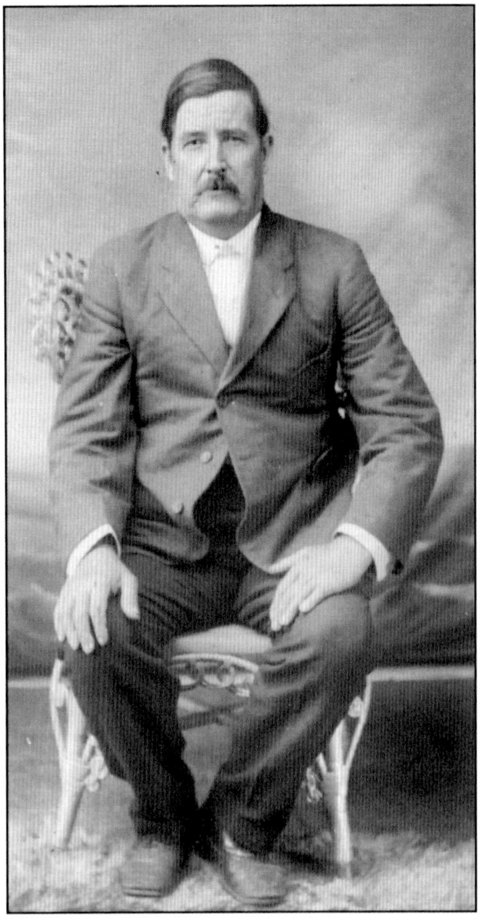

Posing here about 1880 is John Jackson Phillips (1854–1925), a son of Martha Phillips. In 1876, he married Martha Jane Turner (1855–1926), daughter of Augustus William Turner and Martha Jane Dickerson. (Courtesy of Grayson Phillips.)

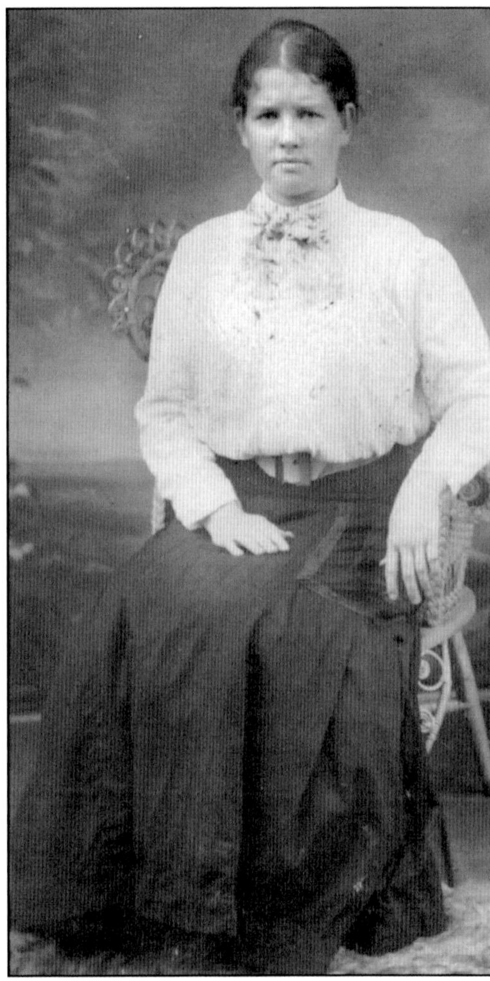

Mary A. "Cissy" Phillips (c. 1892–1979) is pictured in a frilly blouse of the period in this c. 1908 photograph. A daughter of Thomas Jackson "T. J." Phillips and Sarah "Sallie" Wilkes, Cissy married Lonnie J. Hadden, son of James R. Hadden and Sarah Jane Woods. (Courtesy of Grayson Phillips.)

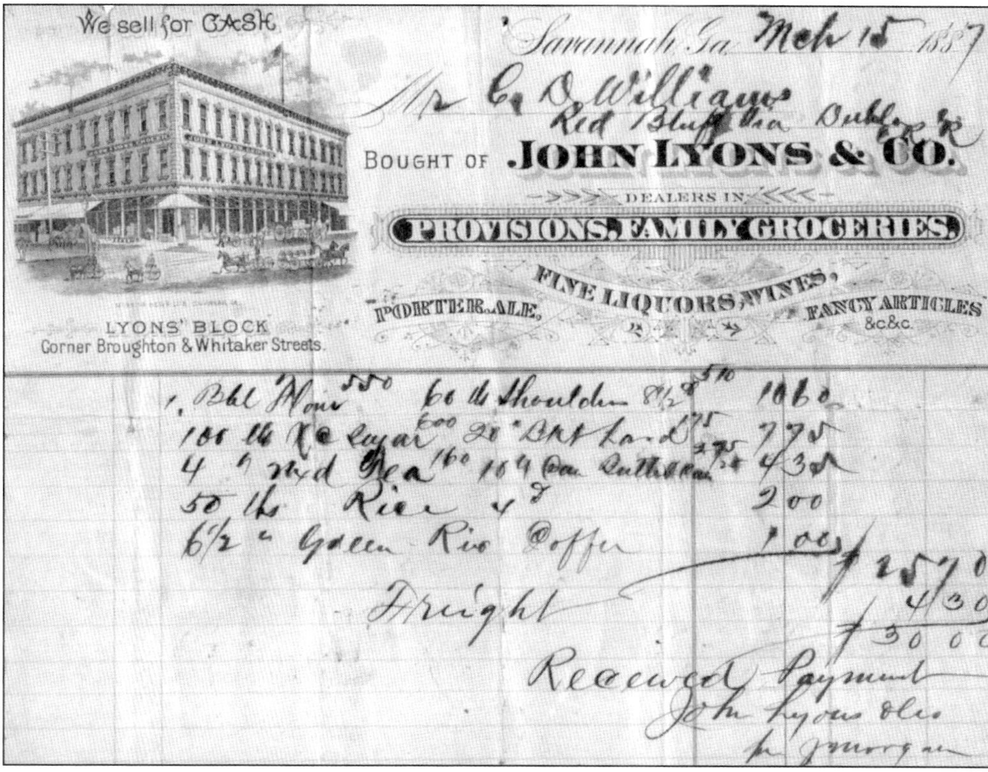

We sell for CASH

Savannah Ga. Mch 15 1887

Mr C. D. Williams

Red Bluff via

Bought of JOHN LYONS & CO.

DEALERS IN

PROVISIONS, FAMILY GROCERIES,

FINE LIQUORS, WINES,

PORTER, ALE,

FANCY ARTICLES &c. &c.

LYONS' BLOCK
Corner Broughton & Whitaker Streets.

50 lbs Rice 4 2 00

Freight

Received Payment

Pictured above is a store receipt for goods bought by Charles Dixon Williams II and his new wife, the former Lillie Mae Miller, after their marriage on March 15, 1887. These items were needed for stocking their pantry as they set up housekeeping. (Courtesy of Buck Crumpler.)

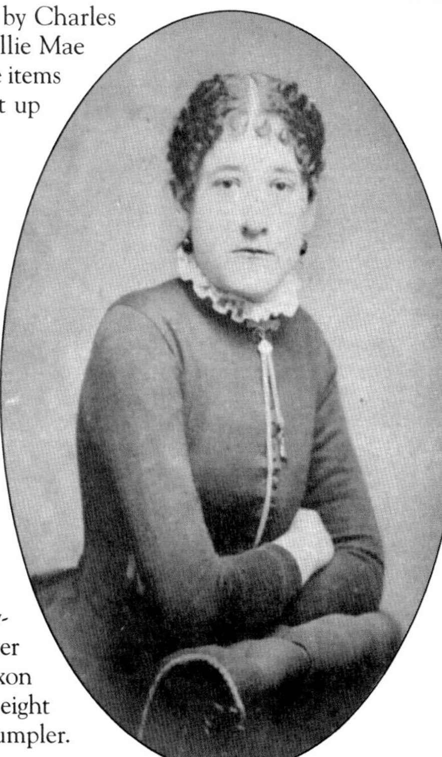

Lillie Mae Williams (1865–1933) poses in this early-1880s photograph. She was a daughter of Abiel Carter Miller and Leonora Moody and married Charles Dixon Williams II (1859–1947). The Williamses reared their eight children in Soperton, including Eva Williams Crumpler. (Courtesy of Buck Crumpler.)

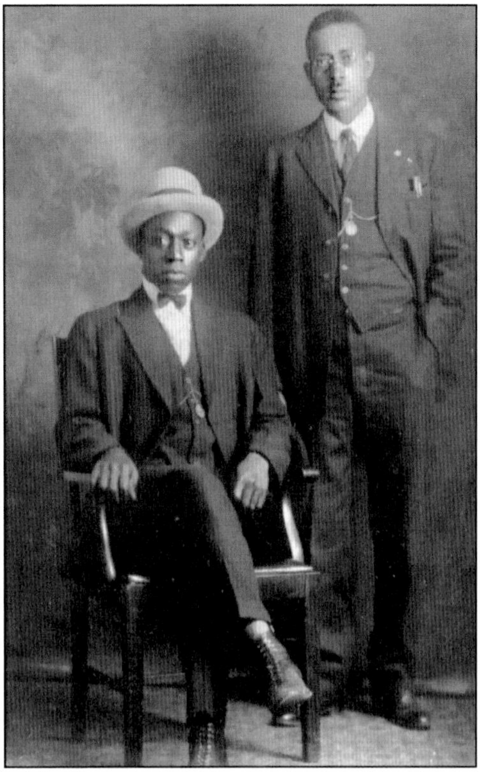

Shown standing is William Barnes "Bill" Baker, who was born and reared in Treutlen County. He moved to Pennsylvania for a time but returned to Soperton and built what is called "the Little Green House" just outside town on Highway 221. The gentleman in the chair is a Mr. Jones. (Courtesy of Vivian Baker Bullock.)

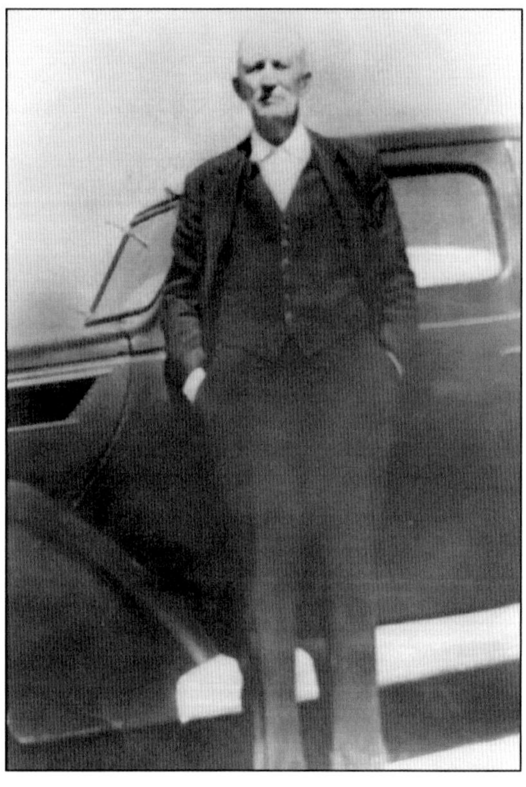

This is George Washington "Crockett" Sammons about 1940. Born in 1872, he first married Frances Black, and after her death, he married Georgia Cooper Hall.

James Vance Daly (1901–1966), son of Herschel V. Daly and Sara Merle Meadows, was a pharmacist in Soperton. He married Pauline Pensy Wheeler (1908–1991), daughter of Shade W. Wheeler and Mary Ouida "Mollie" Woods.

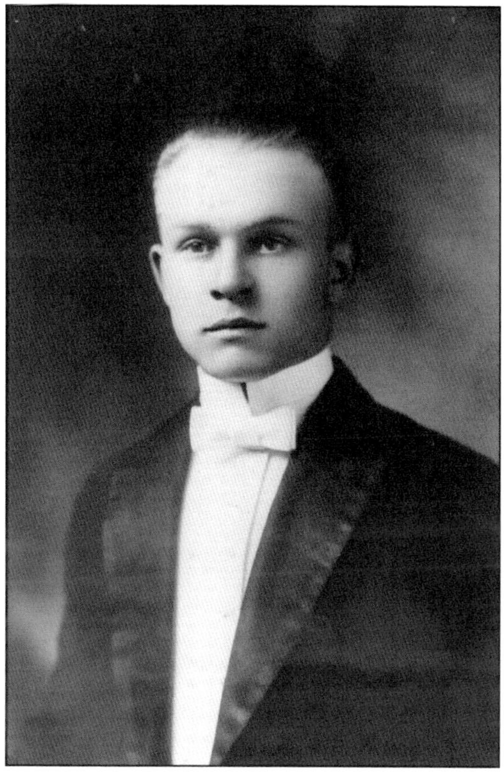

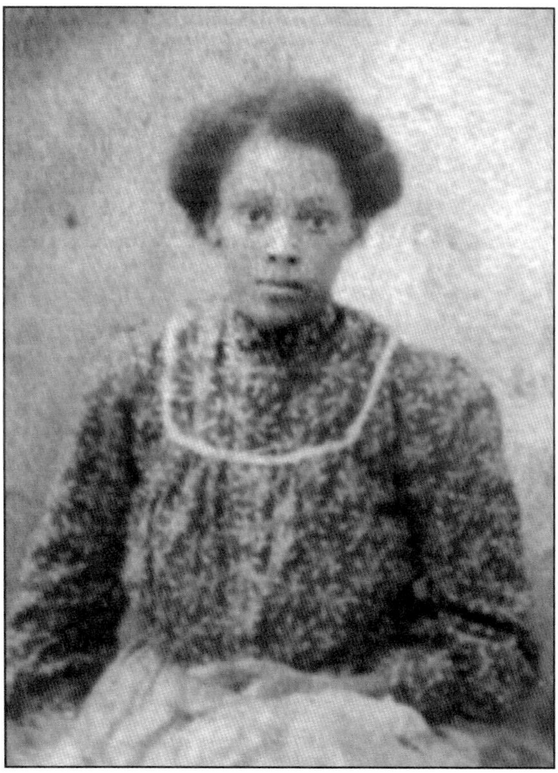

This c. 1890 photograph is of an unidentified young woman, a member of the Love family of Soperton. This was an industrious family, and they were the founders of the Mount Olive Church. (Courtesy of the Love family.)

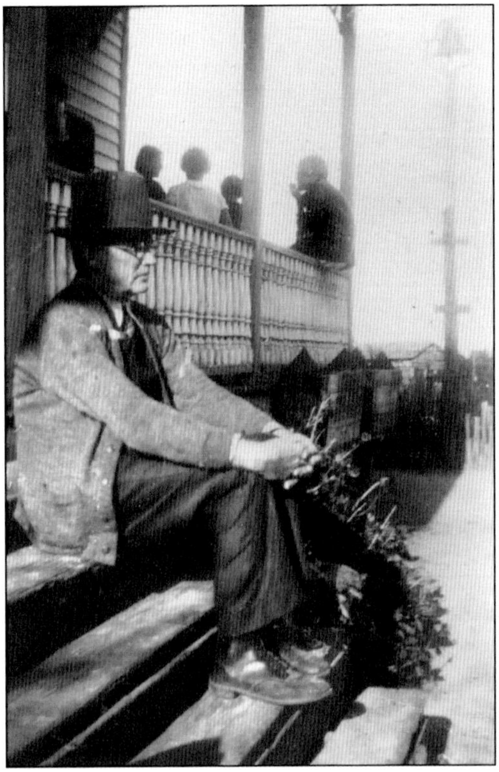

William Henry Moxley stopped to "sit a spell" on the steps of his home near Zaidee in this photograph from about 1940. Henry and his wife, Nancy Mozelle Woods, are buried in the Westview Cemetery in Soperton. (Courtesy of Bill Phillips.)

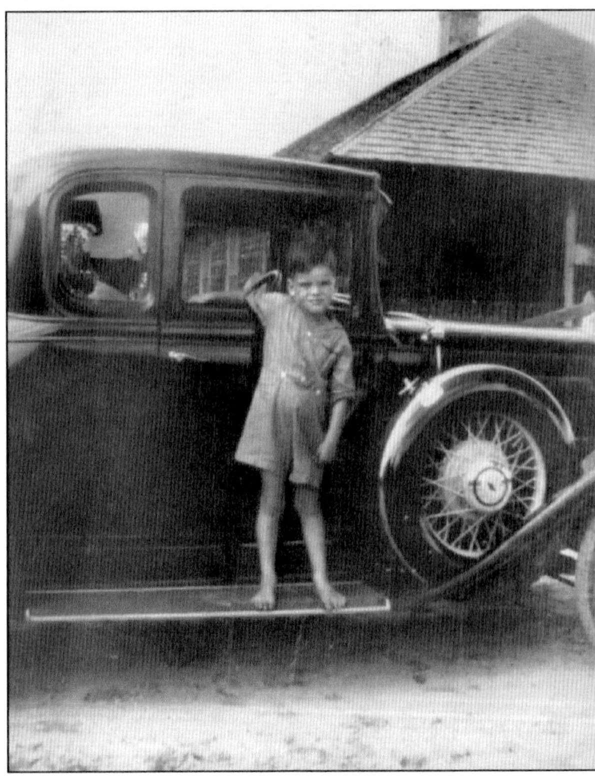

Dressed in a cute playsuit, Thomas Grayson Phillips is waiting on the running board of his father's car in this picture made about 1930. Grayson's parents were Thomas Hilton Phillips and Maggie Phillips, and the house in the background was their home place. (Courtesy of Grayson Phillips.)

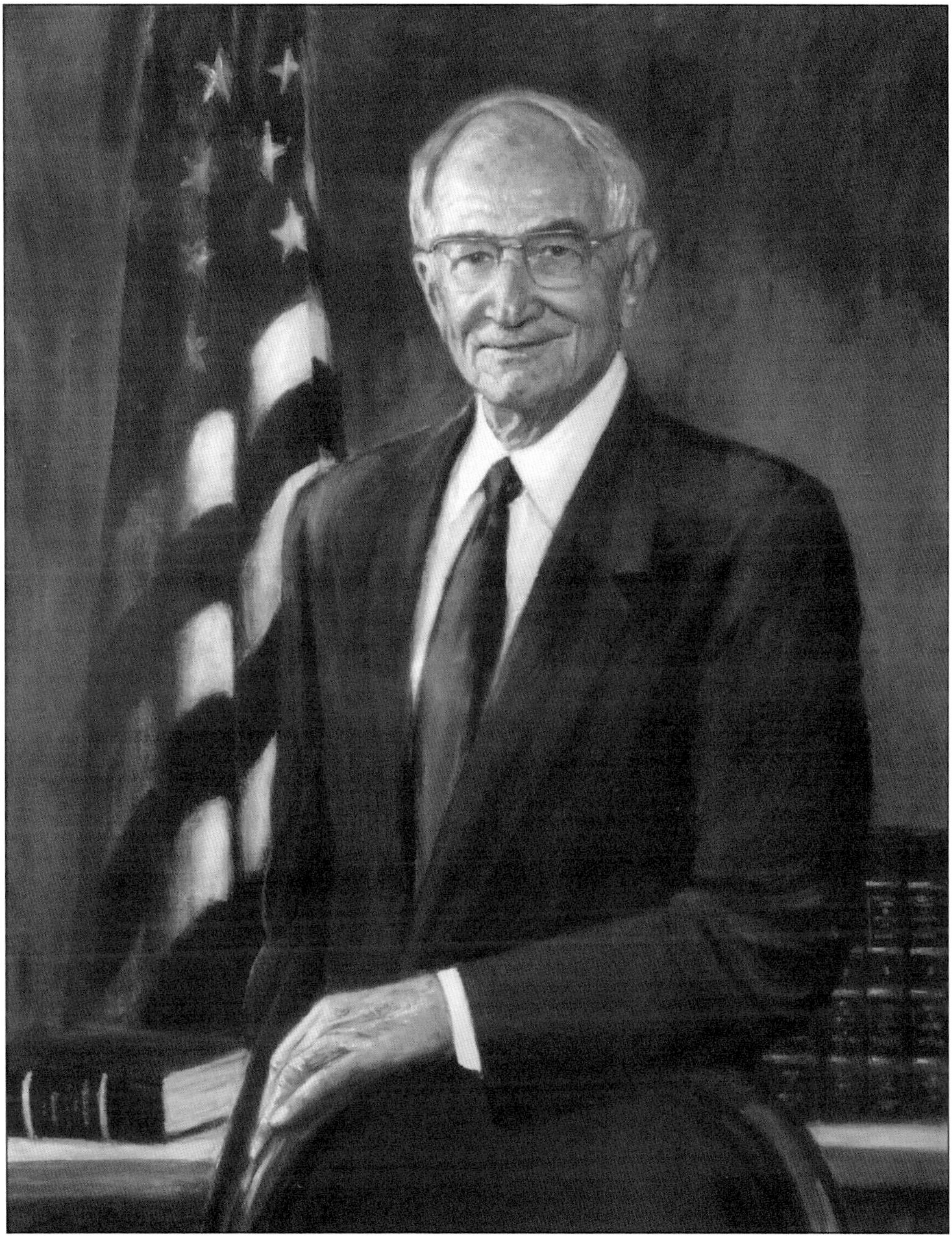

J. Carlton Warnock (1913–2005) was born in Montgomery County to James Tillman Warnock and Dora Braddy. A graduate of Mercer University and the University of Georgia School of Law, he served as the state court judge of Treutlen County for 22 years and as a Treutlen County attorney for 53 years. He was a veteran of World War II and was married to the former Jane Marsh. (Courtesy of Jane Warnock.)

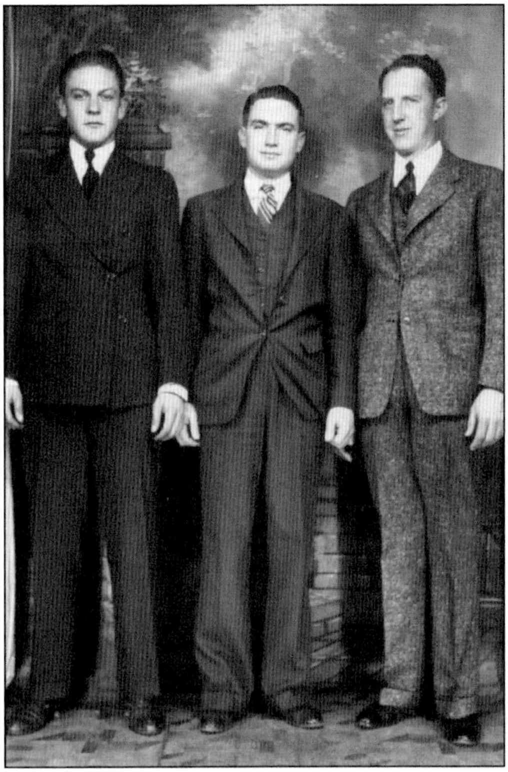

On the left is Jarrett Ned Palmer, son of Edward Clyde "Pat" and Annie Clyde Braddy Palmer, who was killed in an airplane crash in Clarke County, Georgia, in 1947 at the age of 25. The other two gentlemen are unidentified.

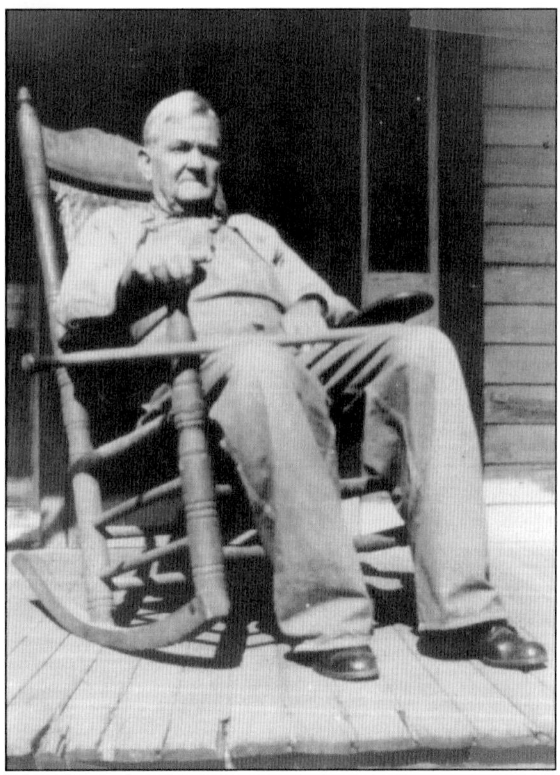

Joseph Thomas "Joe" Moxley (1845–1911) is shown in this c. 1910 picture relaxing on the porch after dinner (the midday meal in the South). He was first married to Martha M. Flanders and later to Sallie Penelope Woods. (Courtesy of Bill Phillips.)

This couple seems to be courting out by the rose vine. This *c.* 1900 picture was taken at the home of Georgann Elizabeth Thompson, who later married Roderick Lonzo Gillis. The young lady is probably her sister. (Courtesy of Hal Jones.)

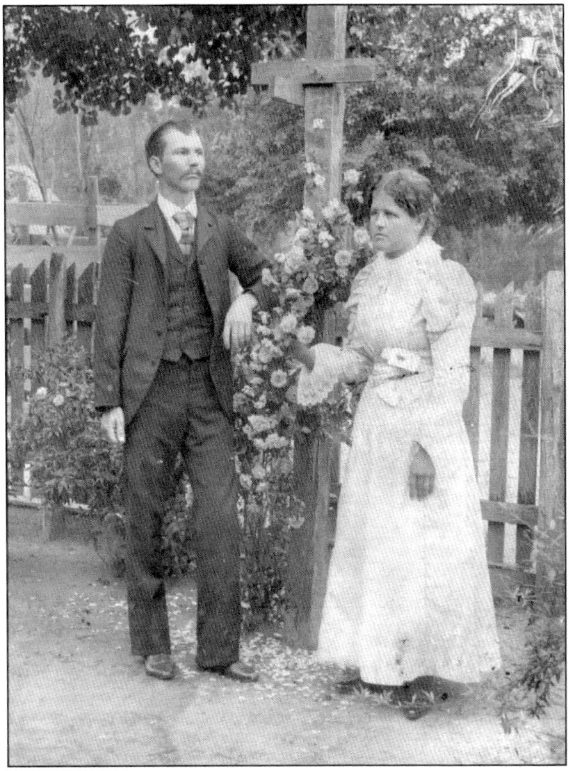

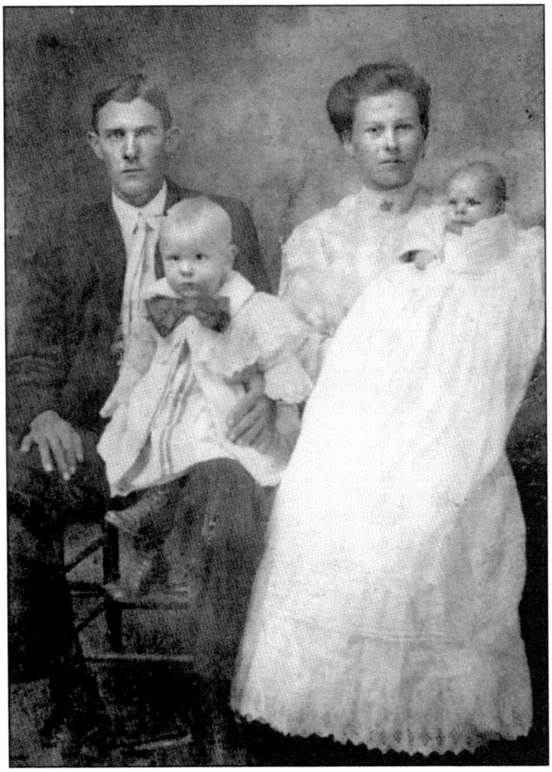

This is an early-1920s picture of Morris Hinton Smith; his wife, Elizabeth Catherine "Lizzie" Mimbs; and their sons, Frank (left) and Johnnie Elmo. Johnnie Elmo Smith married Mary Julia Meeks, a daughter of Matthew Meeks and Nannie Lou Gay.

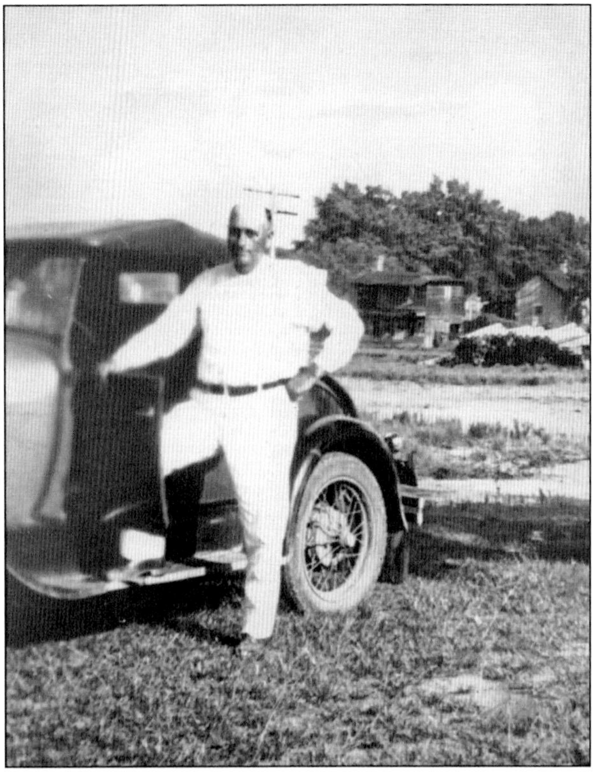

Chappell T. Thigpen (1884–1952) is posing beside his new car. He was a member of Treutlen County's board of education from 1939 until his death.

Norman Gillis (1865–1928) is pictured below about 1910 with his wife, Mary Manning (1880–1966), and their children, from left to right, Thurman, Hazel, Norman Jr., and Rhodus. Norman was a son of Archibald Gillis and Mary Miller. (Courtesy of Patsy Gillis Ware.)

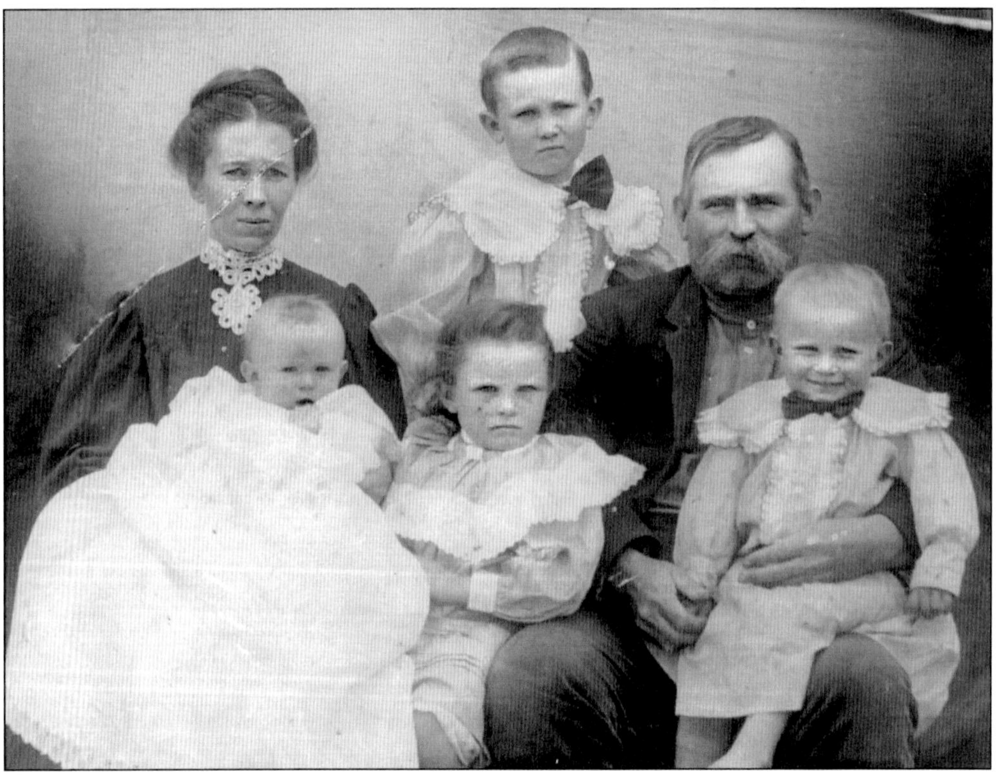

These girls are dressed up and ready to go out. Lash Fowler Hadden (left) and Hayes Fowler Lawton were daughters of James "Jim" and Bessie White Fowler. This photograph was made around 1932 at the Fowler home on Second Street.

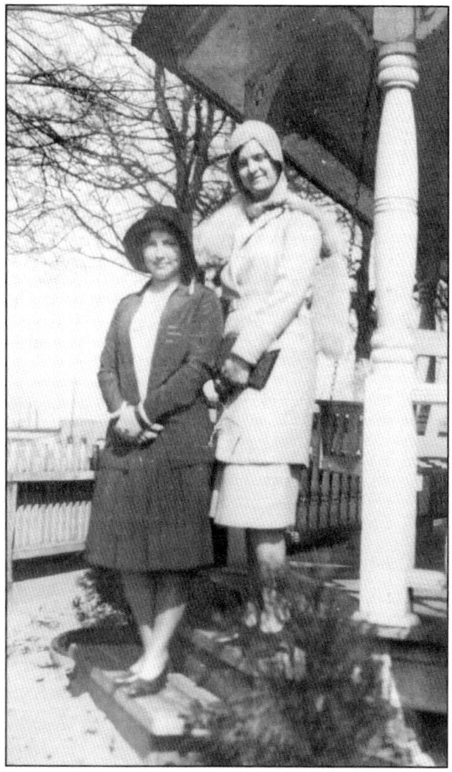

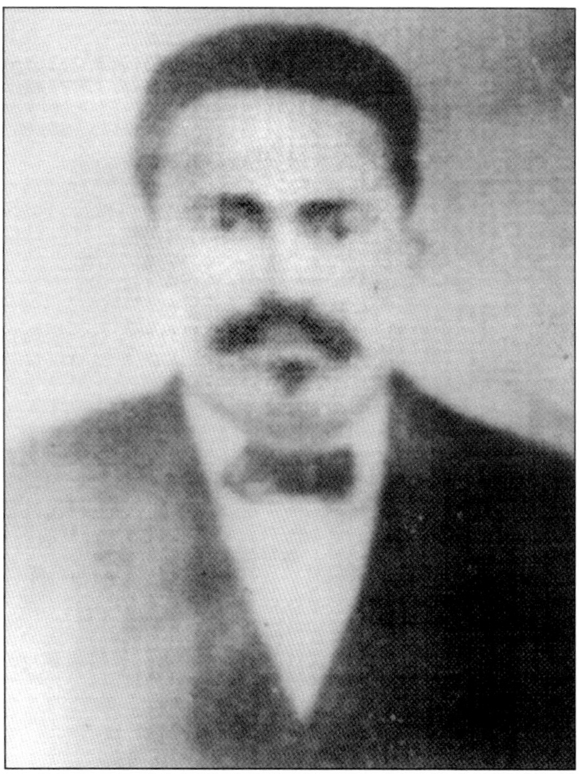

Rev. John A. Love (1875–1961) was a son of Eddie Love and his wife, Florence Hill. He was first married to Nora Smith (1880–1920), and after her death, he married Gertrude Hicks (1896–1951). From these two unions, he fathered 13 children. Reverend Love pastored several churches in the community, including the Mount Olive Baptist Church near Soperton. (Courtesy of the Love family.)

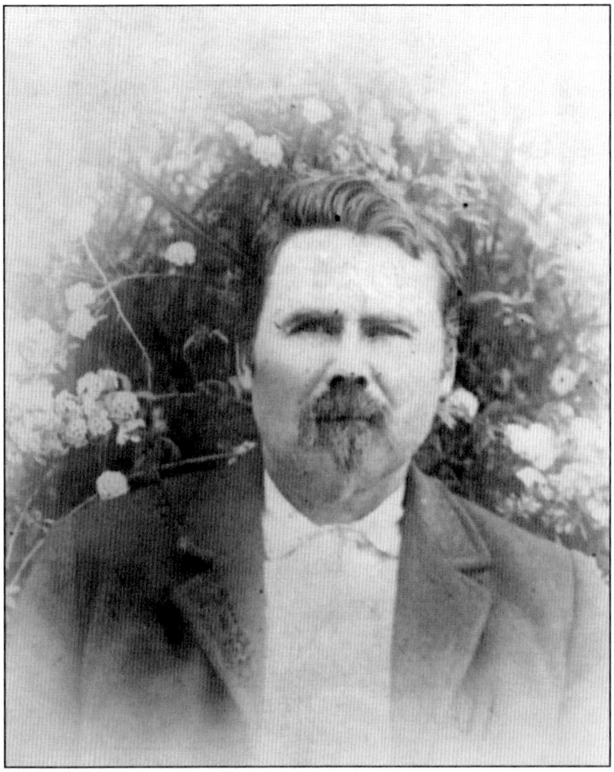

Pictured around 1880 is Brantley A. Mosley (1847–1919), who lived in the Lothair community. He was a son of Clement Angelsly Mosley and Anna "Nancy" Prevatt. In 1870, he married Lydia A. Currie (1848–1920), daughter of John Jackson Currie and Sarah Elizabeth Johnson.

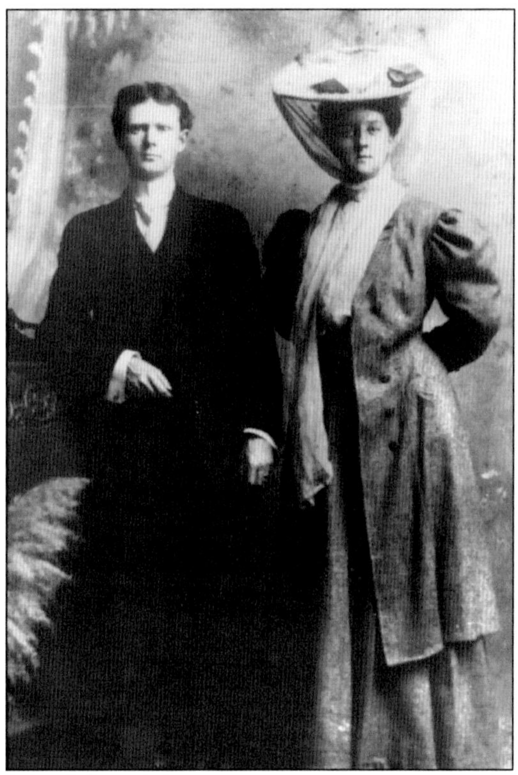

William Daniel Green and his wife, Eugenia Ward Green, are pictured together here. They were headmaster and teacher respectively at Crooked Run from 1920 to 1927, and both had long and distinguished careers in public school teaching.

Two

Town Life

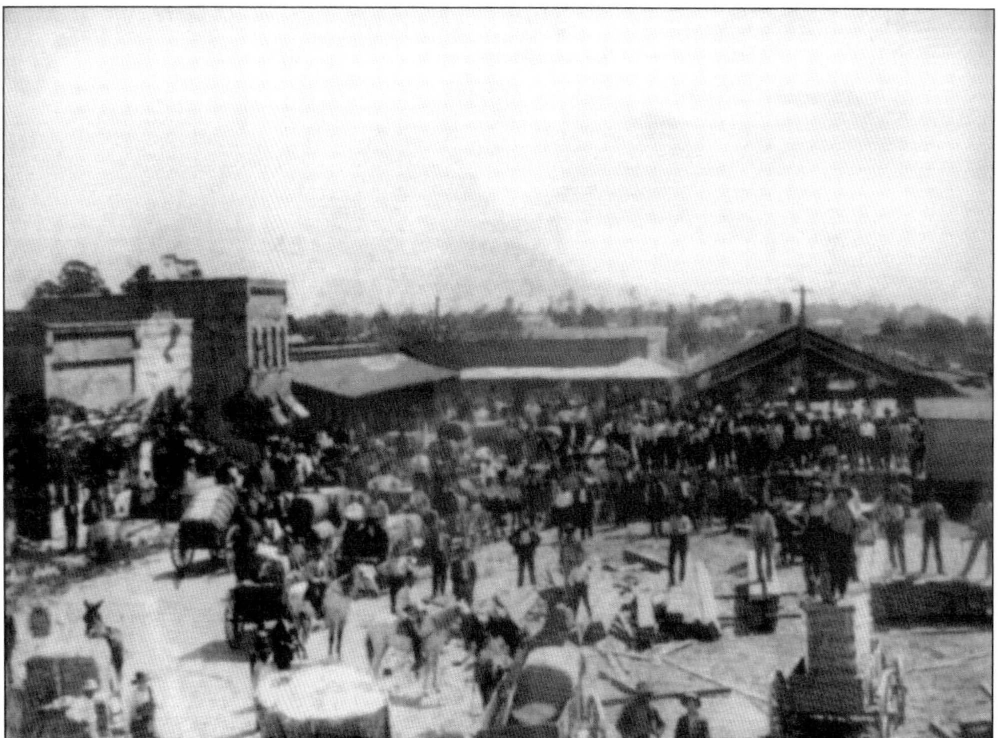

This 1908 scene in the new town of Soperton, Georgia, shows the streets filled with people bringing in their cotton for ginning and to be shipped out of town by rail. The railroad depot served as a gathering place and the hub of commercial activity in early-20th-century Soperton. (Courtesy of Patsy Gillis Ware and Lena Moring Wiley.)

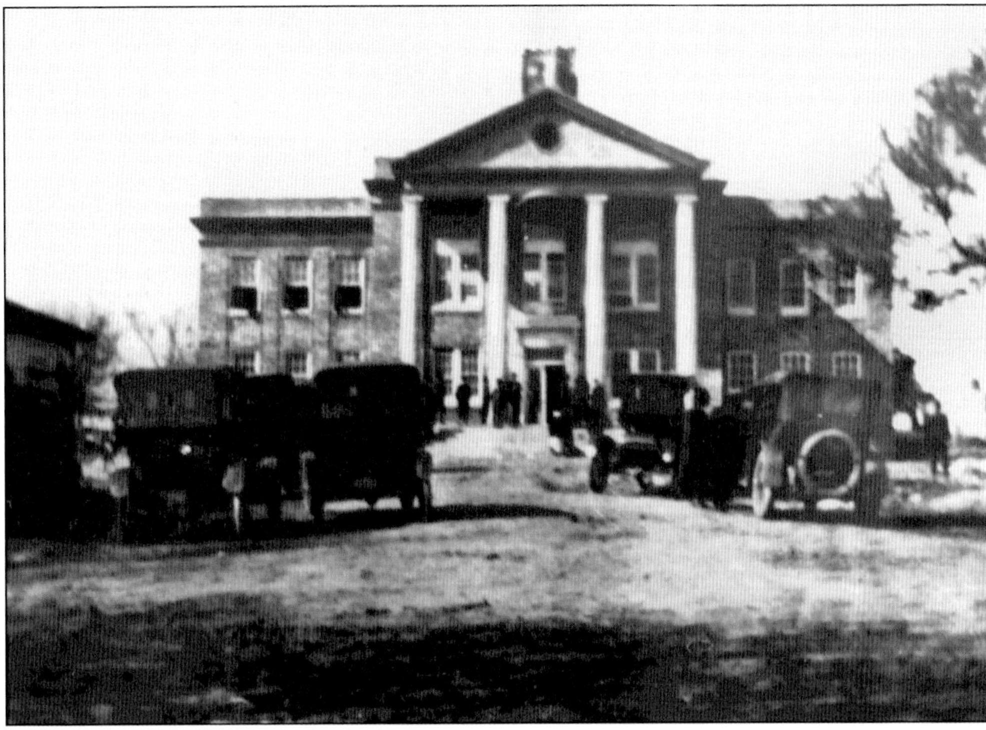

The Treutlen County Courthouse is shown here as it appeared in the 1920s. This is the original building, constructed shortly after the creation of the county in 1917.

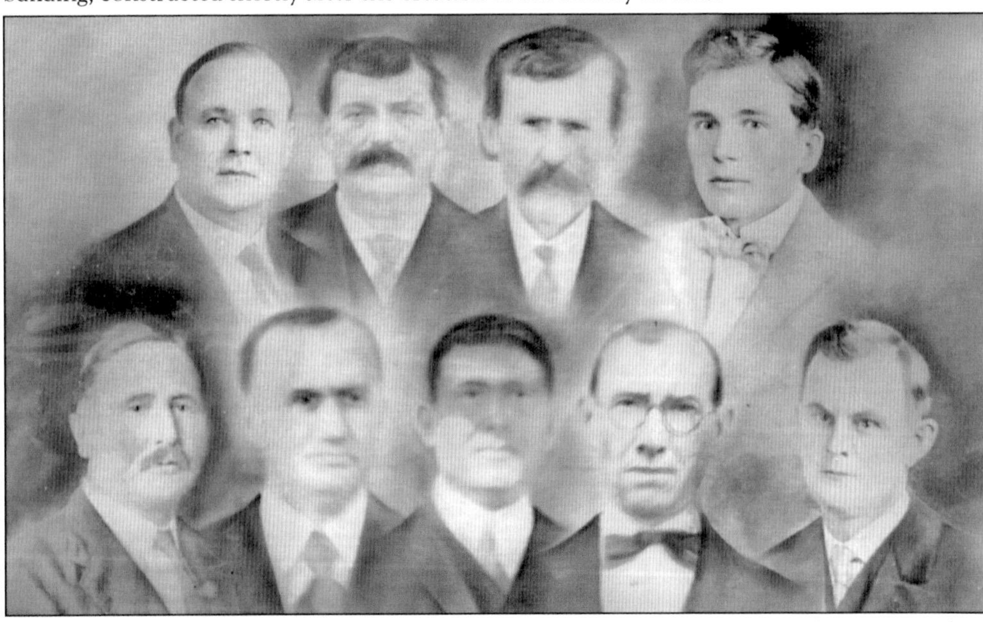

This is an old composite picture of the original officers of Treutlen County. The men are, from left to right, (first row) Dr. G. M. Barwick, state senator; R. E. Ward, school superintendent; M. B. Ware, sheriff; Joel Mullis, clerk of courts; and J. E. Tharpe, tax receiver; (second row) Neil Gillis Sr., ordinary; W. M. Courson, tax collector; Wiley Davis, coroner; and Jim L. Gillis Sr., House of Representatives.

Dr. O. B. Moye (left) is taking a ride with Soperton's first mayor, Benjamin Gillis, who served during the year 1902. Dr. Moye became the mayor in 1905 and served through 1906.

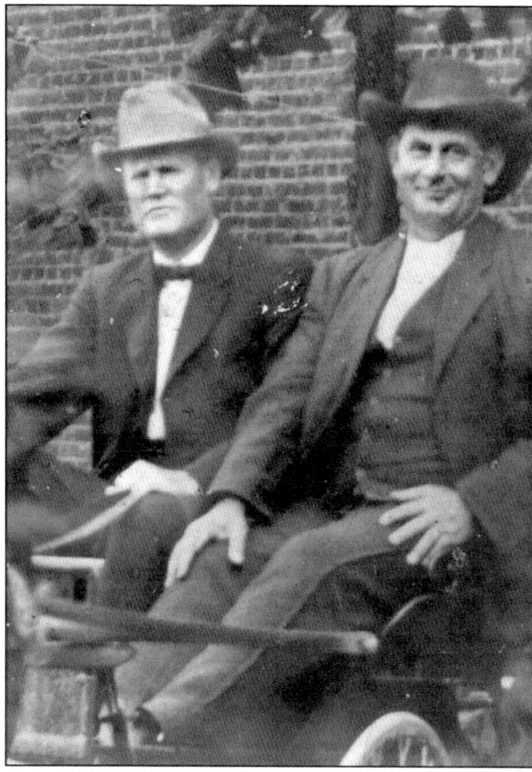

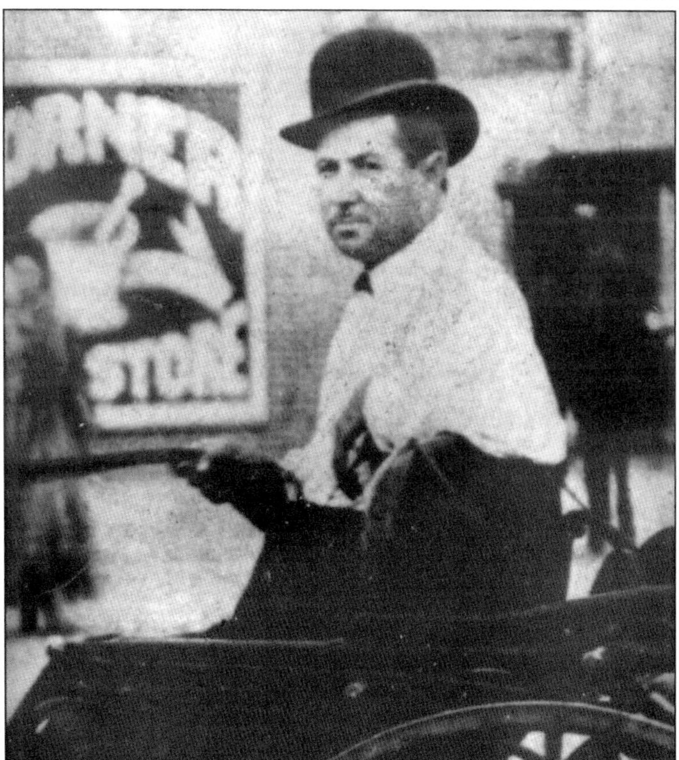

A son of Noah and Isabella Mishoe of Horry County, South Carolina, Wiley Mishoe and his wife, Georgianna, and their three children, arrived in Soperton in 1903. He was elected mayor that year, the same year he appeared in this photograph.

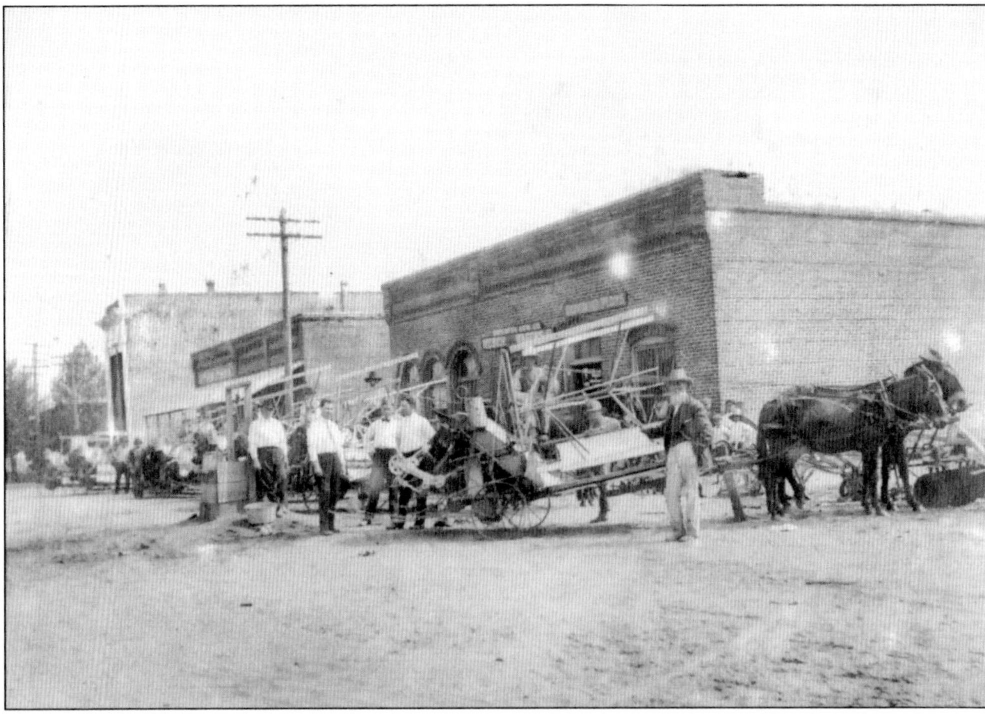

This 1913 scene depicts the Soperton Hardware Company receiving a delivery of a carload of Deering Binders. Notice the mules being used to pull them.

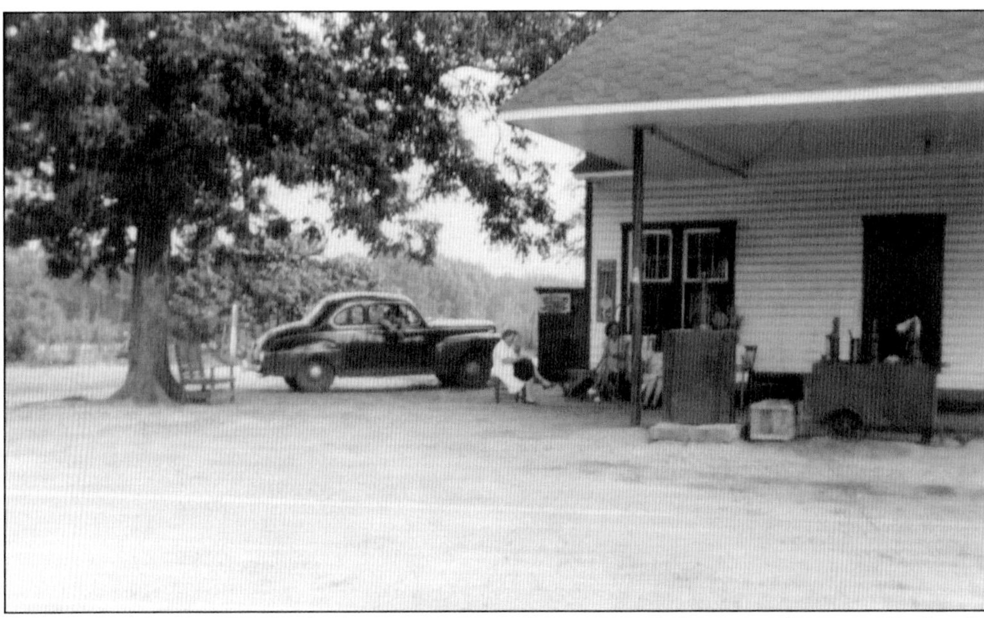

Clyde Phillips and his wife, the former Mary Moxley, operated this general store in Zaidee for several decades in the mid-20th century. In addition to groceries, meats, and hardware items, they sold gasoline and kerosene. (Courtesy of Bill Phillips.)

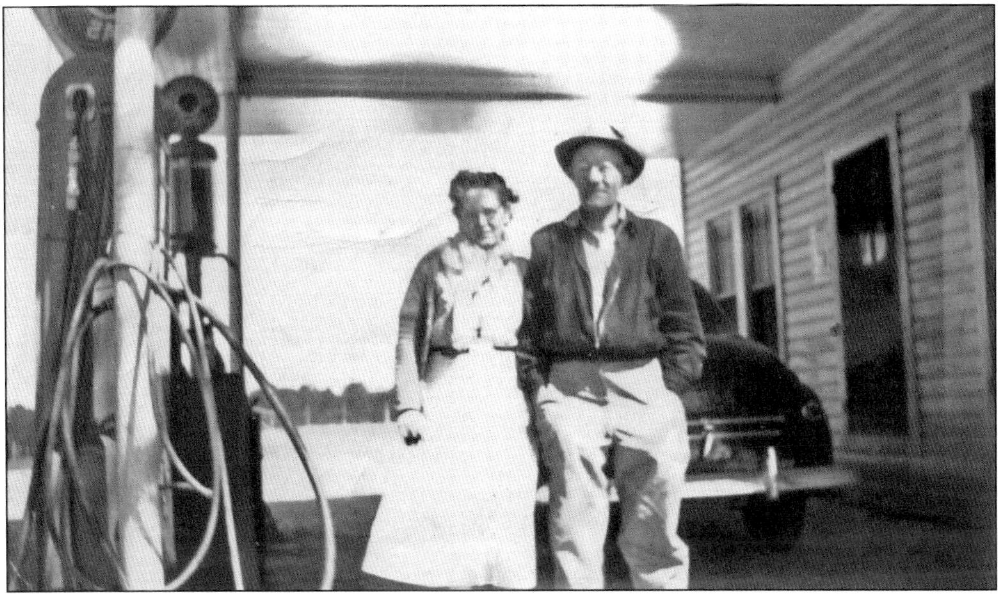

Shown standing in front of their store in Zaidee are Edward Clyde "Pat" Palmer (1899–1973) and his wife, the former Annie Clyde Braddy (1900–1973), around 1940. The Palmers operated their store for several decades during the mid-20th century. It served as the hub of activity in the Zaidee community.

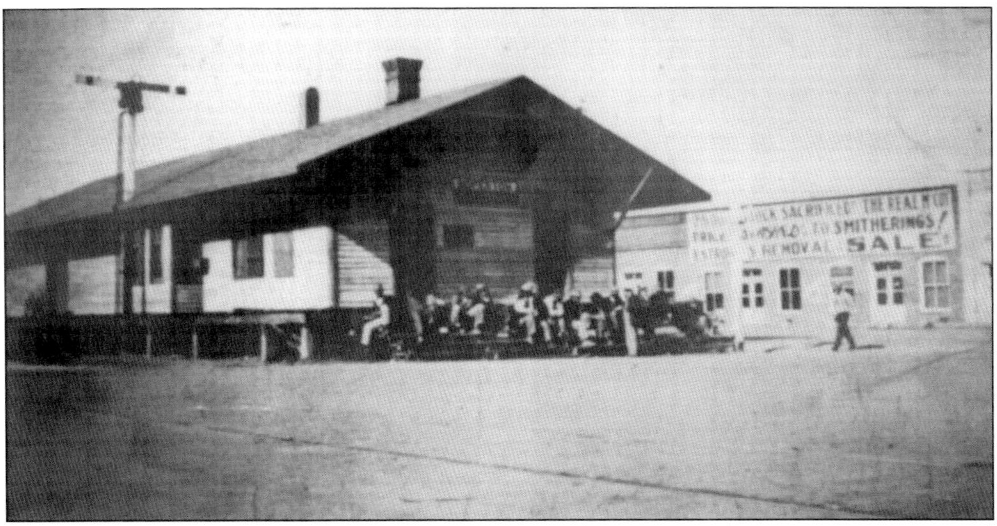

The old railroad depot was moved from the central part of Soperton. In later years, it was renovated and used as the city hall. It is currently on Martin Luther King Street.

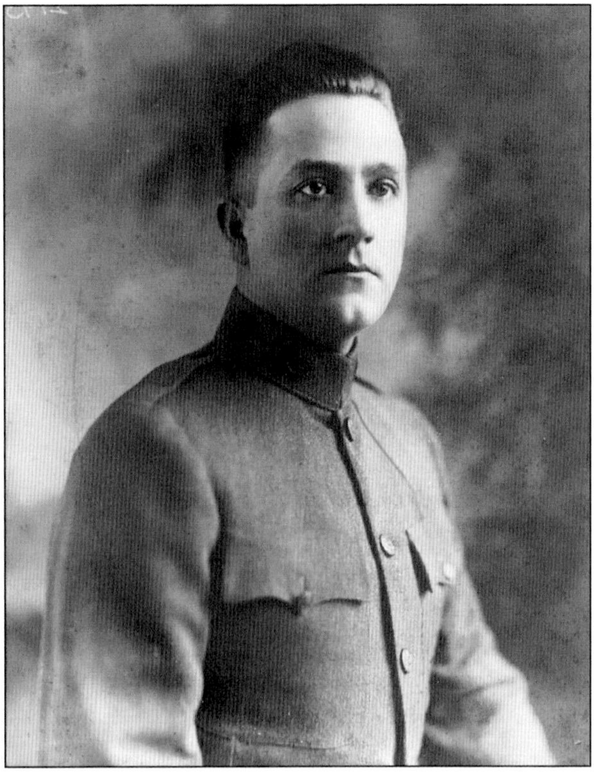

Posing in his World War I uniform is Neil Lee Gillis Jr. (1894–1934). A son of Neil Lee Gillis and Lougenia Youmans, he married Jennie Belle Perry (1895–1987), and they were the parents of Lougenia (Gabard), Neil Lee III, and Benjamin Kennon. (Courtesy of Kennon Gillis.)

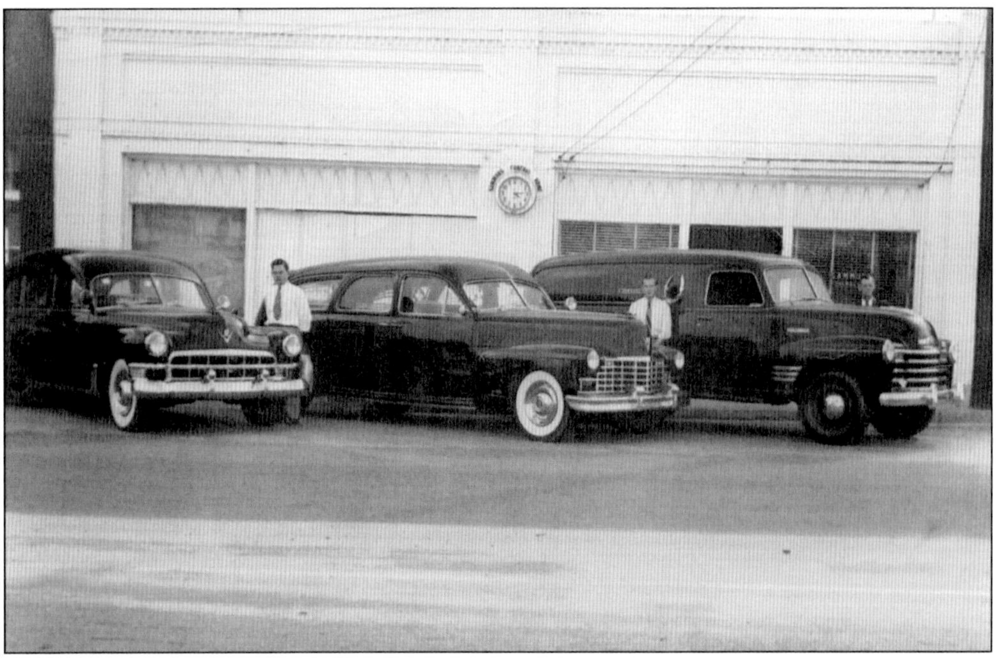

The Sammons Funeral Home had its beginning in January 1917, when the late W. W. Sammons purchased a stock of caskets from Charlie Peterson, who was selling his hardware business. The caskets were housed in this store building in Soperton. In 1919, he bought his first hearse and began a full-scale funeral business.

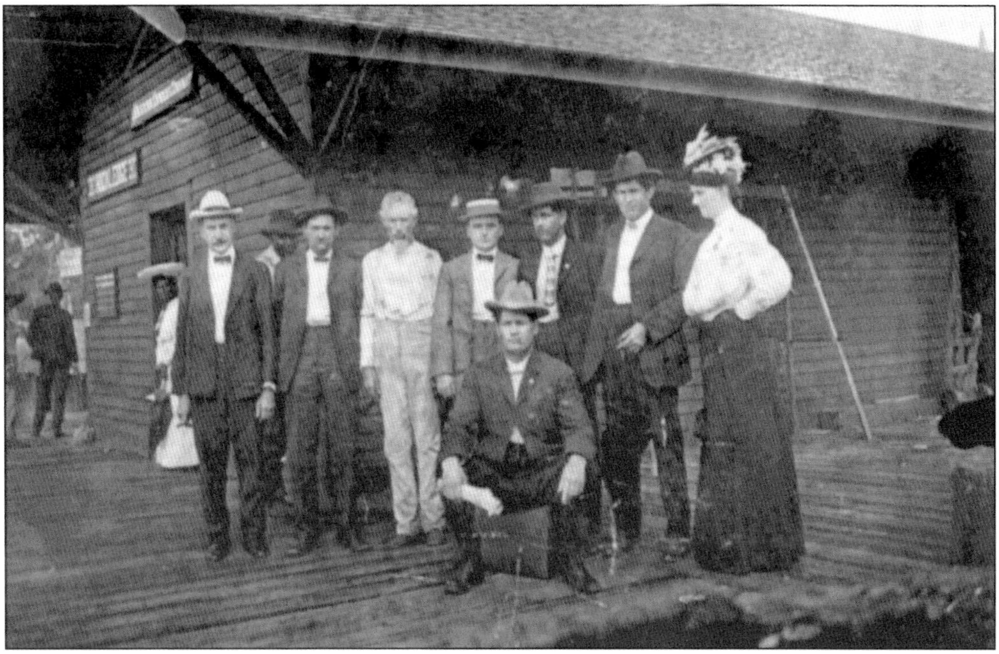

People are waiting for the train at Rockledge Depot in this photograph, taken before 1911. Among those identified are Noah and Clara Thompkins (far left), William "Bill" Greenway (without a hat), James M. Thigpen (seated), and Mr. and Mrs. John Thigpen (far right). The man wearing a straw hat is Jesse Jordan, the depot agent.

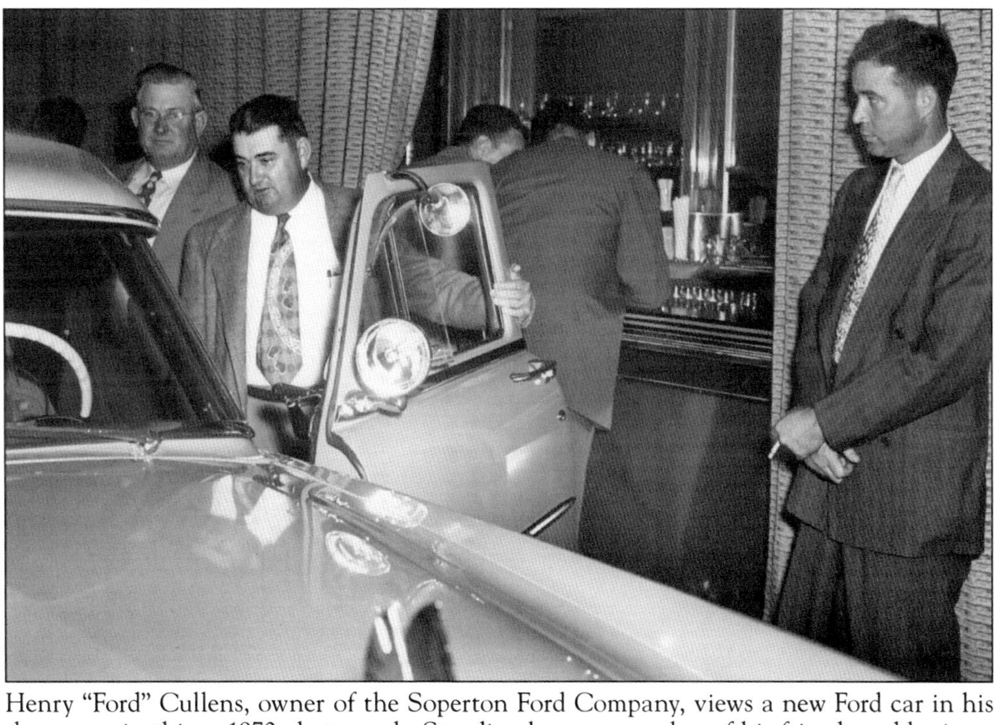

Henry "Ford" Cullens, owner of the Soperton Ford Company, views a new Ford car in his showroom in this c. 1970 photograph. Standing by are a number of his friends and business partners. (Courtesy of Tommy Cullens.)

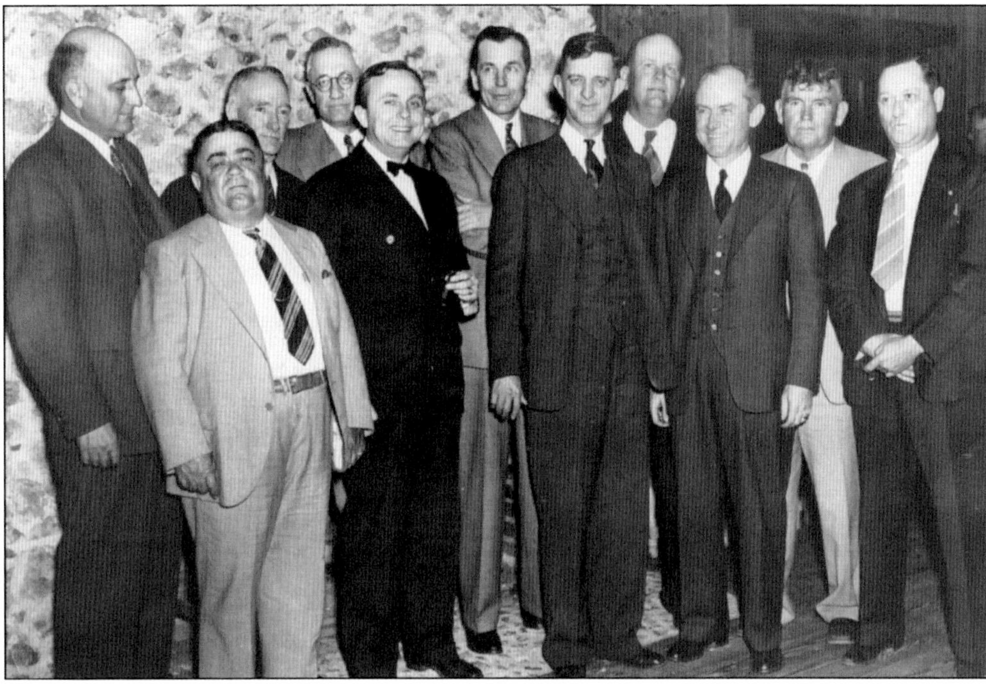

James C. "Jim" Fowler, James "Jim L." Gillis Sr., Hilton Phillips, and Thomas Cullens are some of the men included in this group of civic leaders. They are standing in front of the fireplace in the Community House, which was built by the WPA during the 1930s. (Courtesy of Tommy Cullens.)

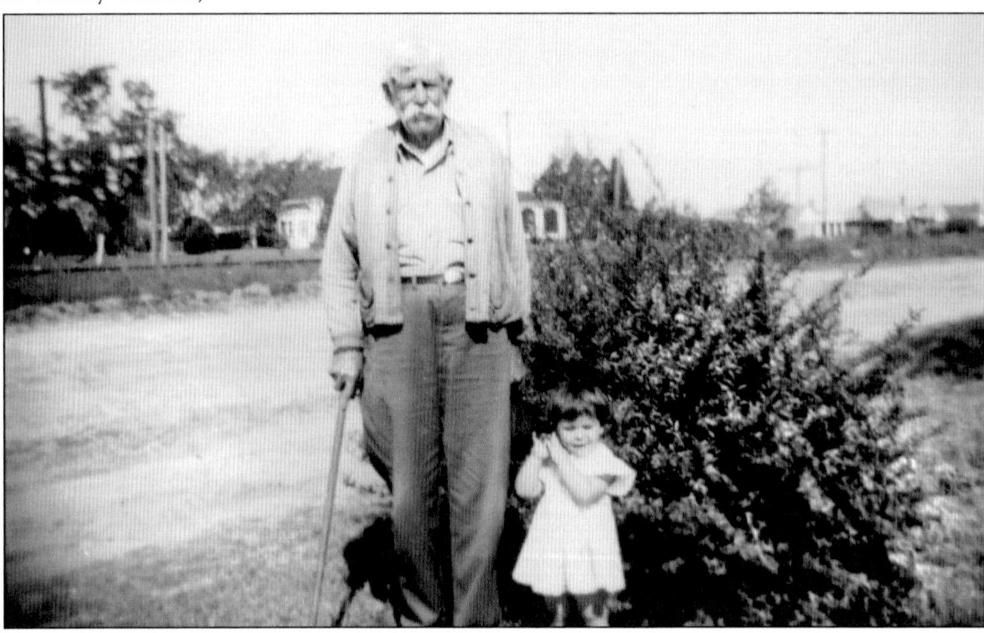

James D. "Jim" Calhoun (1861–1955) takes a stroll in the late 1950s on Railroad Avenue near his home with his great-granddaughter, Terrie Smith. Jim was a son of James Rufus Calhoun and Mary Eleanor Phillips. In 1896, he married Sarah J. Palmer (1875–1927), daughter of Dr. William Tootle "Bill" Palmer. (Courtesy of Reba Calhoun.)

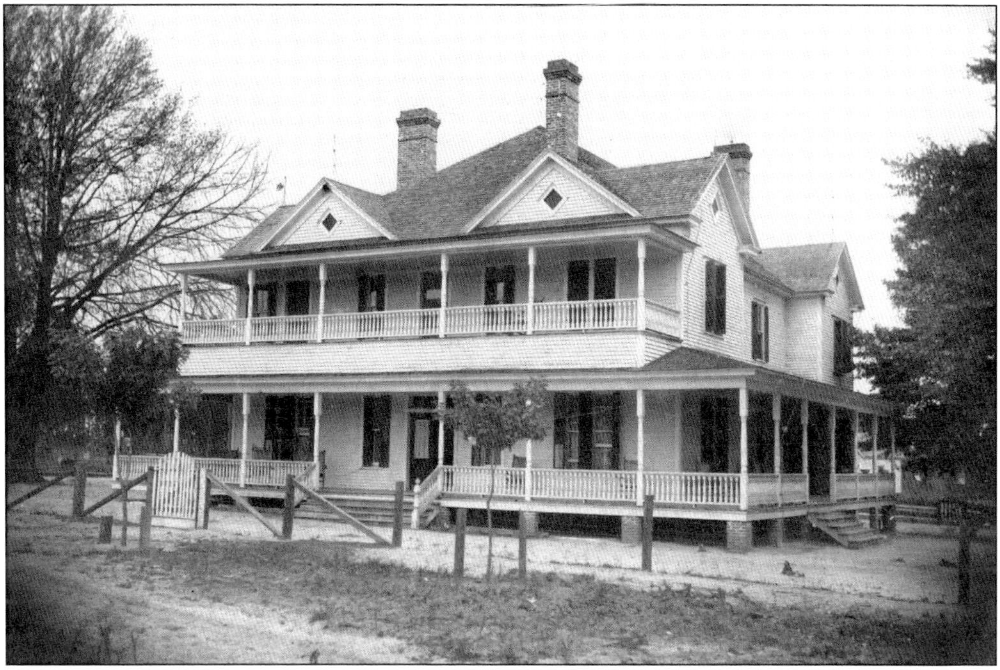

The Gillis Springs Hotel is shown here about 1920. The Gillis Springs Recreational Resort was begun by Roderick Gillis in 1902 and was in operation about eight years. People who came to the springs to bathe in the mineral waters were housed here. (Courtesy of Hal Jones.)

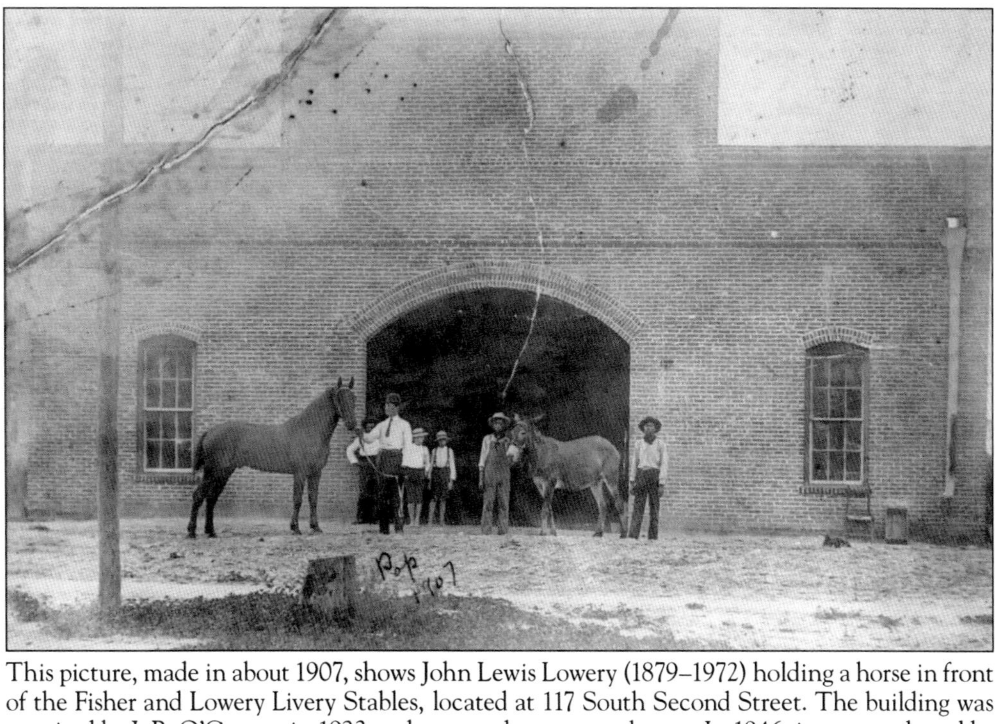

This picture, made in about 1907, shows John Lewis Lowery (1879–1972) holding a horse in front of the Fisher and Lowery Livery Stables, located at 117 South Second Street. The building was acquired by J. B. O'Conner in 1923 and was used as a general store. In 1946, it was purchased by Webb's Firestone Store.

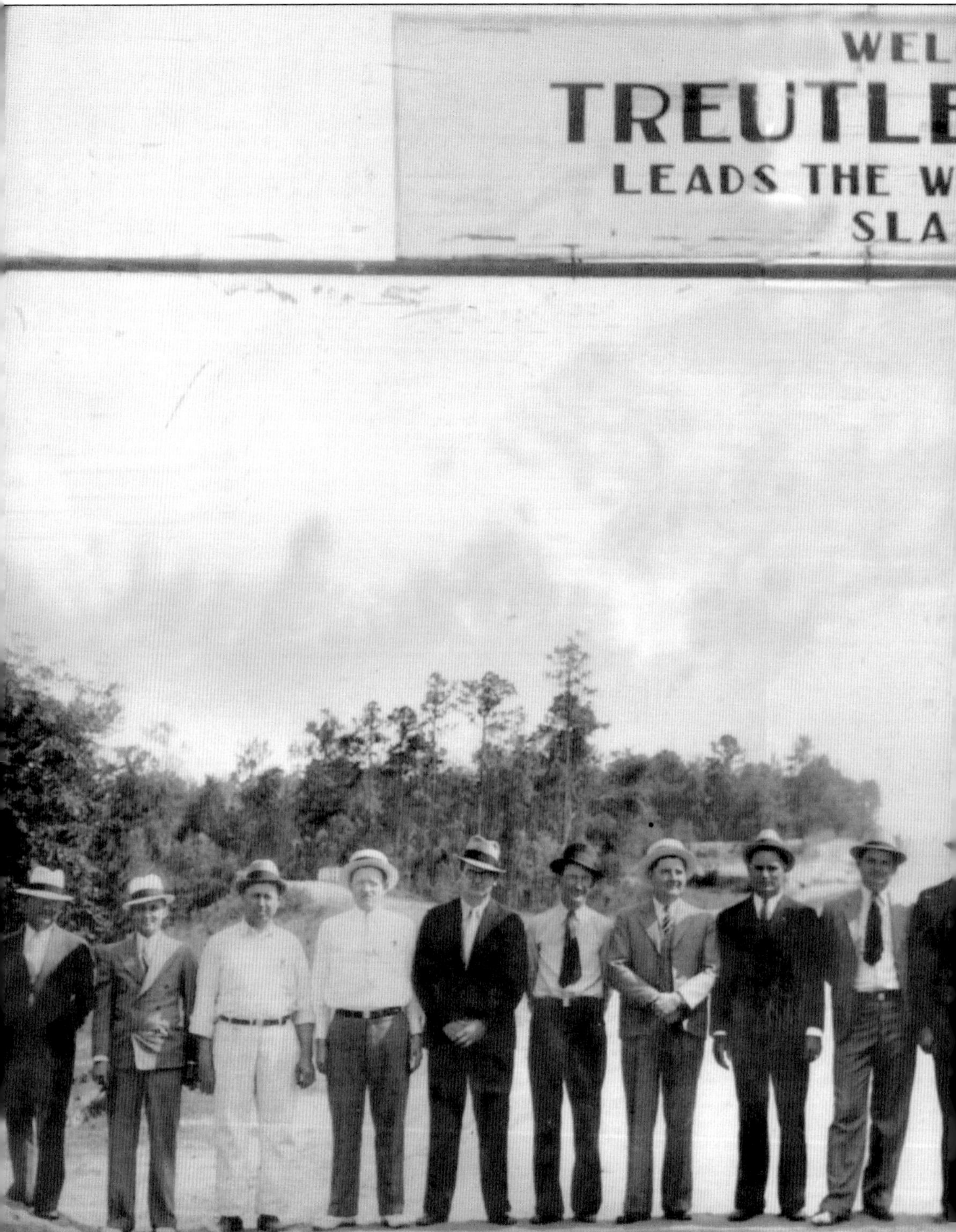

This photograph was made in Treutlen County in the 1930s. The Soperton Lions Club erected the sign, which spanned the unpaved road leading from Dublin to Soperton, to welcome visitors

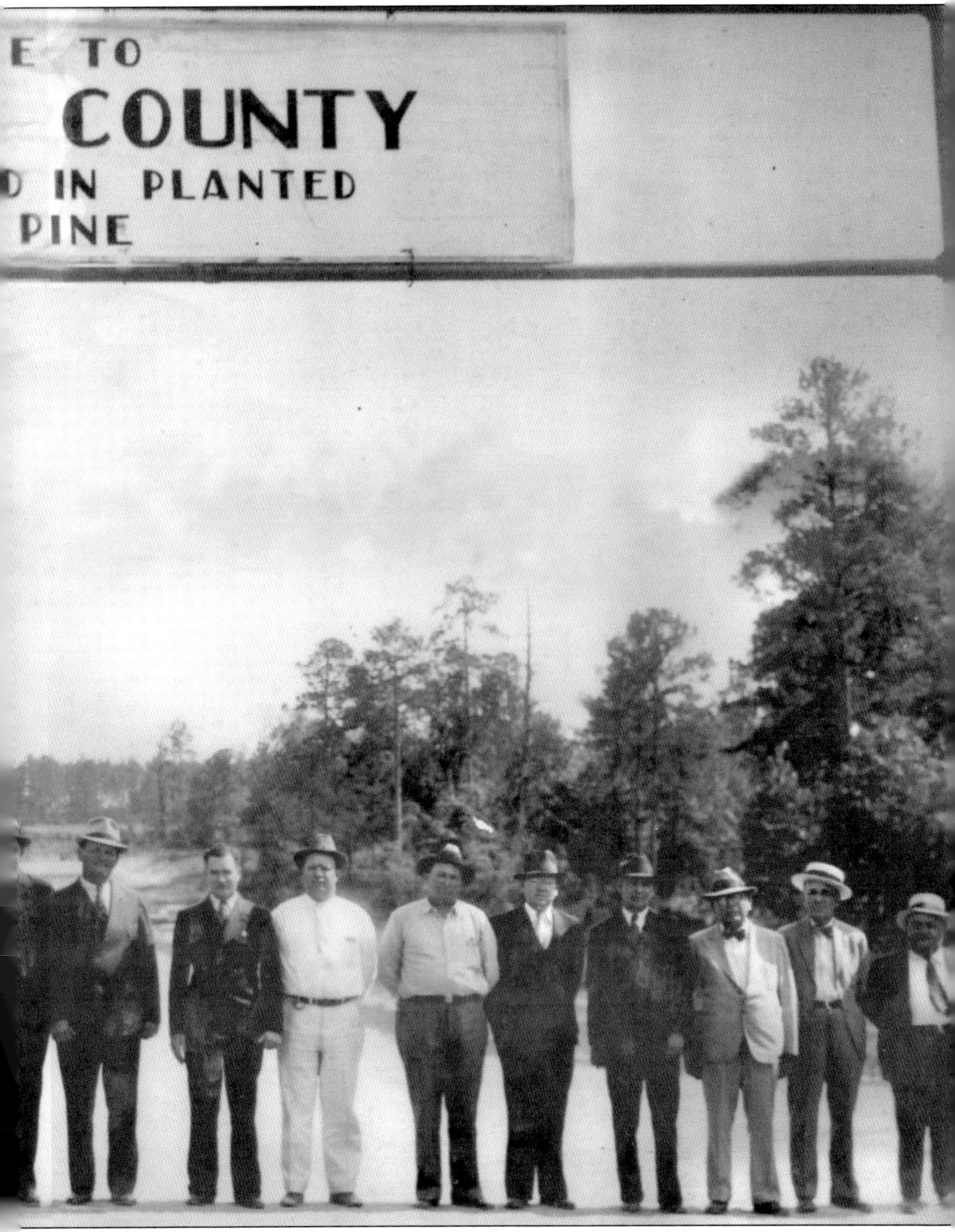

to the county and to inform them of the county's leadership in reforestation.

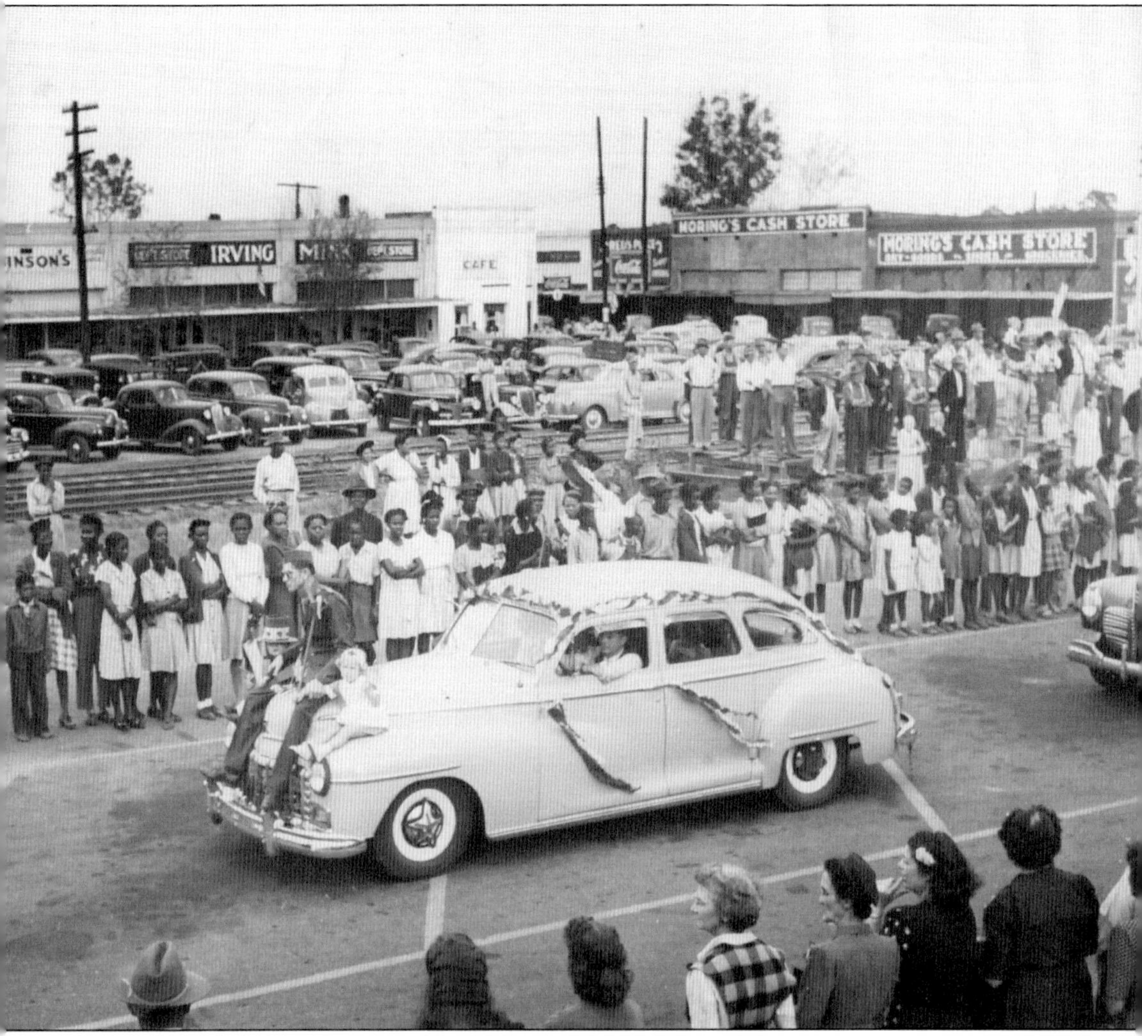

This is a picture of the famous 1947 Veterans Parade in Soperton. Riding on the car are Julian Warnock (center), Sandra Calhoun Odom, and Henry G. Shuman III; Marion L. Calhoun is the driver. (Courtesy of Sandra Calhoun Odom.)

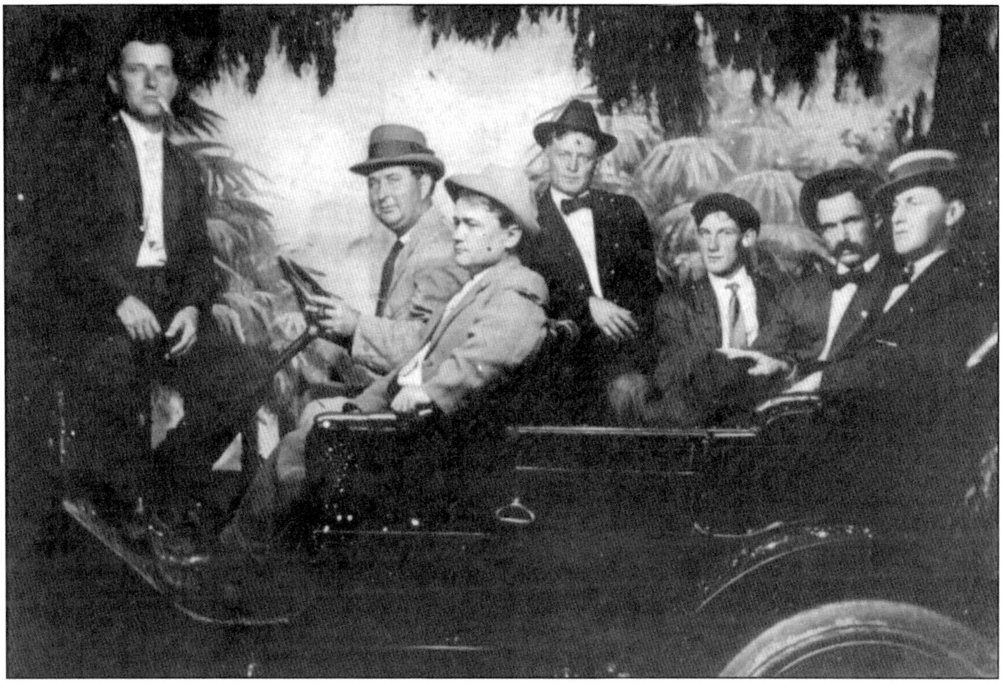

This picture, made about 1902, shows Soperton's pioneers—(in no particular order) Herschel Daly, James Pullen, Thomas Cullen, Willis Wade, John Gillis, Thomas Pritchett, and John Fisher. They were all instrumental in the founding of the town of Soperton and held different city offices during their lifetimes.

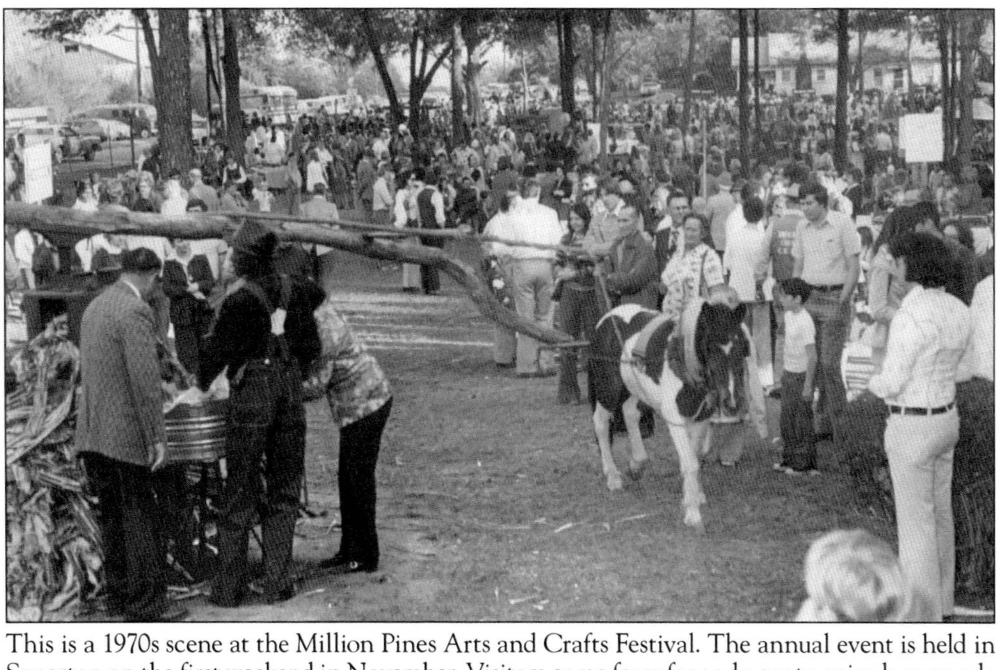

This is a 1970s scene at the Million Pines Arts and Crafts Festival. The annual event is held in Soperton on the first weekend in November. Visitors come from far and near to enjoy homemade crafts, exhibits, food, and live entertainment. A Shetland pony has replaced the traditional mule to turn the cane grinder.

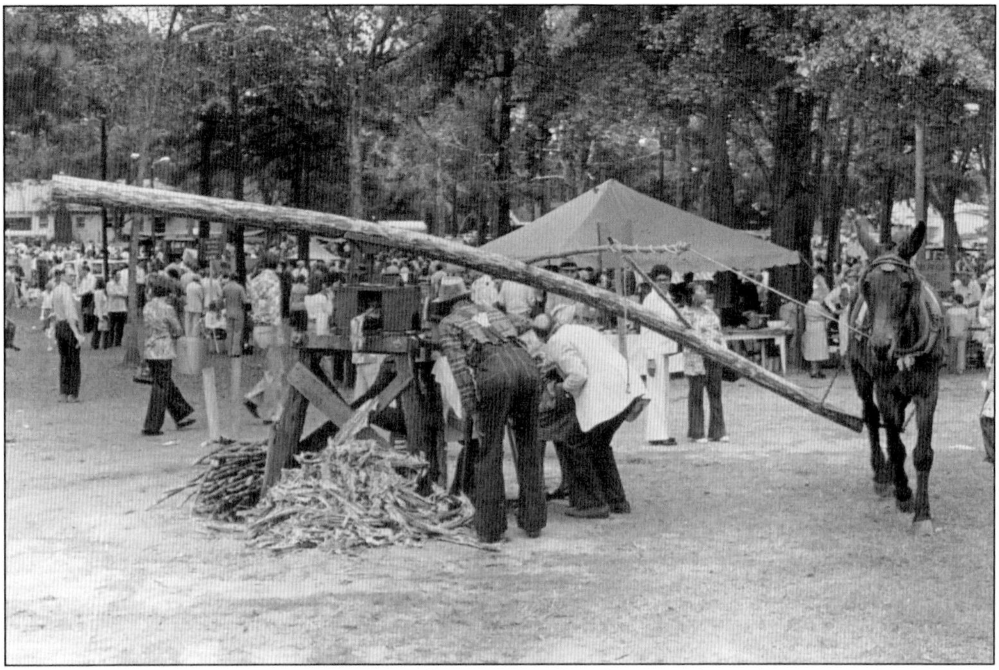

These people are grinding cane with the help of a mule. The juice from the cane is then cooked in a large iron kettle to make syrup, a staple in the South. This is just one of the many exhibits at the annual Million Pines Arts and Crafts Festival held at Iva Park in Soperton.

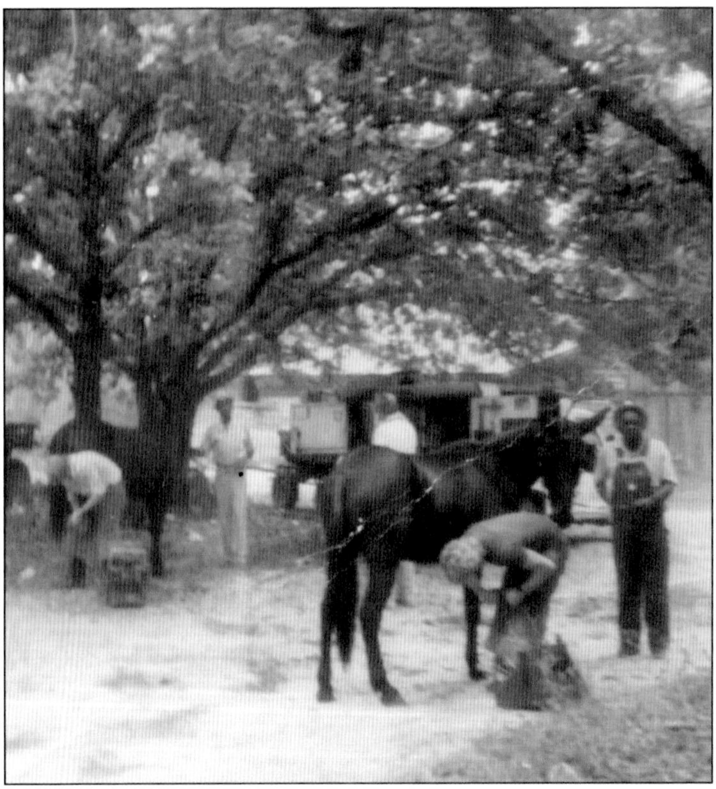

These men are shoeing mules at Million Pines, the farm of James C. "Jim" Fowler, located near Soperton.

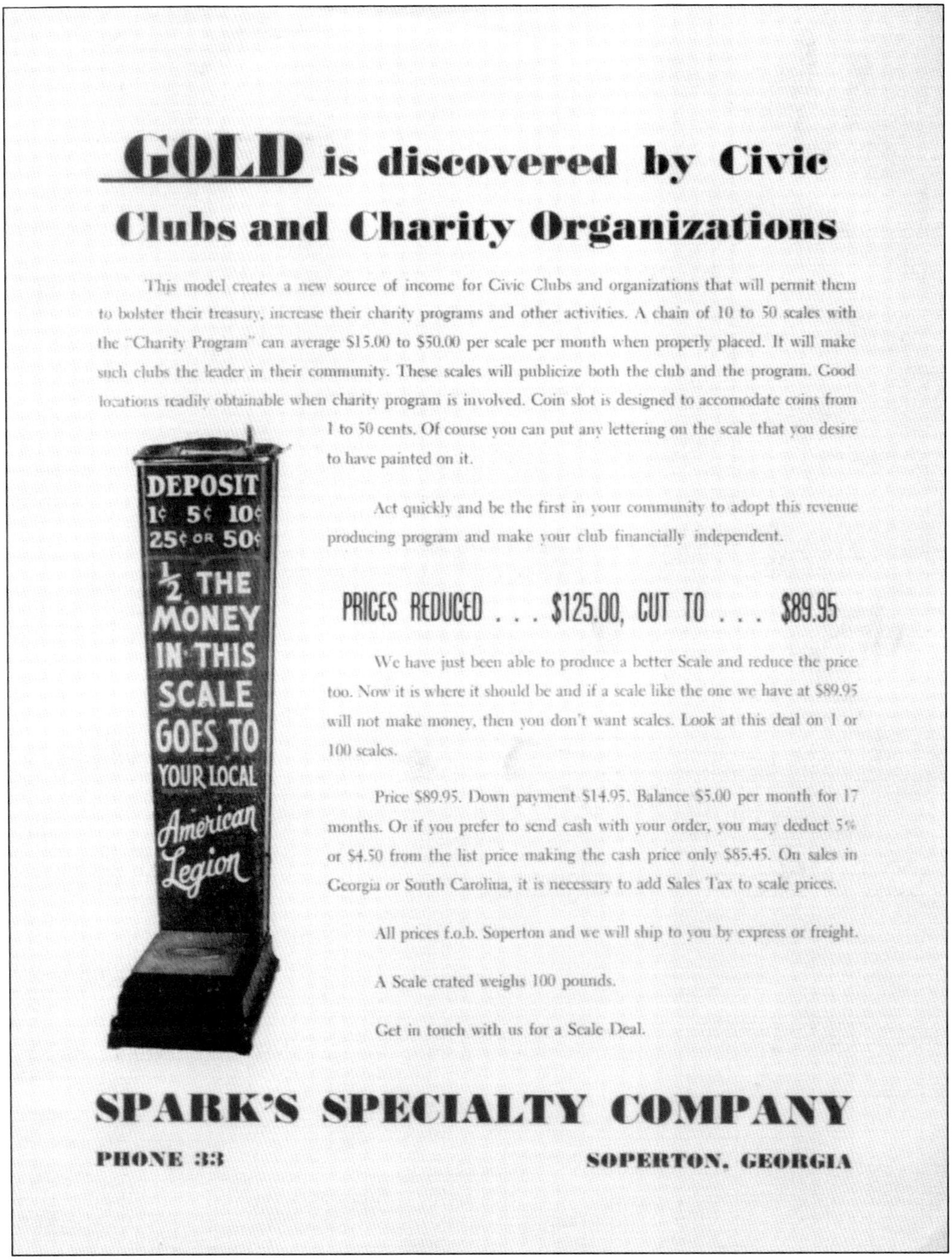

Many will remember the tall scales that once stood on the streets of every town in the early to mid-20th century. This is an advertisement for Spark's Scales as a fund-raiser for civic clubs. This company was located in Soperton.

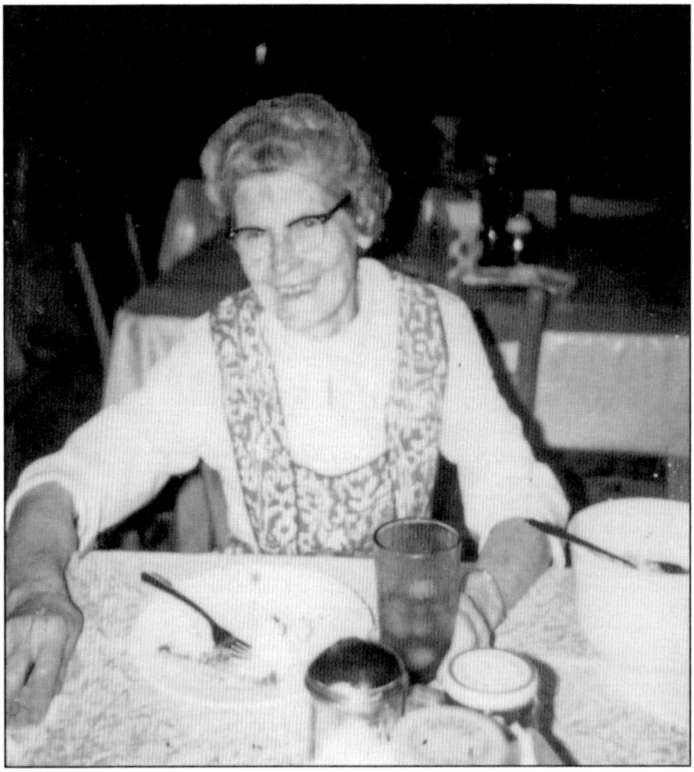

Mamie Braddy Ricks (1896–1985) is pictured sitting at one of the tables in her boardinghouse, which she operated in Soperton for approximately 40 years. Mamie was the 12th of 14 children born to Moses Algerine Braddy and Florence Herndon. She married George M. Ricks (1894–1951).

This 1910 photograph below shows the Soperton Post Office. Radford Cleaners and attorney Carlton Warnock later used this building, and the *Soperton News* was located on this same block. Note the boardinghouse in the background.

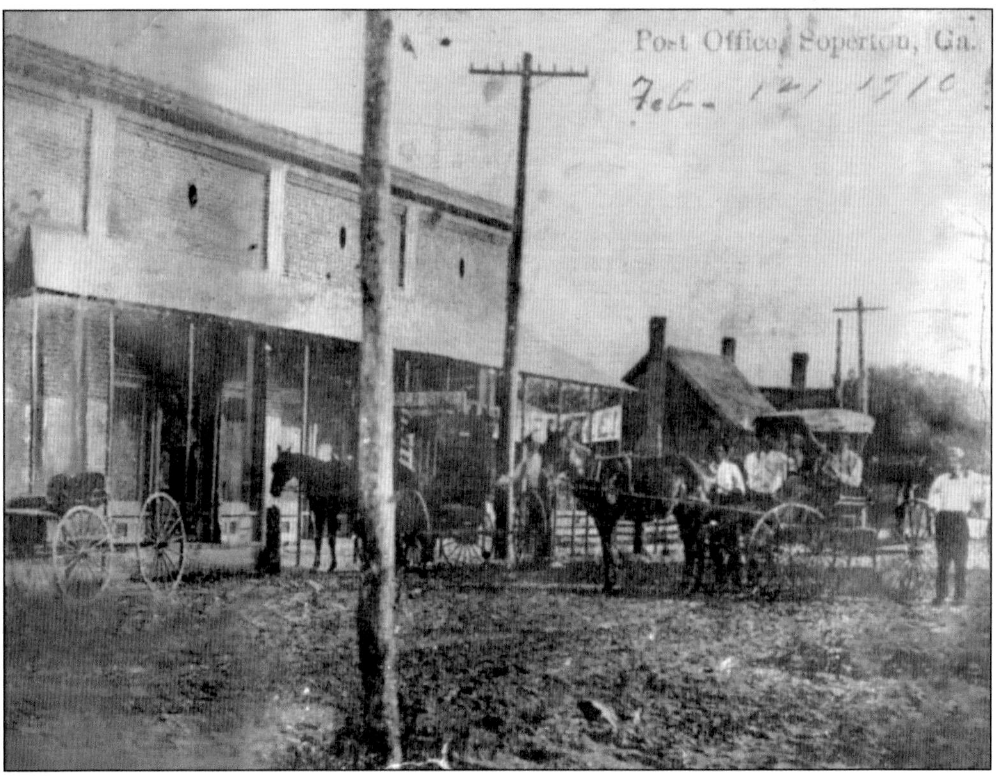

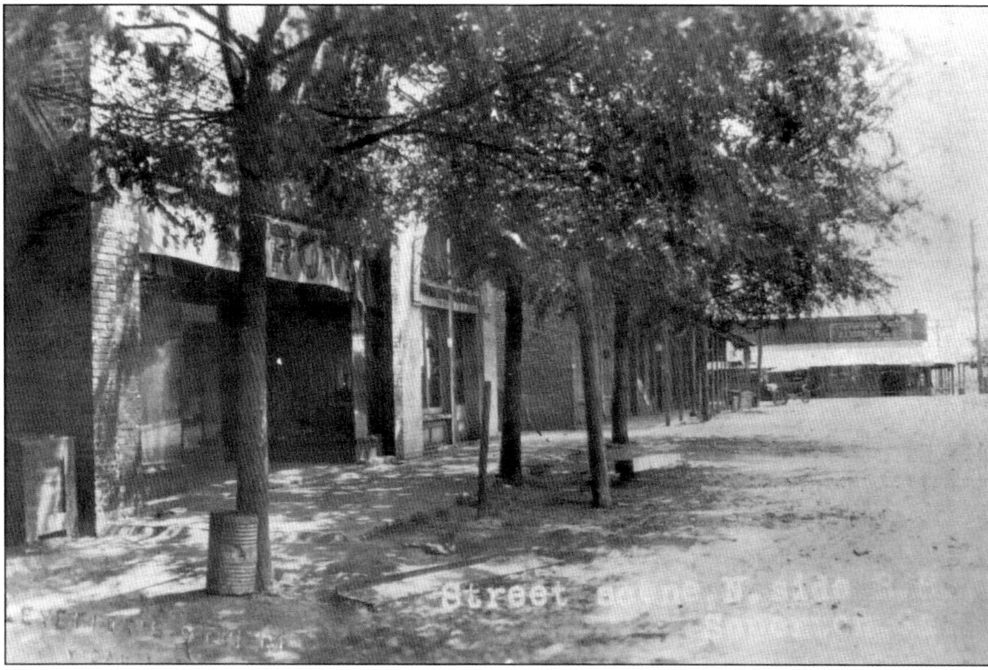

Soperton was incorporated as a town on December 17, 1902. It is the county seat and the only incorporated town in Treutlen County. The town was named for Benjamin Franklin Soper, a construction engineer with the Macon, Dublin, and Savannah Railroad (MD&S). This is a view of an early street scene.

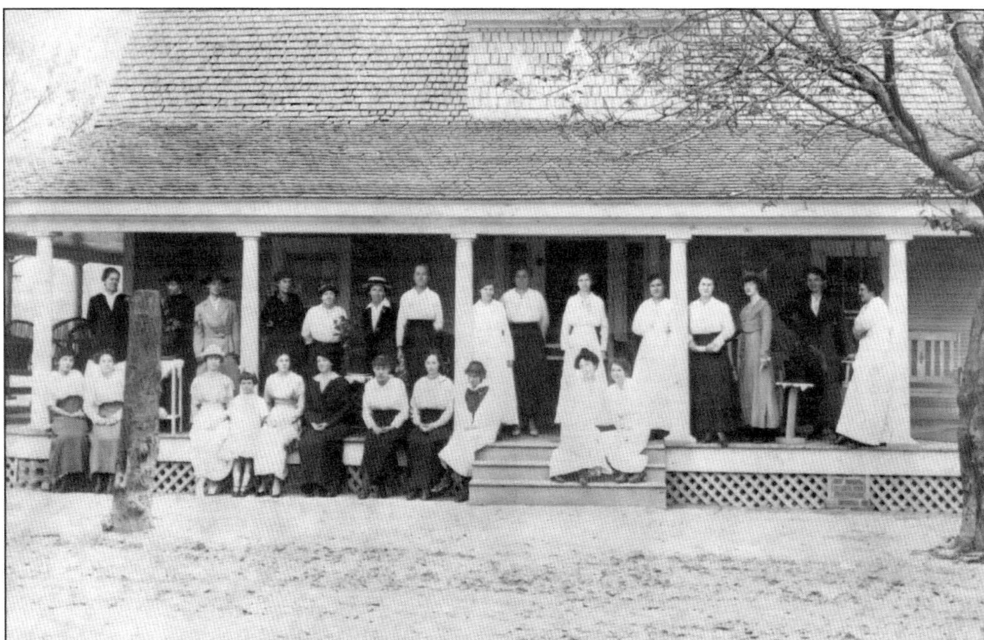

This is the home of Dr. and Mrs. W. H. Worrill in Soperton in 1916. It was located on Second Street South and Georgia Avenue. The ladies on the porch are enjoying a bridal tea given in honor of Pearl Gillis, who soon married John A. Thigpen.

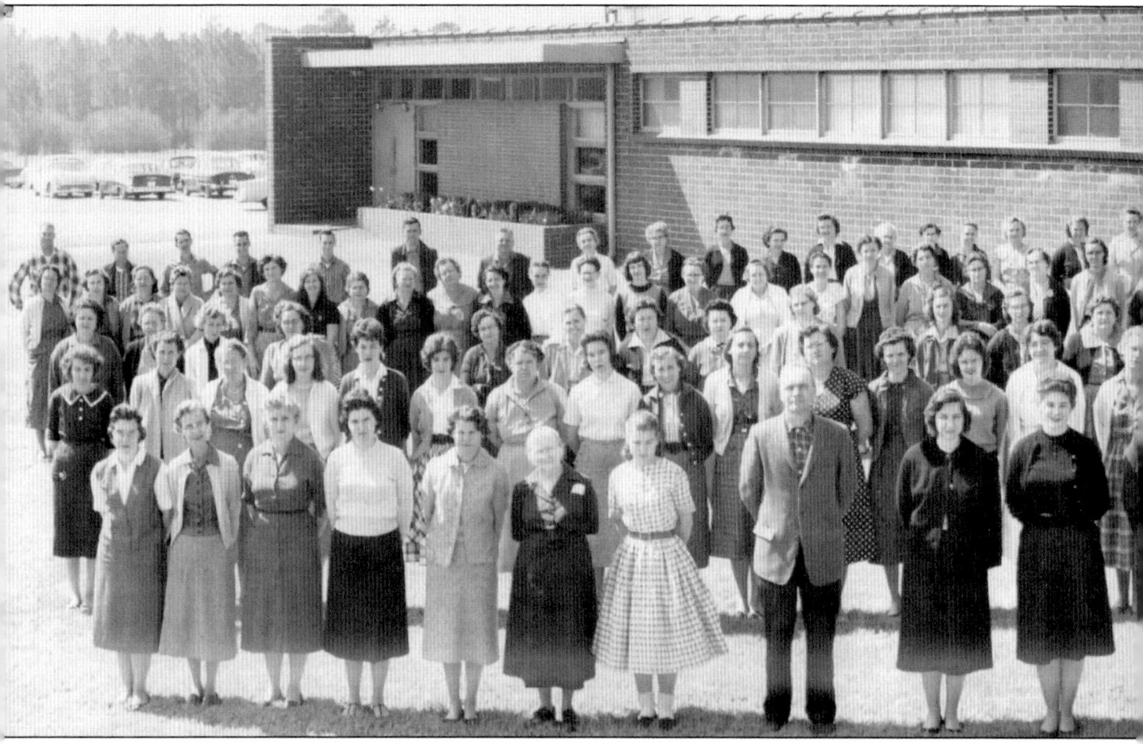

In this *c.* 1960 photograph, Will Peterson, founder, owner, and manager of the Soperton Manufacturing

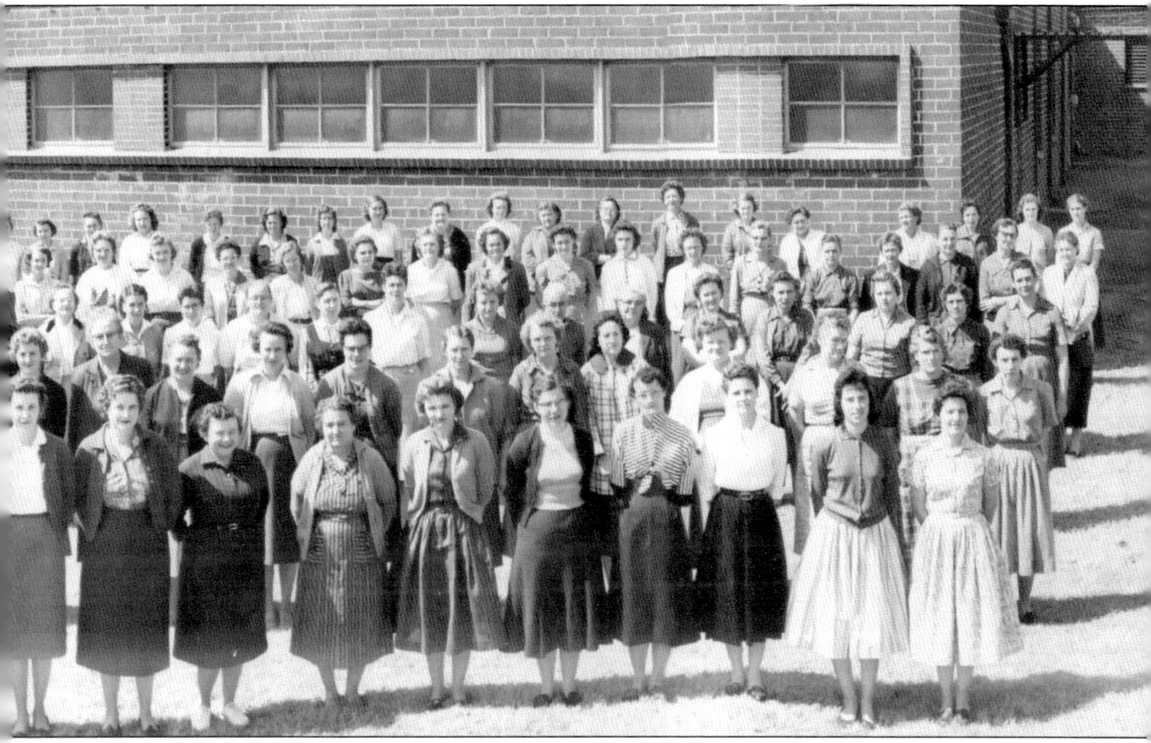

Company, is shown in front of the factory with his employees (first row, eighth from the left).

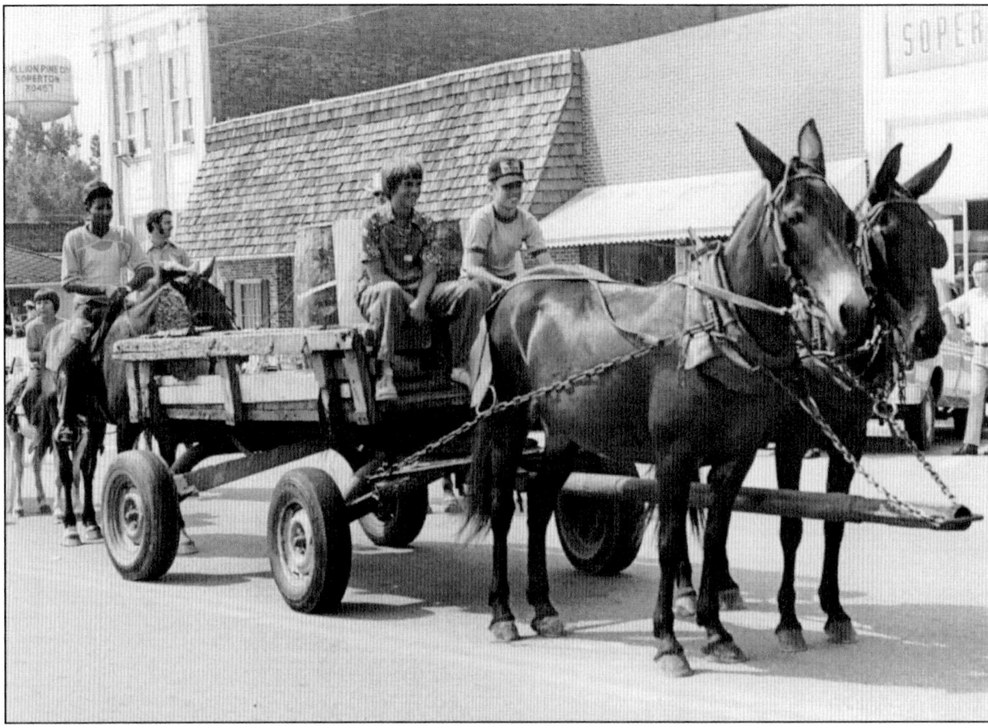

These boys are enjoying a ride in a Fourth of July parade in downtown Soperton, the "Million Pines City." Jim Ellington (left) and an unidentified friend are shown sitting on a mule-drawn wagon that was used to harvest tar (sap) from pine trees. (Courtesy of Jack Ellington.)

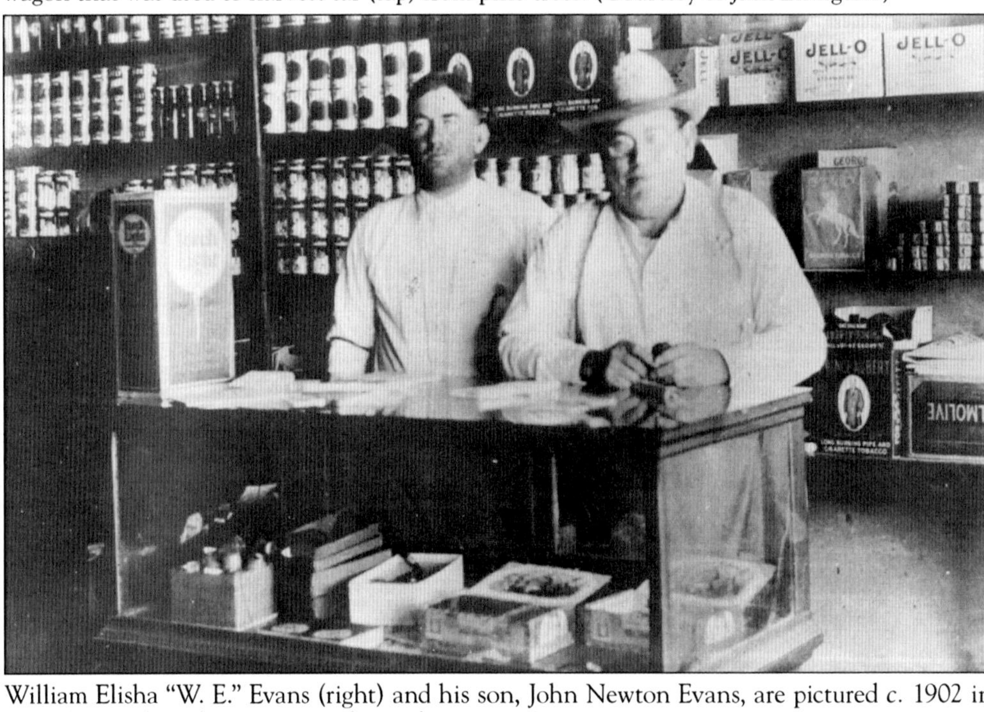

William Elisha "W. E." Evans (right) and his son, John Newton Evans, are pictured *c.* 1902 in their dry-goods and grocery store located on Main Street in Soperton.

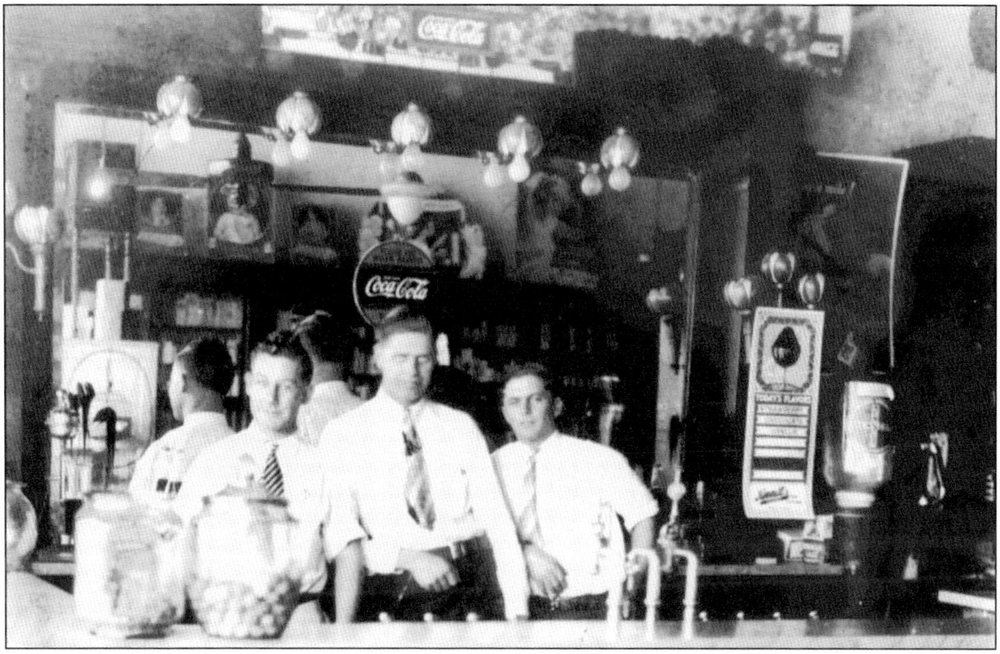

This picture shows the interior of the Soperton Pharmacy around 1925. From left to right are James "Jim" Barwick, Meadie W. Williamson, and Fred Chivers. This drugstore remains in business today in the original building.

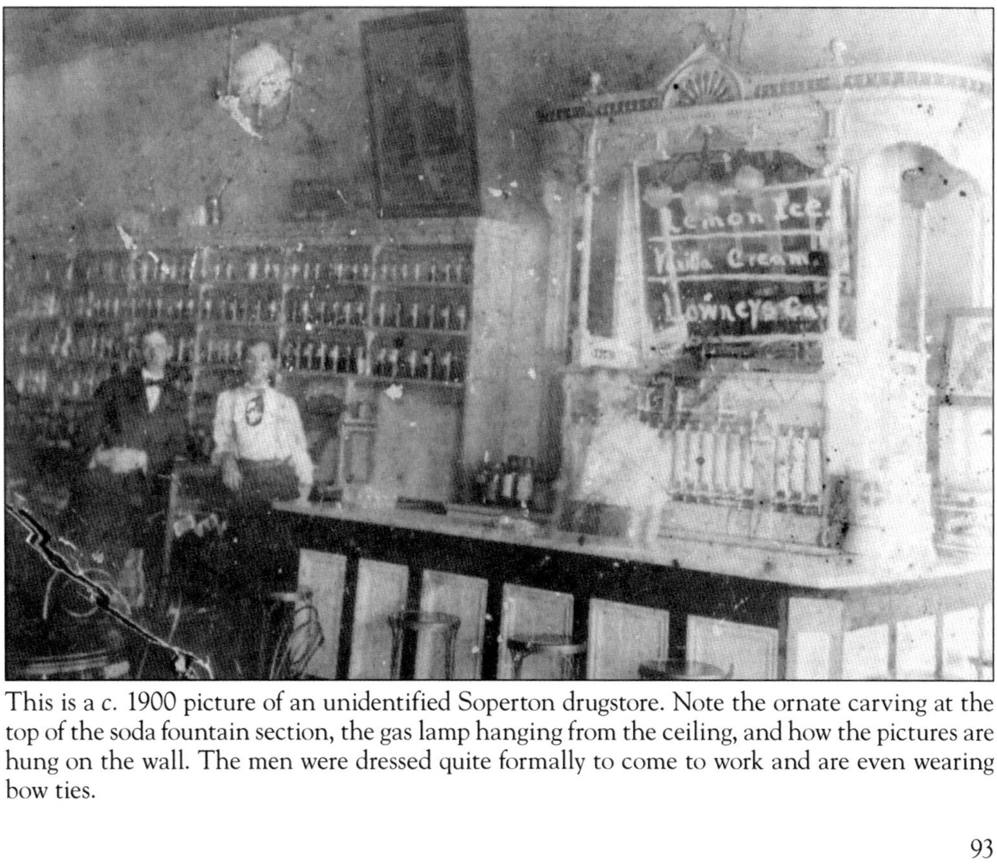

This is a *c.* 1900 picture of an unidentified Soperton drugstore. Note the ornate carving at the top of the soda fountain section, the gas lamp hanging from the ceiling, and how the pictures are hung on the wall. The men were dressed quite formally to come to work and are even wearing bow ties.

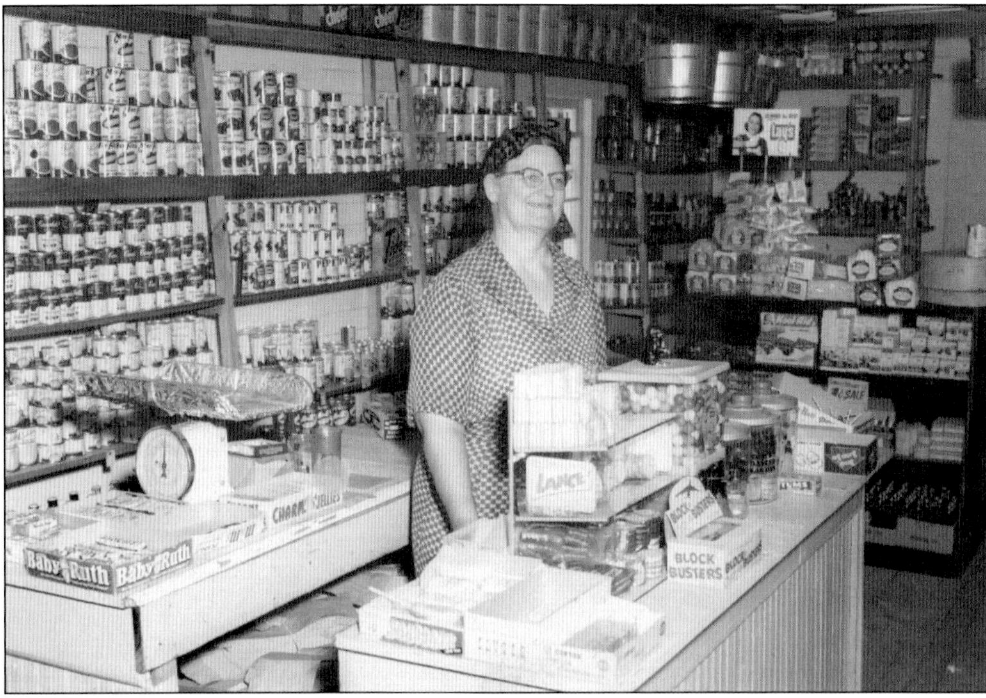

Thelma Ricks Herrmann is shown tending the family store, known as Herrmann Villa, located in Blackville. Thelma was a daughter of Daniel Tilton "D. T." Ricks and Arrilla Youngblood. She is remembered as always having her long, thick hair braided and wrapped neatly around her head. (Courtesy of Tracy Manning Gillikin.)

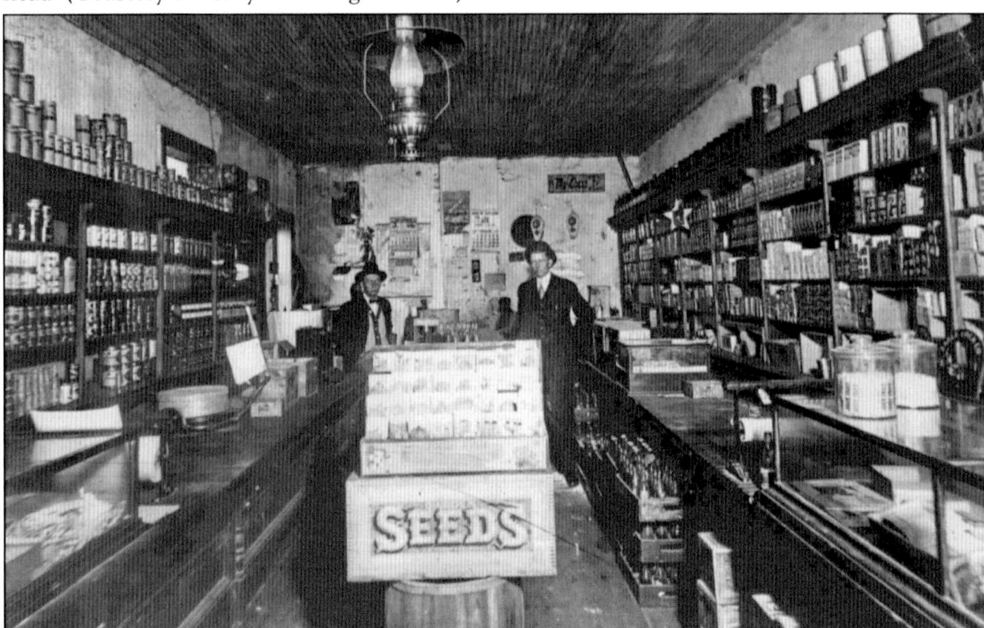

J. A. Thigpen's store is pictured here around 1915. It was located at 111 West Railroad Avenue. Tending the store are J. A. Thigpen (right) and his assistant, a Mr. Savage. This store sold a wide variety of merchandise. Notice the hoop of cheese on the counter at left.

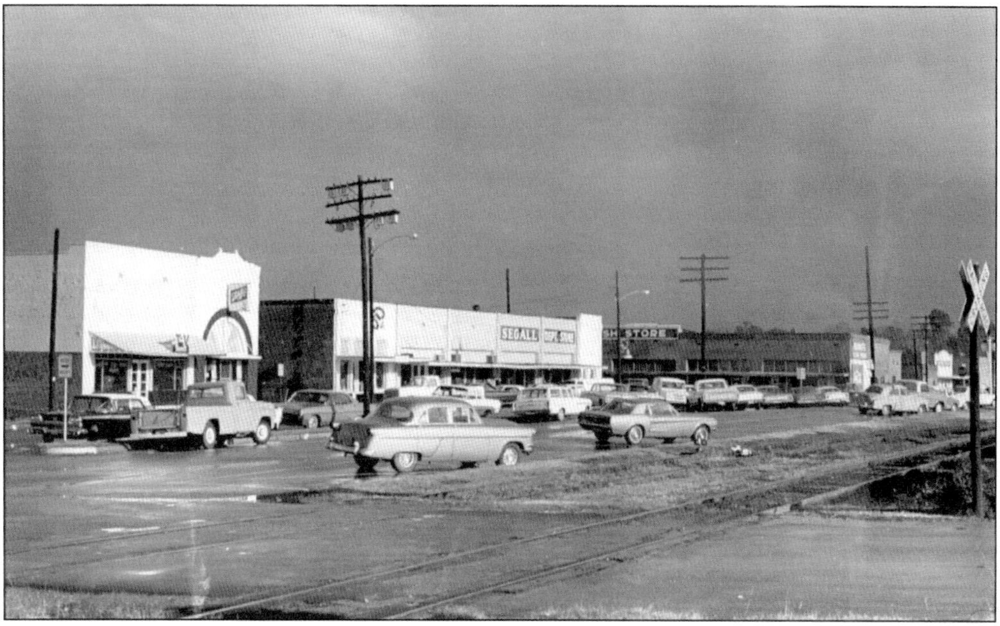

This is a view of downtown Soperton about 1960, apparently right after a rainstorm. Notice the difference in the way cars were parked then. The picture was taken several years before the beautification work was done in the area of the railroad tracks.

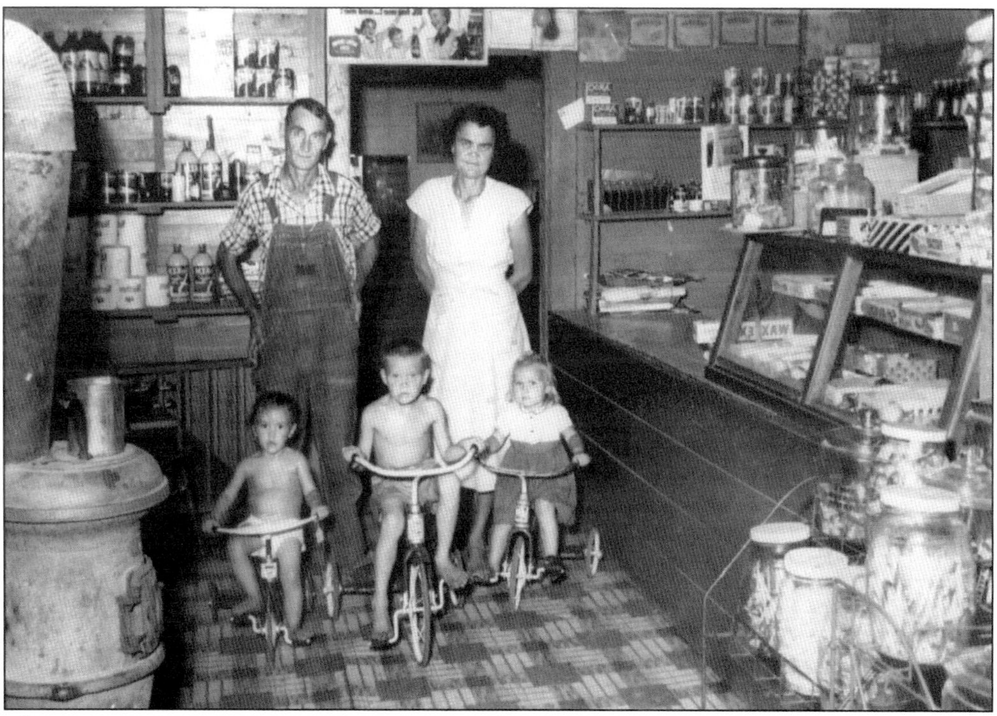

This is a c. 1950 interior view of Cox's General Store, which served the neighborhoods on the Eastman and Miller Pond Roads for decades prior to the age of convenience stores. Kerosene, grocery staples, ice cream, and candy were among the items sold. Olan and Burta Rea Cox are pictured with their son, Dreben (left), and nephew and niece, Billy Joe "Bobo" and Jewell Harrison.

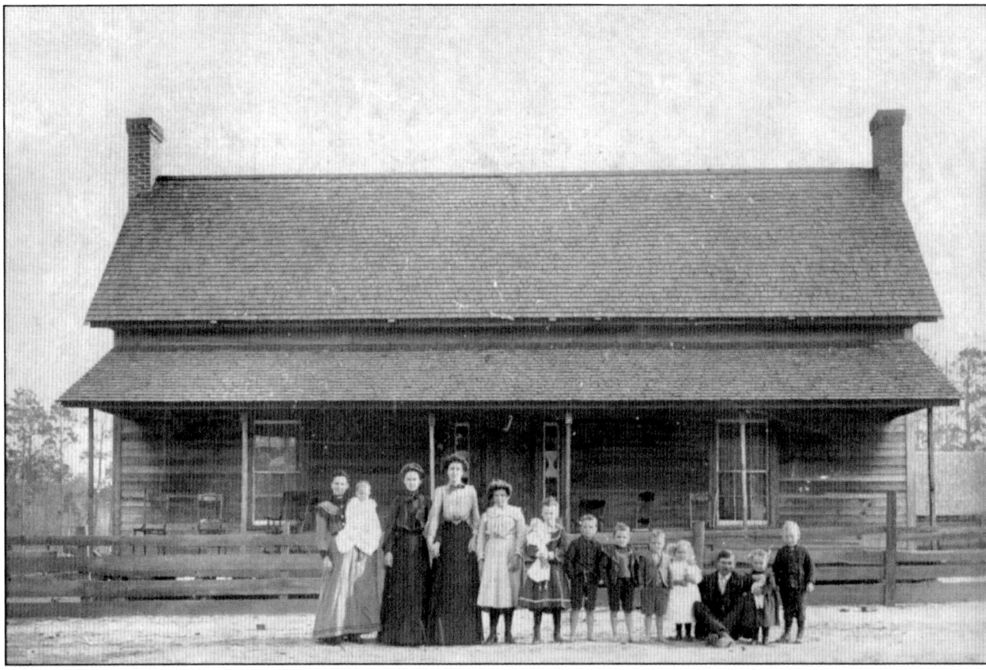

Mrs. Lizzie Johnson's Hotel is pictured here in the early 1900s. It was located on 203 Second Street in Soperton.

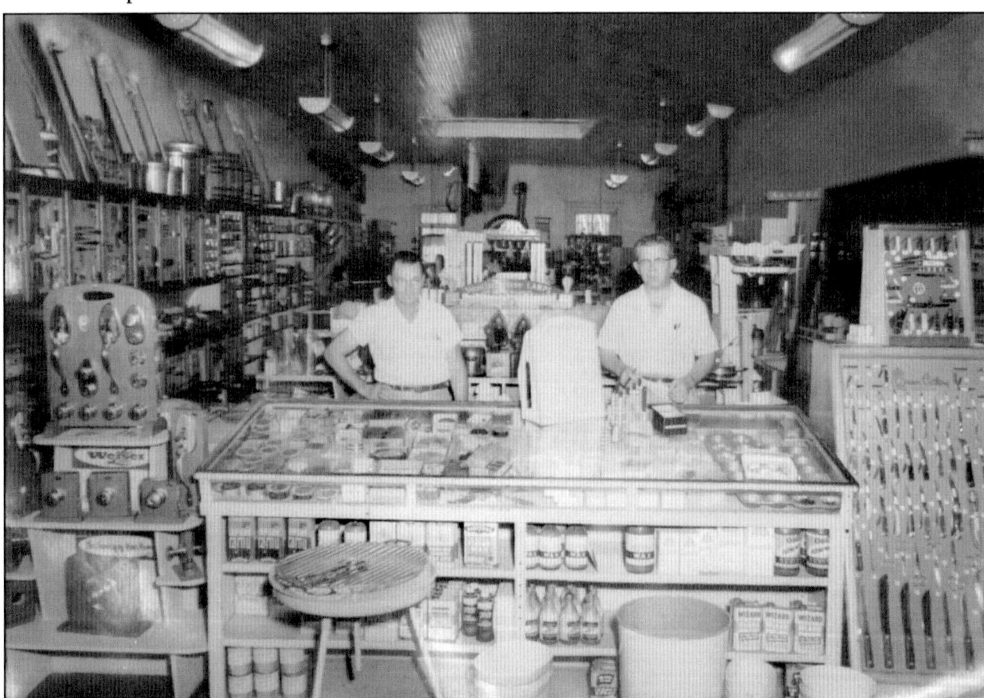

Cecil Jennings Sr. (left) and Charles Herbert Sumner are shown inside the C. A. Sumner Hardware and Furniture Store, which was established shortly after 1906. (Courtesy of Shirley Jones Sumner.)

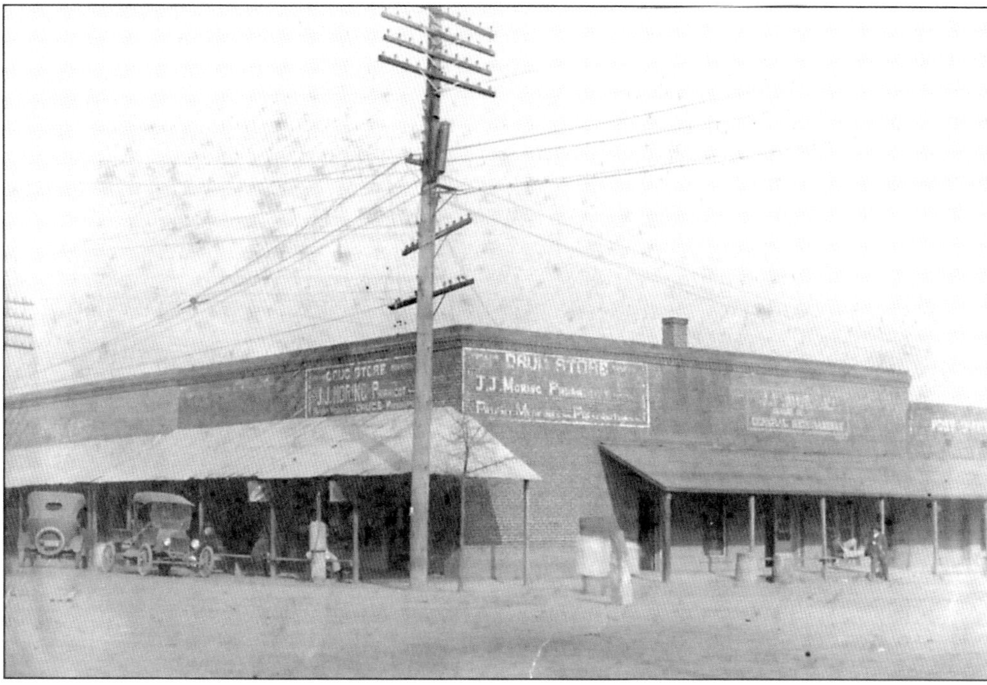

Moring's Corner Drugstore is pictured here in 1912. The interior of the store had burned that year, but it was rebuilt and expanded. Mullis' Mercantile is shown at the far right. (Courtesy of Lena Moring Wiley and Quinn Mullis.)

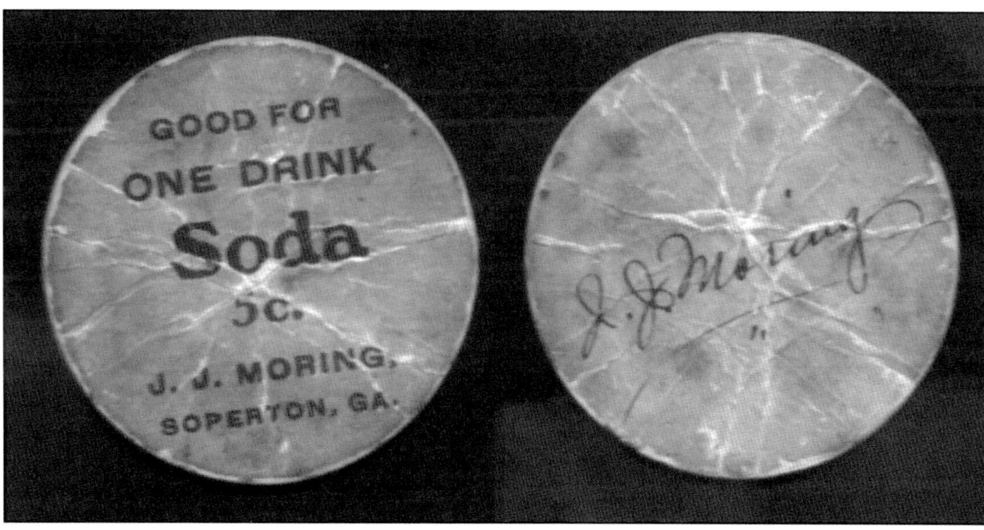

Pictured are the front and back of a soda token from Moring's Store. It was signed by Joel J. Moring. A soda fountain was added to the store in 1912, and according to Lena Moring Wiley's *The Moring/Rabun Family Tapestry* (1998), "They were now in the business of making their own tonic drinks—peach, strawberry, cream soda, and root beer—and bottling them in custom made bottles with 'JJ Moring' and the year molded into the glass bottle."

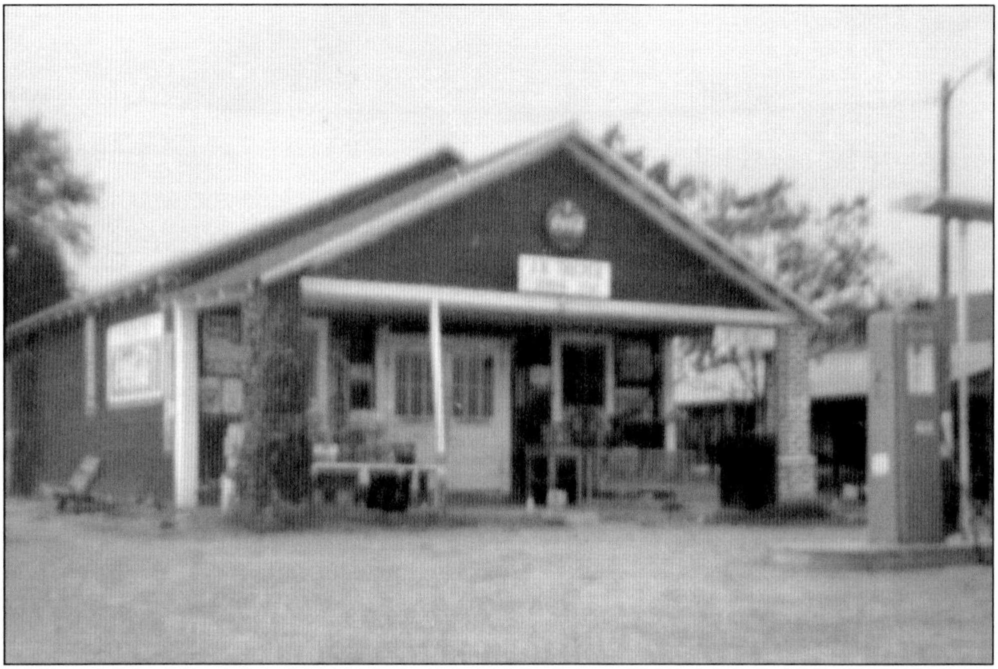

In 1937, J. B. Thigpen opened a mercantile store a block from the Orianna School. The next year, he married Jessie Kate Lacey, and they continued to operate this store until about 1946, when they built a new store, J. B. Thigpen's General Store. This store was a landmark for 33 years, with people coming long distances to purchase items that could not be found in the surrounding counties. (Courtesy of Frances Hussey Watts.)

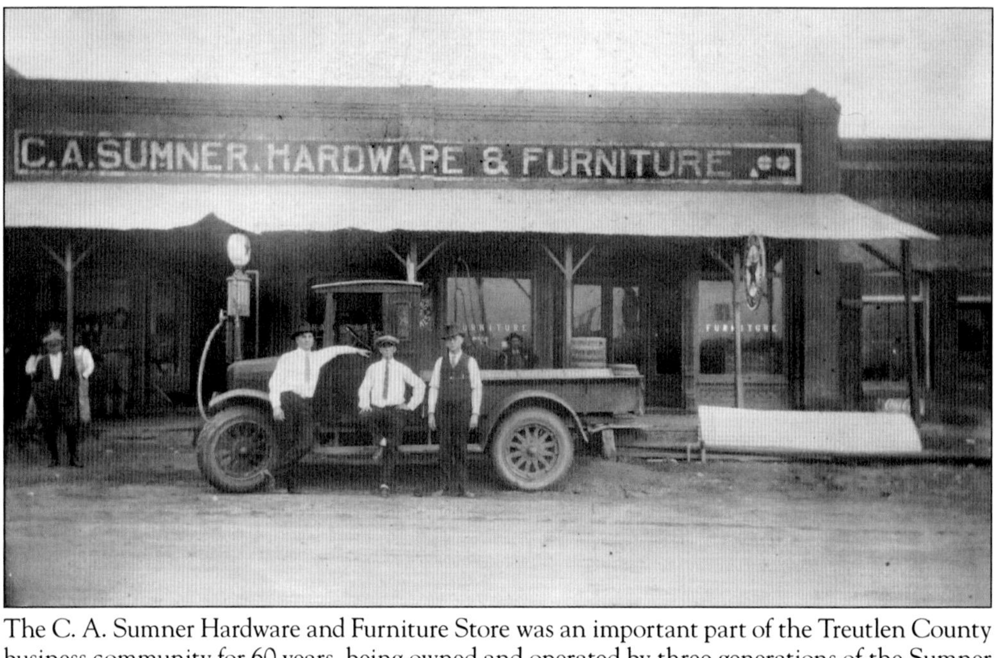

The C. A. Sumner Hardware and Furniture Store was an important part of the Treutlen County business community for 60 years, being owned and operated by three generations of the Sumner family. Standing in front of the truck in this 1925 picture are, from left to right, J. B. Curry, Charles Herbert Sumner, and Charles Augustus Sumner.

Three

Country Life

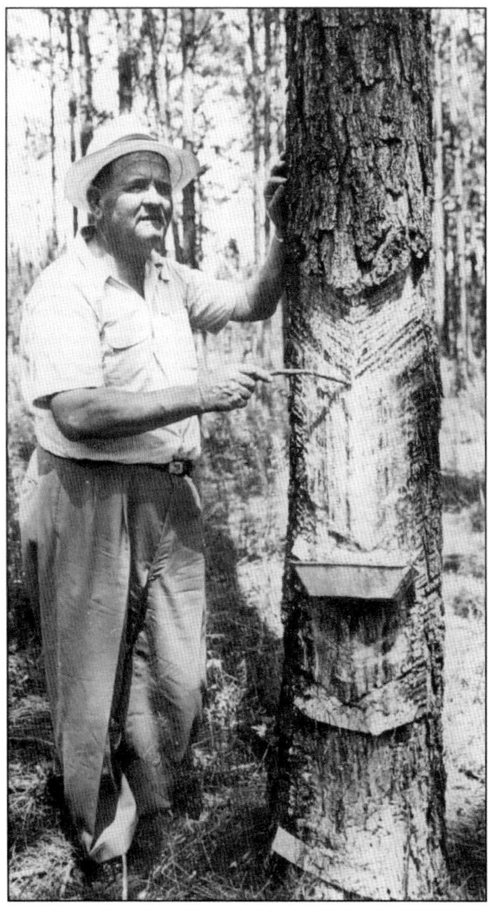

James C. "Jim" Fowler is shown here with one of the millions of pines that he planted during his lifetime. The first paper made from Fowler's trees was used to publish the *Soperton News* of March 31, 1933. He received many honors for his faith in the potential of the Southern pine. Pine by-products are now an important part of the local economy. (Courtesy of Jack Ellington.)

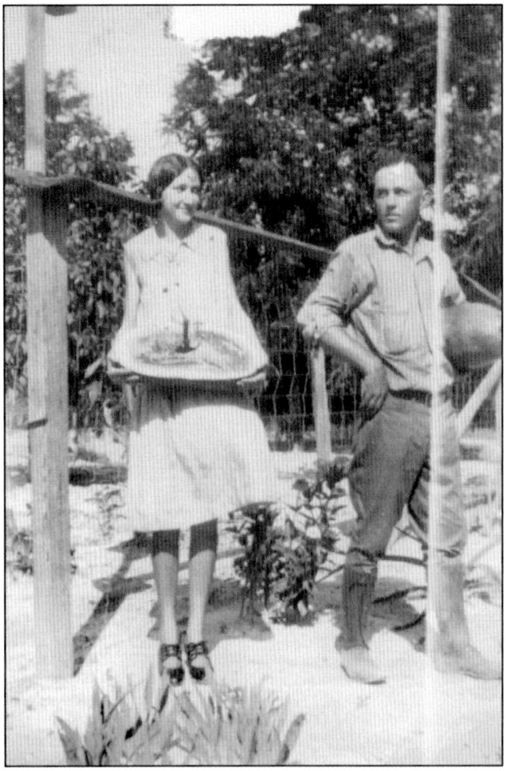

It is watermelon-eating time at the Peebles home near the O'Hoopee River. In this 1920s photograph are Lou Gillis Raley (1911–2004) and her uncle, Leon Peebles (1904–1995). (Courtesy of Jones Peebles.)

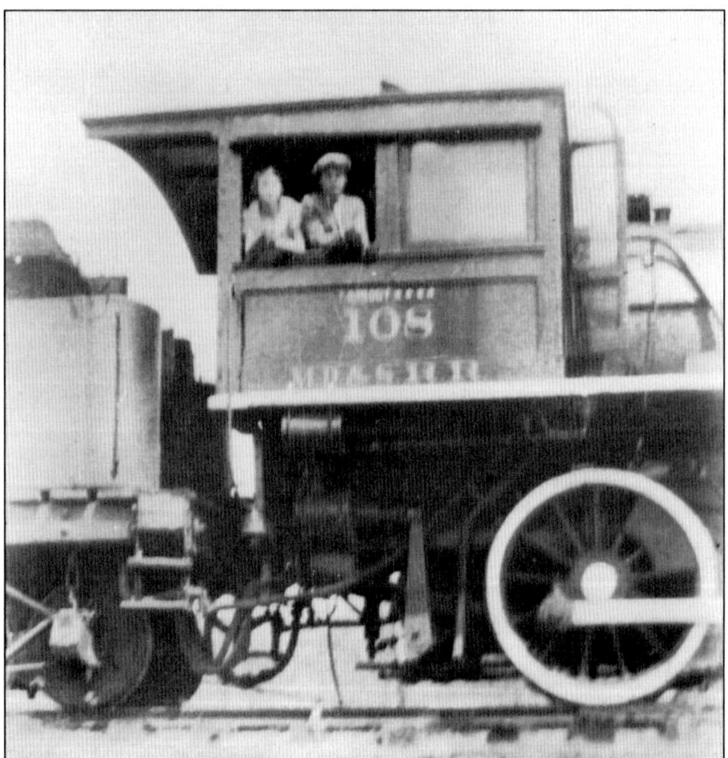

Charlie Mae Davis Landers (left) and her sister Mildred went up to the engineer's cab to have their picture made back when the MD&S was an active line in the early 1900s.

This is the grave of Morris O'Brien in the O'Brien-Cooper Cemetery near Lothair. He was born in Ireland in 1839 and died in Treutlen County, Georgia, in 1907. He fought in the War between the States in Company H, 1st Regiment of Connecticut Volunteers. He is the only Union soldier buried in Treutlen County whose service is documented on his headstone.

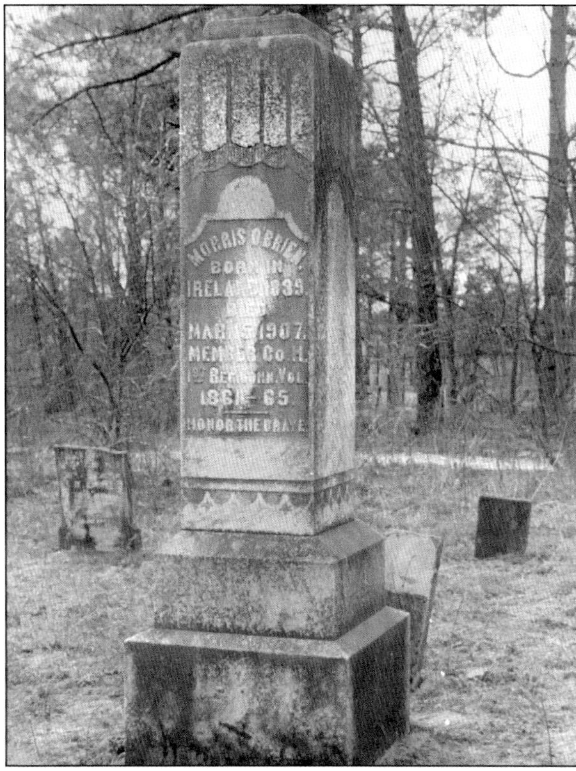

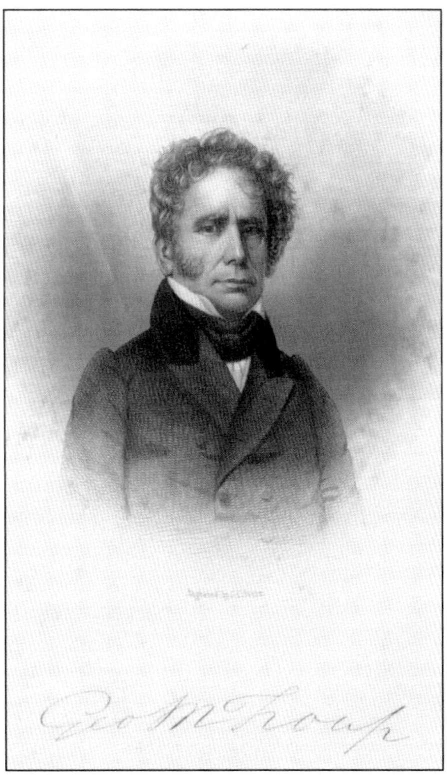

George Michael Troup (1780–1856) served in the Georgia Legislature, U.S. Congress, and U.S. Senate; he was twice governor of Georgia. Although he was the first cousin of the Creek chief Gen. William McIntosh, Governor Troup was instrumental in having the Native Americans removed from Georgia during the 1820s and 1830s. He died while visiting Rosemont, one of his plantations, located off Highway 46 in present-day northern Treutlen County, and is buried there.

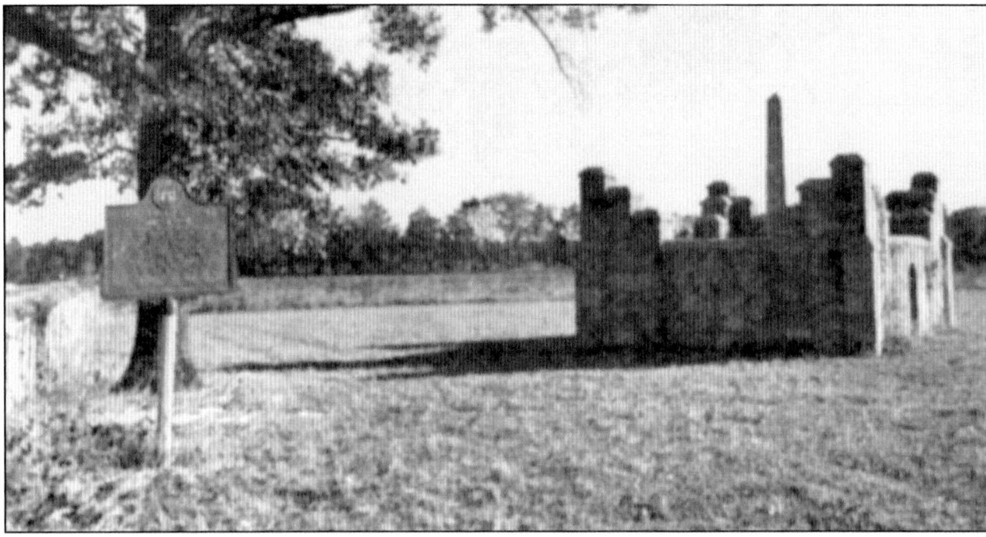

One of Treutlen County's most interesting historical sites is the tomb of Gov. George M. Troup. Surrounding the grave is a wall of sandstone quarried from nearby Berryhill Bluff on the Oconee River, in the center of which stands a shaft of Georgia granite. The tomb is easily accessible to sightseers; markers are located on Highways 46 and 199.

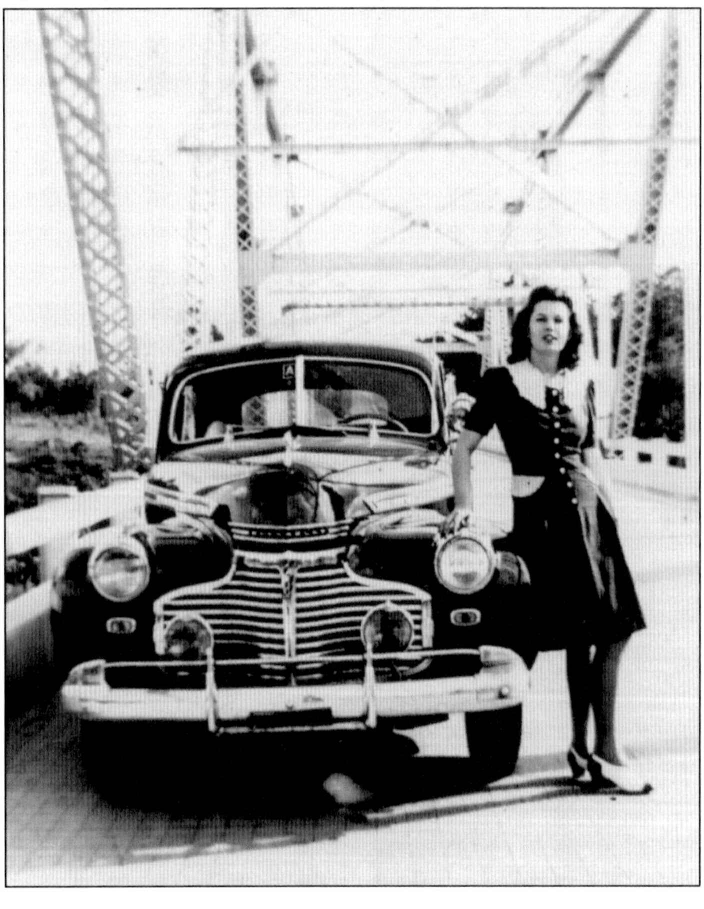

Shown in this 1950s picture is Maureen Gillis Calhoun (1923–2006), standing on the old bridge that spanned the distance across the Oconee River between Treutlen County and Wheeler County. At the time, Maureen was dating her future husband, Marion L. Calhoun. (Courtesy of Sandra Calhoun Odom.)

This old log cart recalls the days of mule power. It was made entirely by hand by Francis Marion Calhoun (1865–1939), son of James Rufus Calhoun and Mary Ellen Phillips. Pictured is his grandson, Marion L. "M. L." Calhoun (right), and his great-grandson, Marion Calhoun. (Courtesy of Sandra Calhoun Odom.)

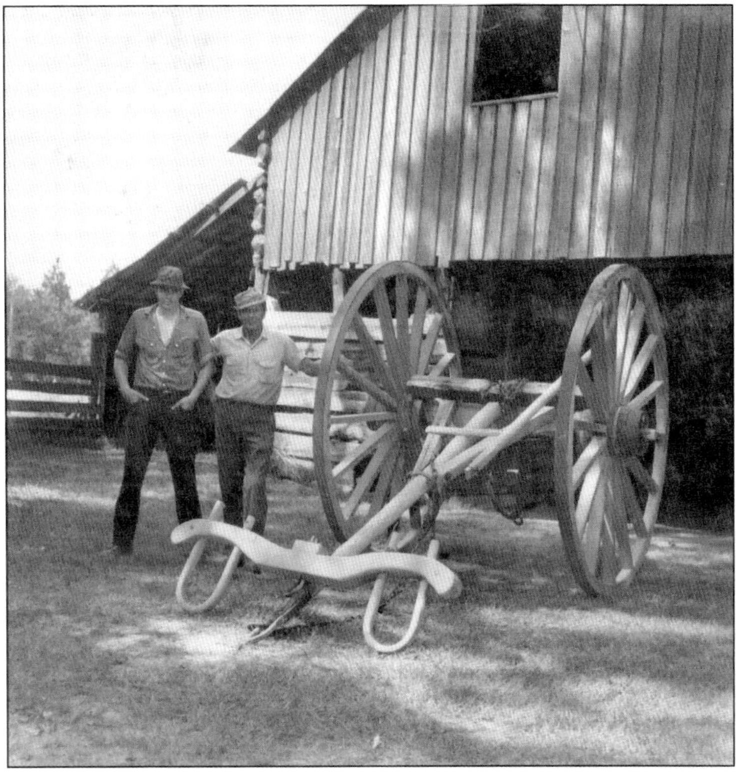

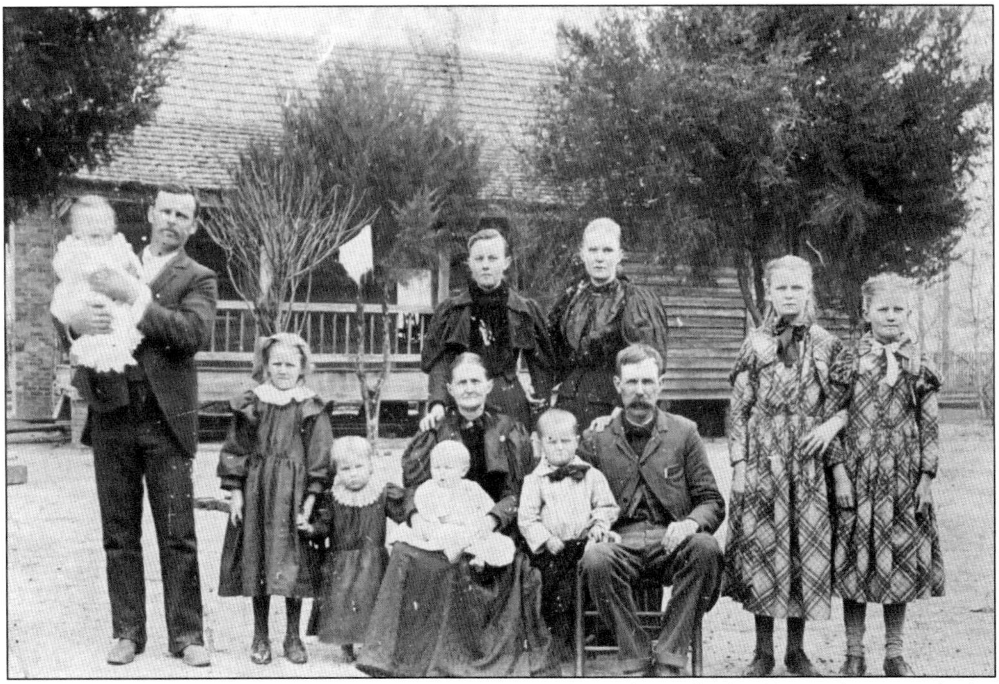

The Angus A. Gillis family is pictured here. Angus Alexander Gillis (1855–1920), a son of John Gillis and Mary Ann Gillis, married Mary Jane Barwick (1856–1922), daughter of Curtis Manning Barwick and Mary Ann "Polly Ann" Kea. (Courtesy of Marvin Gillis.)

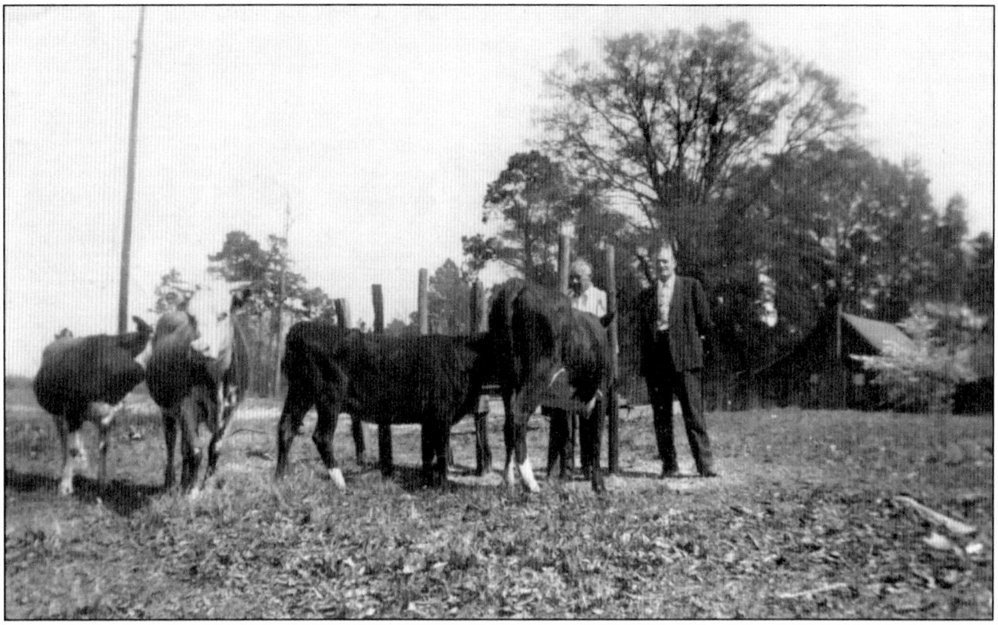

Daniel Tilton "Babe" Ricks is shown at left in this c. 1925 picture out in the pasture looking over some of his cows. The other gentleman is unidentified. In the background is Ricks's home. (Courtesy of Tracy Manning Gillikin.)

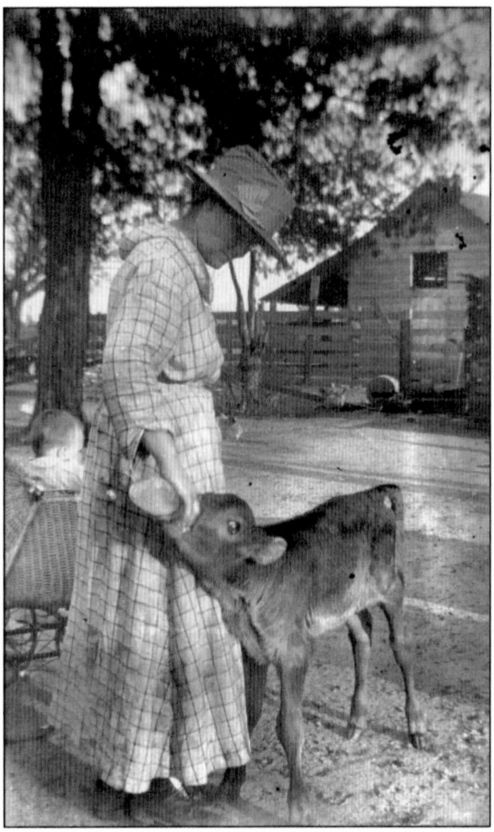

In this 1919 photograph, Onie Calhoun Williamson is shown out in the muddy lot in her husband's old boots feeding a bottle of milk to her calf. Her husband, Gaston Williamson, was in the armed forces and was stationed overseas at the time. Beside her in his wicker carriage is their son, Gaston Benjamin "G. B." Williamson.

The Gillis Springs Recreational Resort was a favorite not only of people in the Emanuel-Treutlen area, but also with people who came here from far-off places to picnic and bathe in the springs, which were said to have great medicinal value. This is an early picture of the gazebo that was built over the spring, which had been welled up. (Courtesy of Hal Jones.)

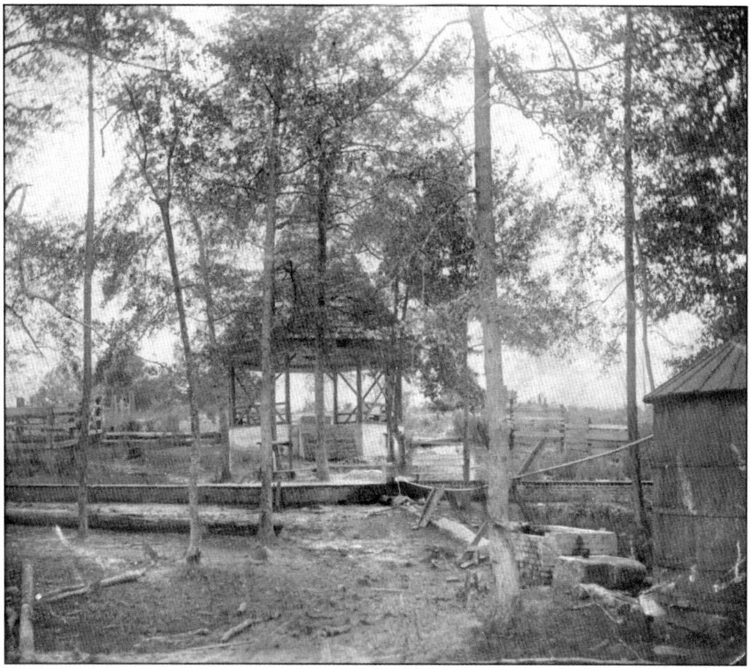

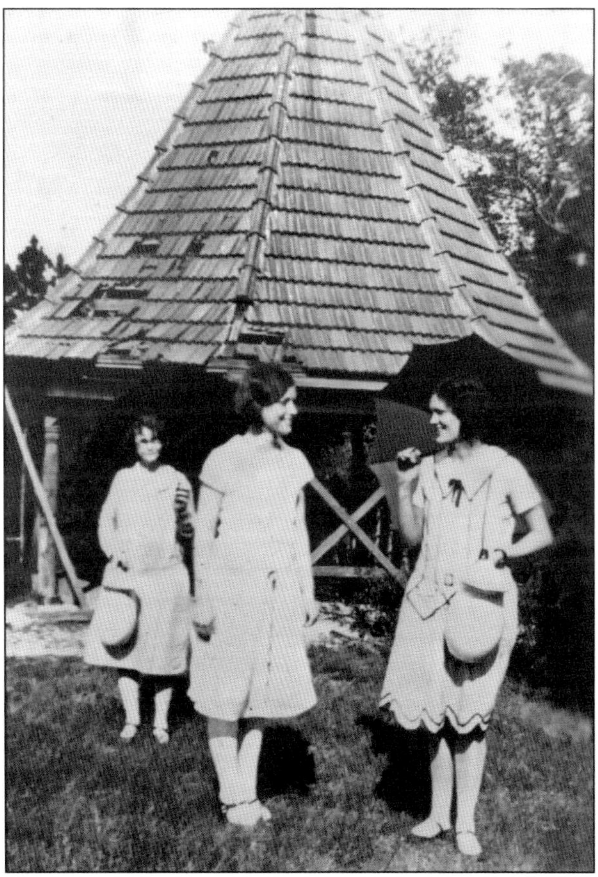

Shown is the Gillis Springs gazebo in 1929, located across the road from the Gillis Springs School. The teachers pictured are, from left to right, Ana Rizer, Annie Lou Courson, and Myrtle O'Brien. Note the odd water carriers being used to transport the spring water.

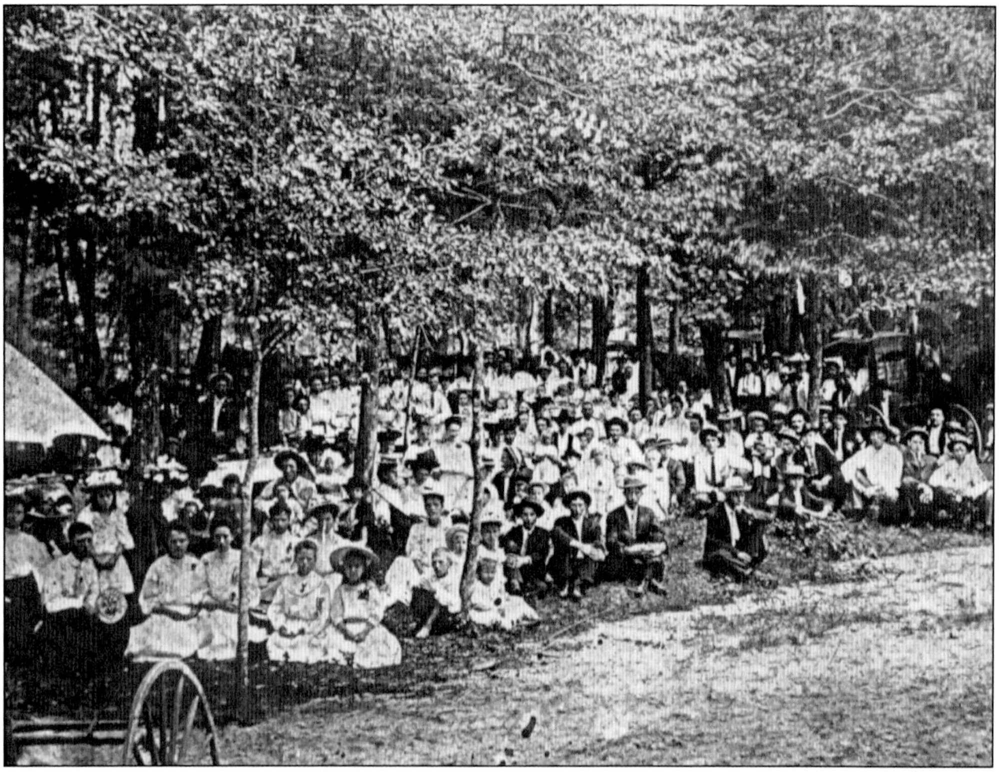

This is a rare *c.* 1908 scene of a large group enjoying an outing at the famous Gillis Springs Recreational Resort. The people posing are unidentified.

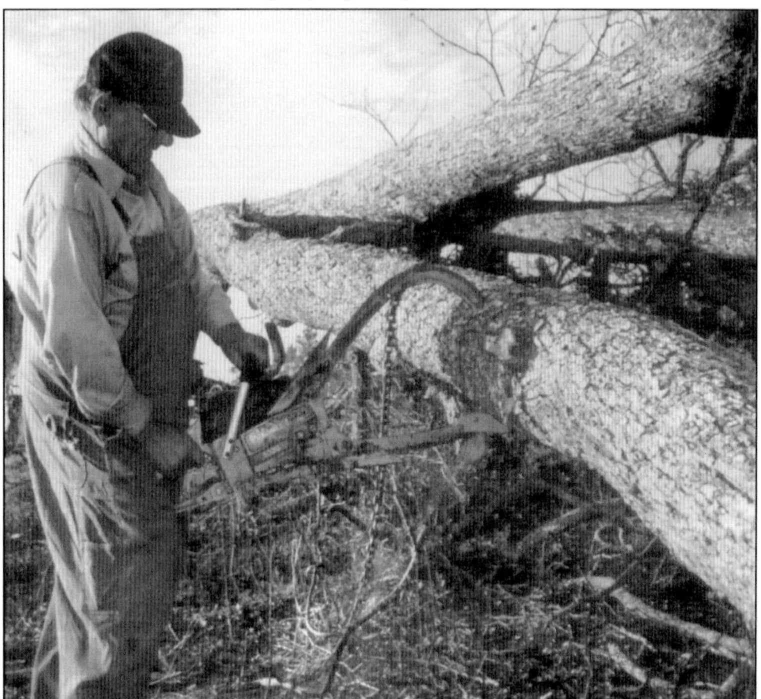

M. A. Braddy (1917–2008) was well known for his skill at felling trees. He is shown here later in life taking down a big one—a 100-year-old water hickory at the Phillips-Braddy home near Zaidee. It is said there was a huge tree on Louisiana Avenue in Soperton that needed to come down, but no one wanted to tackle the job. At the age of 72, M. A. brought it down single-handedly, to the astonishment of bystanders.

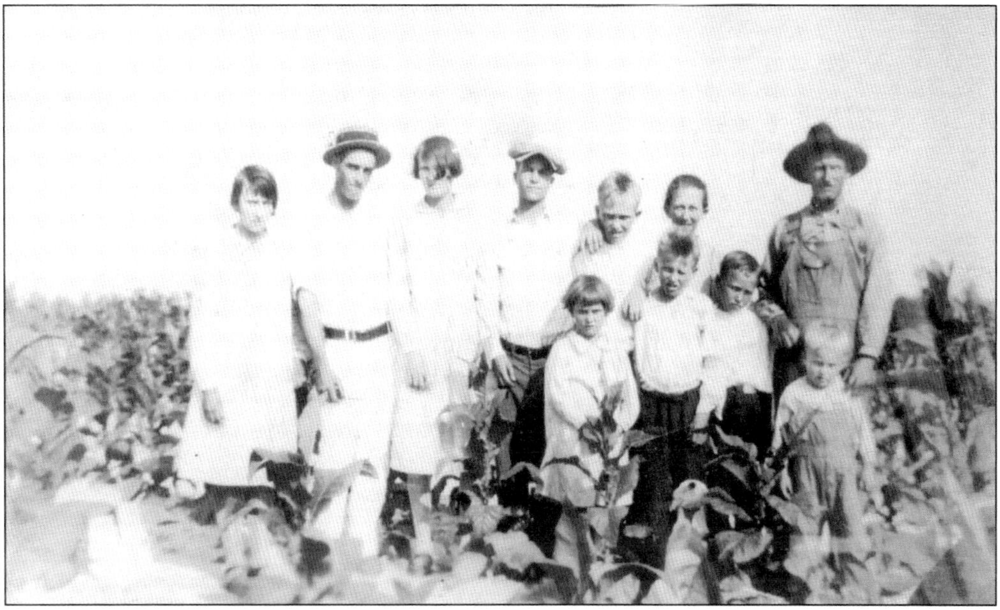

In this 1920s picture, the John Wickstrom family is taking time out from their work to pose in their tobacco field. Working in tobacco was a family affair. The men and boys picked the tobacco and brought it by mule and sled to where the women and girls were gathered to hand and tie it, usually under a big shade tree. (Courtesy of Kay Wickstrom.)

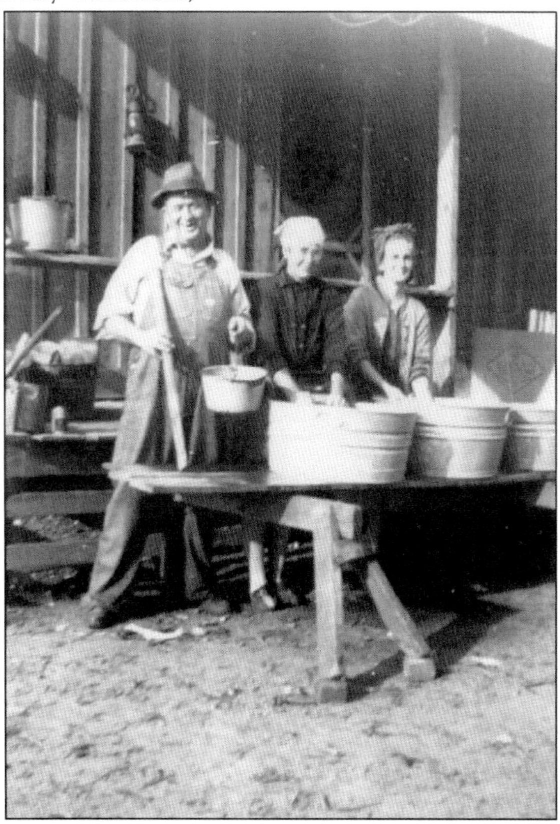

Hog-killing time was a real chore in the rural South. It was customary to use nearly every part of the animal. John and Mary Page (center) are being assisted by Irene Spivey in cleaning "chit'lins" (chitterlings) in this c. 1940 snapshot. (Courtesy of the Page family.)

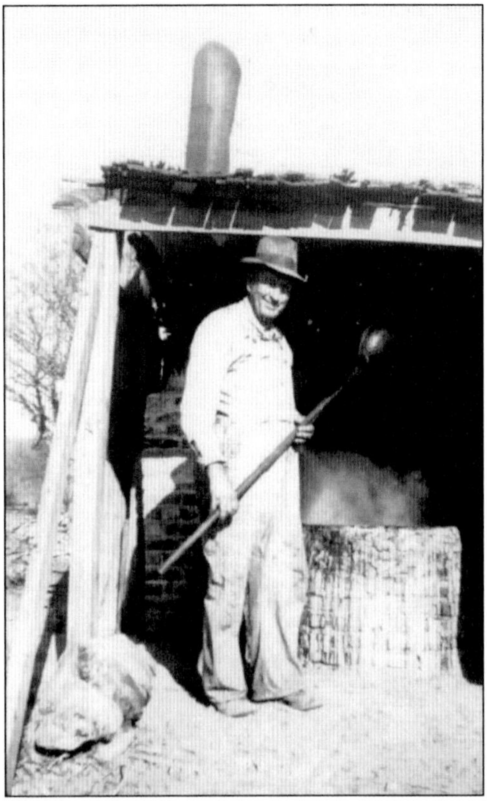

John Allen Page is shown making syrup in the early 1900s. The syrup kettle is a huge iron bowl or kettle set in a brick framework attached to a chimney. A fire is kept burning underneath the bowl, and cane juice is cooked in the kettle until the syrup is the right consistency. Page is holding a skimmer, used to scoop foam from the top of the syrup. (Courtesy of the Page family.)

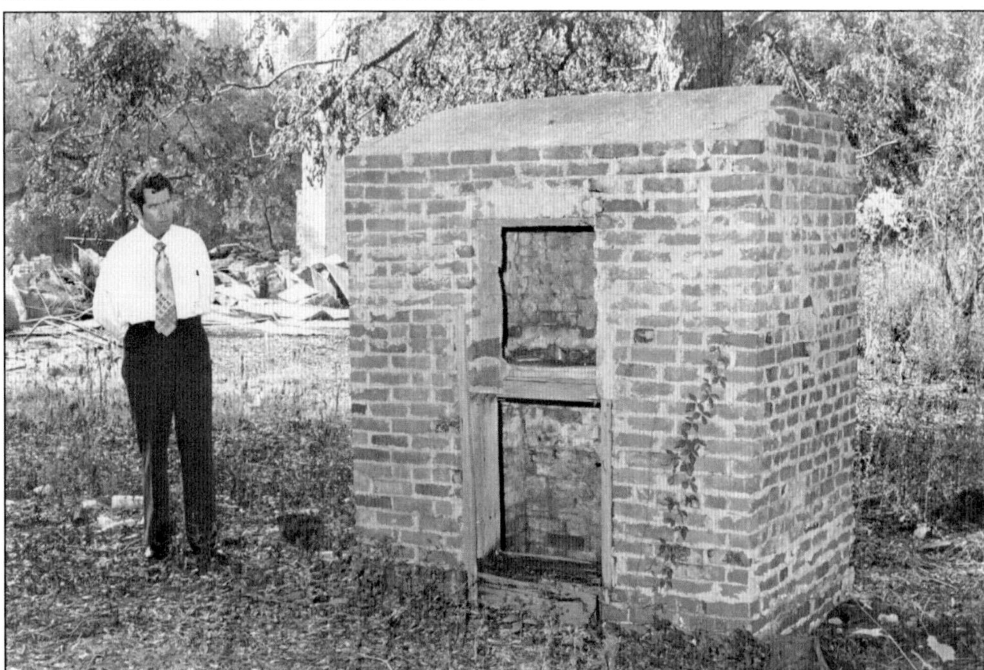

In this 1970s photograph, noted Treutlen County historian J. Clayton Stephens Jr. is standing beside a brick meat curer at the recently burned Roderick Gillis home.

Merida Norris Hutcheson (1868–1944) is shown here with his wheat crop. The photograph was made about 1930 at the Hutcheson place, east of Soperton. (Courtesy of Norris Hutcheson.)

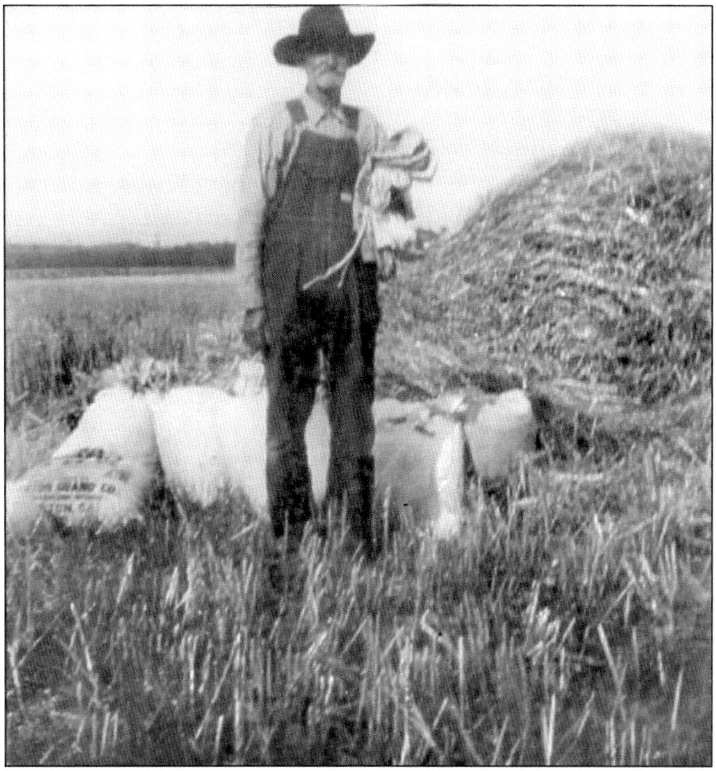

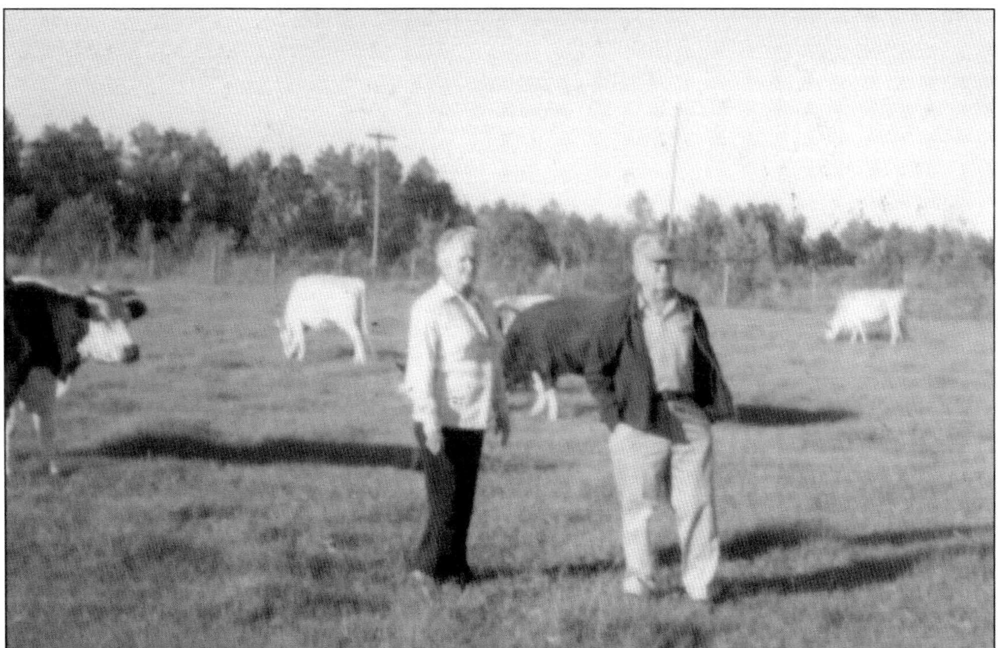

Shown taking a walk in their cow pasture in the 1960s are Joseph David "J. D." Palmer Jr. and his wife, Helen Mixon. Their home was on the Thompson Pond Road near Zaidee. (Courtesy of the Mixon family.)

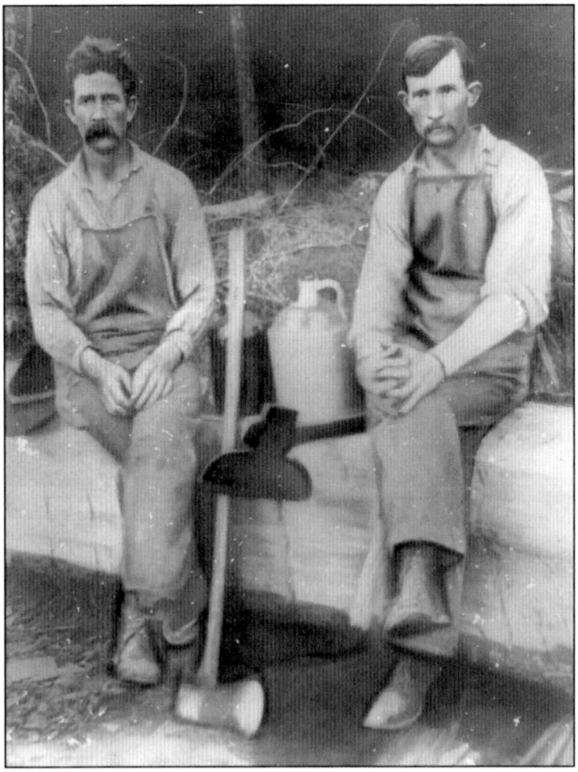

This *c.* 1900 picture illustrates the early timber industry when trees were felled and rafted down the Oconee River. Taking a break from their work are Richard Arthur Ricks (left) and Charles Crumley.

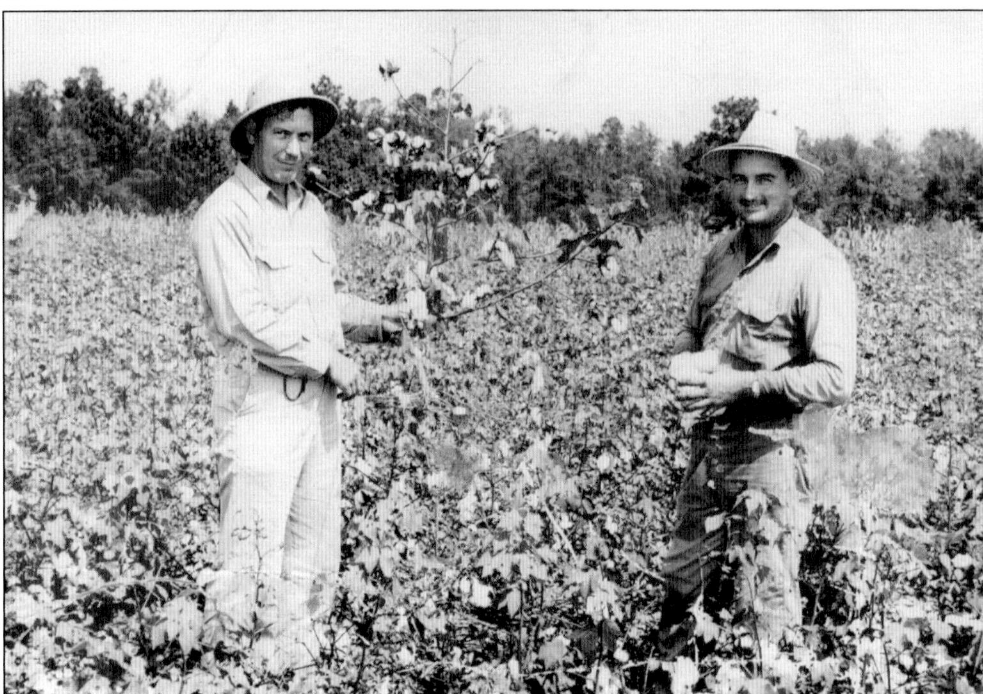

Standing in a beautiful field of snowy white cotton are Robert A. Kight (left) and Roger Brinson. This picture was made in the late 1950s. (Courtesy of Joy Kight McLendon.)

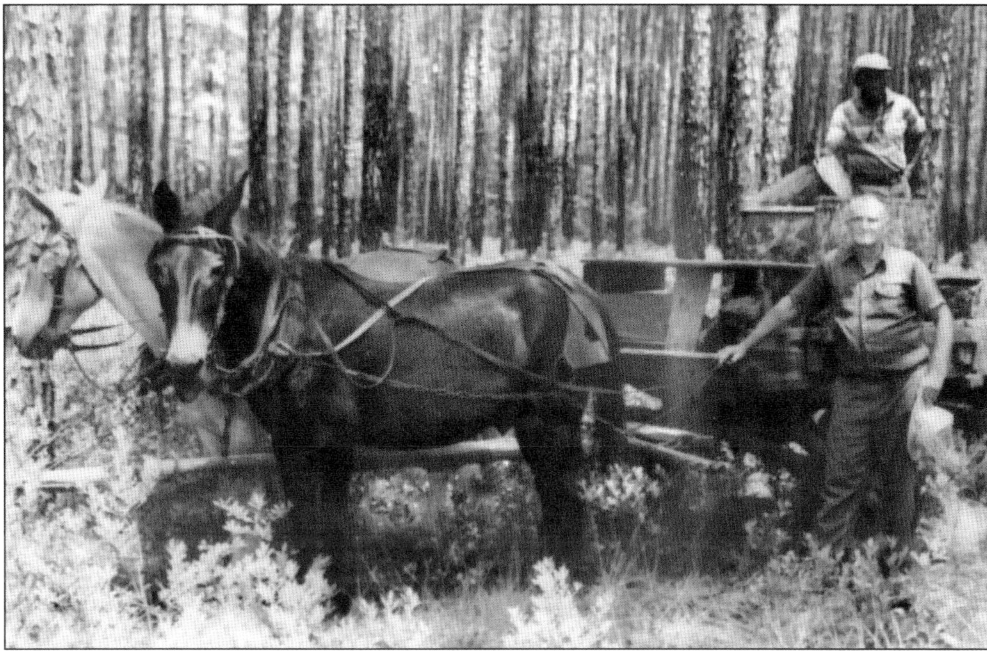

Jim L. Gillis's mules were photographed around 1940 while being worked in the woods. Willie Mitchell is sitting in the tar wagon, and Lawton Beck stands beside the wagon. Mules were used extensively in all farming and timber operations for many decades. (Courtesy of Jim L. Gillis Jr.)

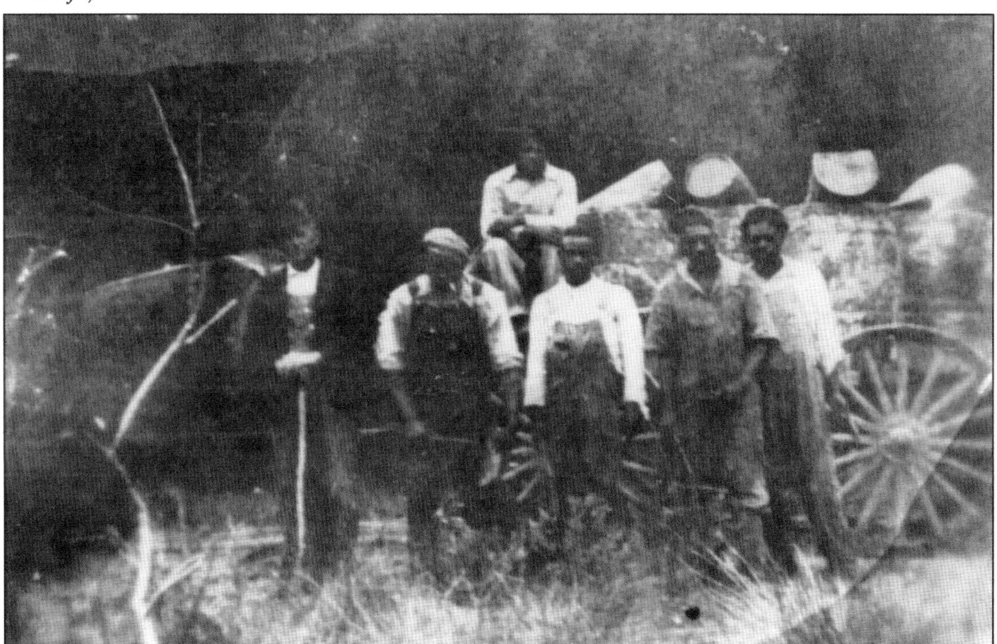

Mules are shown here being used in dipping turpentine. Pictured from left to right are Columbus Carter, dip walker; H. K. McKever, Hezekiah Overtree, Adam Wise, and Milton Roberson, dippers; and Bud Linder, wagon driver. Columbus Carter died between 1943 and 1945. (Courtesy of Jones Peebles, Jim L. Gillis Jr.)

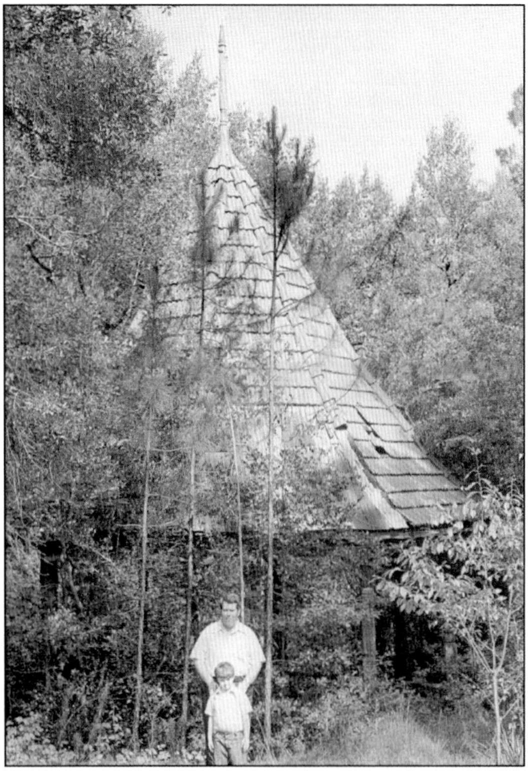

J. Clayton Stephens Jr. (1941–1997) is pictured here with his son, William, after touring the area that was once an important recreational center at Gillis Springs. Behind them is the gazebo, built around 1908 over the welled-up springs.

In this picture, made near Lothair about 1890, are Selma Higgs (left) and Arnold Spivey. This is typical of the large log carts pulled by teams of oxen, which were used for hauling out timber from the dense forests. Logging the ample virgin pine timber growing in the area provided livelihoods for many families during the 1800s and early 1900s.

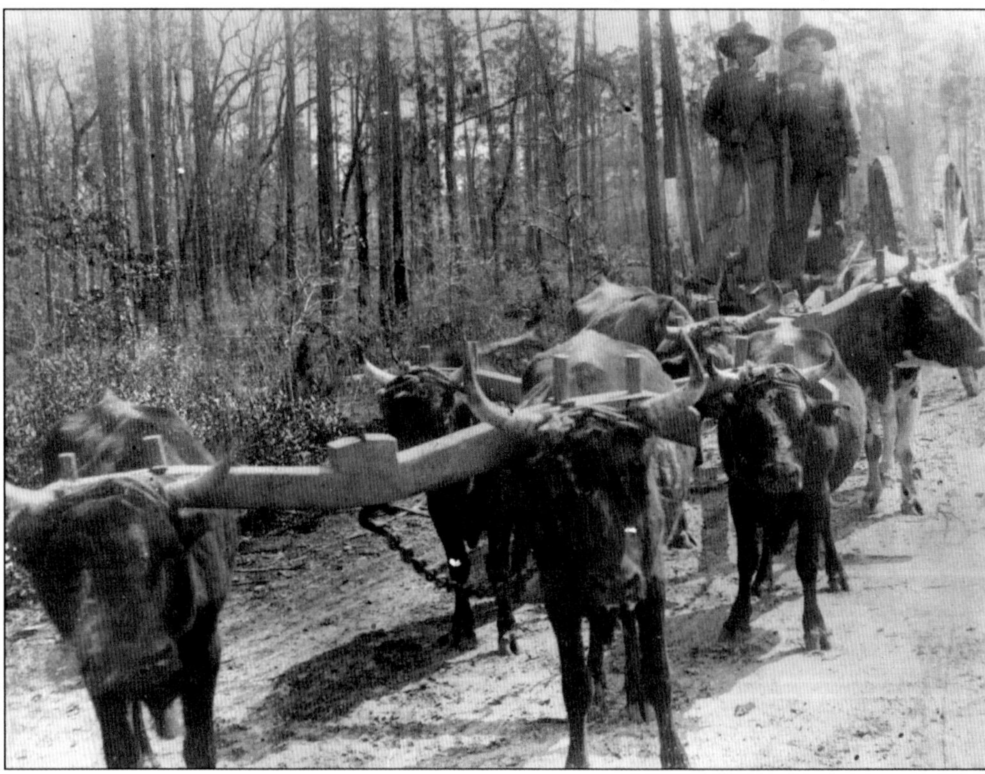

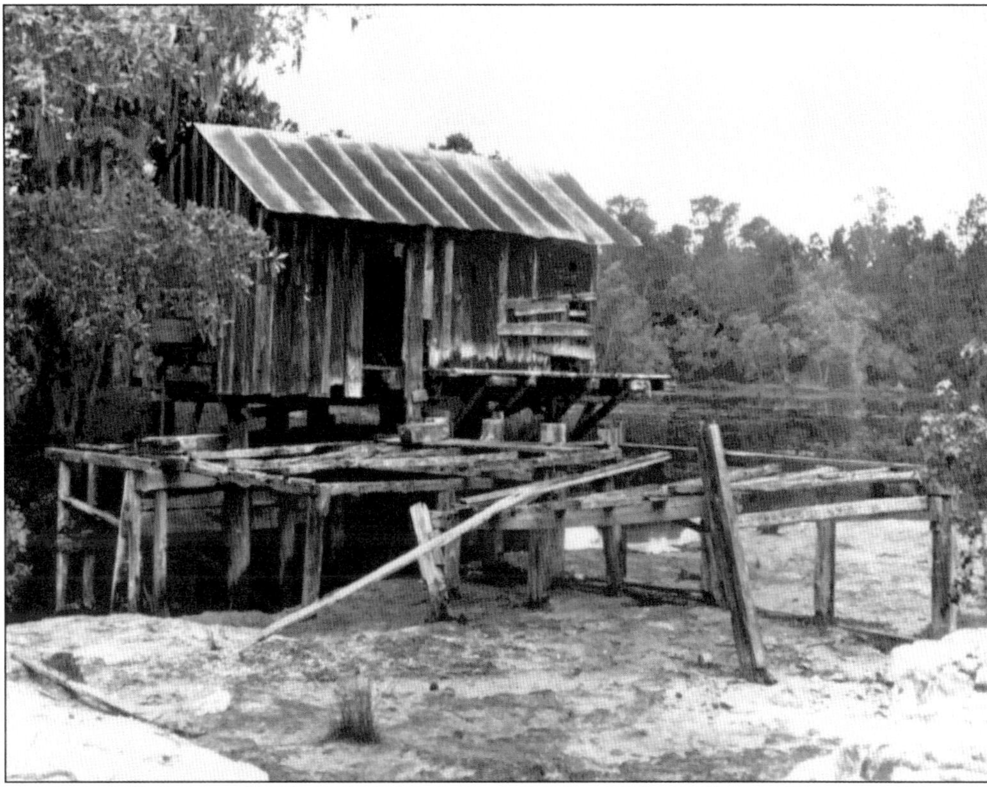

Shown are the ruins of Miller's Mill House near Lothair. John Miller Jr. (1818–1904) was the owner of Miller's Mill in the late 1900s.

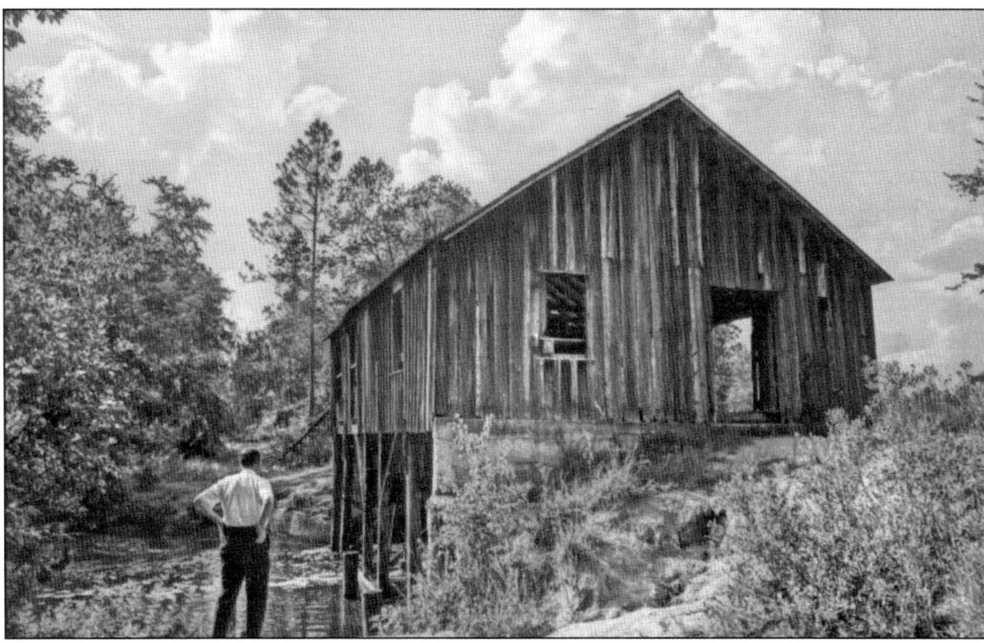

Pictured here is all that remains of the Sterling Mill near Highway 29 North. Having withstood the ravages of so many years, it proves that it was built of quality materials.

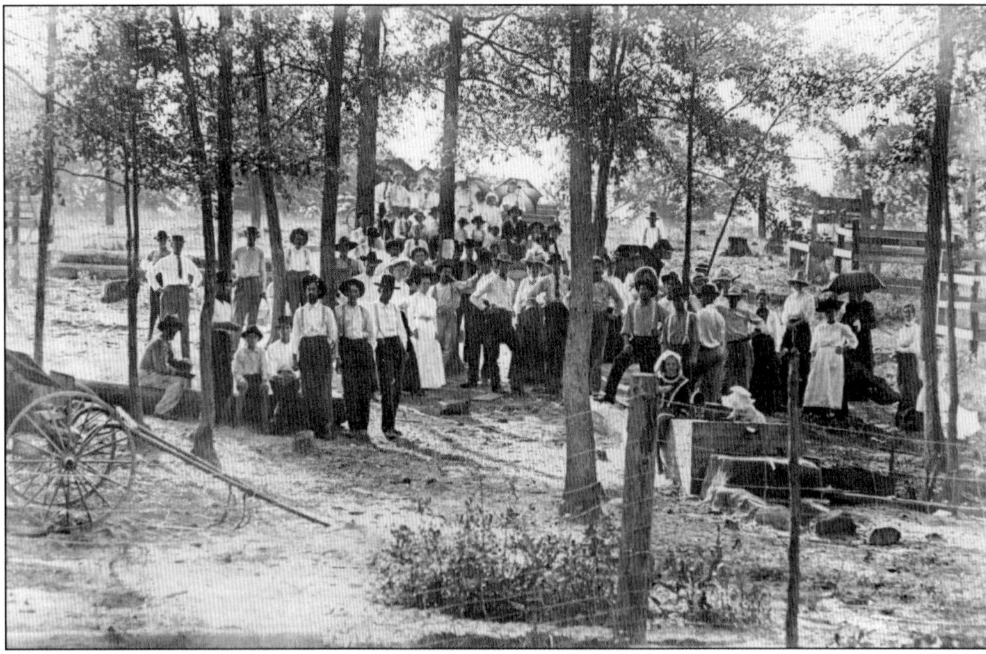

This is the earliest known photograph of the spring known as Gillis Springs. Roderick Gillis discovered the spring prior to 1902 while chasing cattle in the woods. This picture was taken before the gazebo was built; therefore, it was probably about 1905. Note the large umbrellas at the back that the women are holding. A woman is pouring water from a pitcher onto the lady in the bonnet. (Courtesy of Marvin Gillis.)

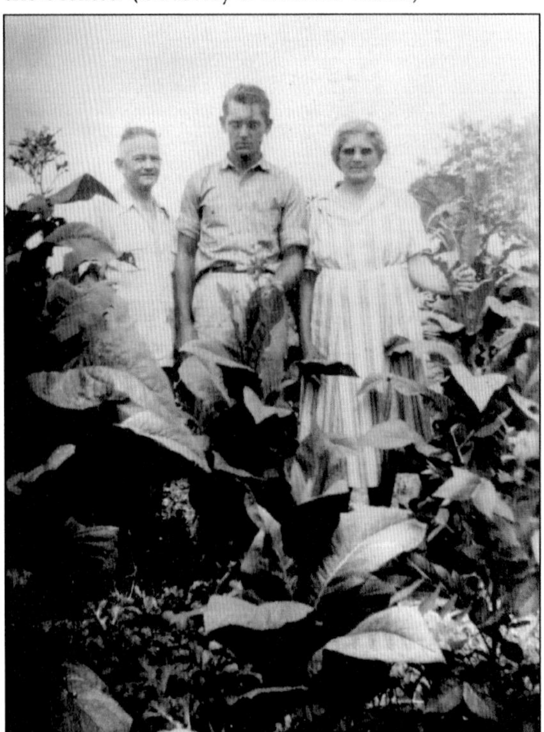

This family was proud of its tobacco crop. Standing in the tobacco patch are Bill Blue (left), his brother-in-law, Athel Braddy, and his mother-in-law, Stella Collins Braddy. "Putting in" tobacco was a time for family and friends to come together and have conversations while working. (Courtesy of Billy Wade Jr.)

Four

WHERE WE LEARNED AND WORSHIPPED

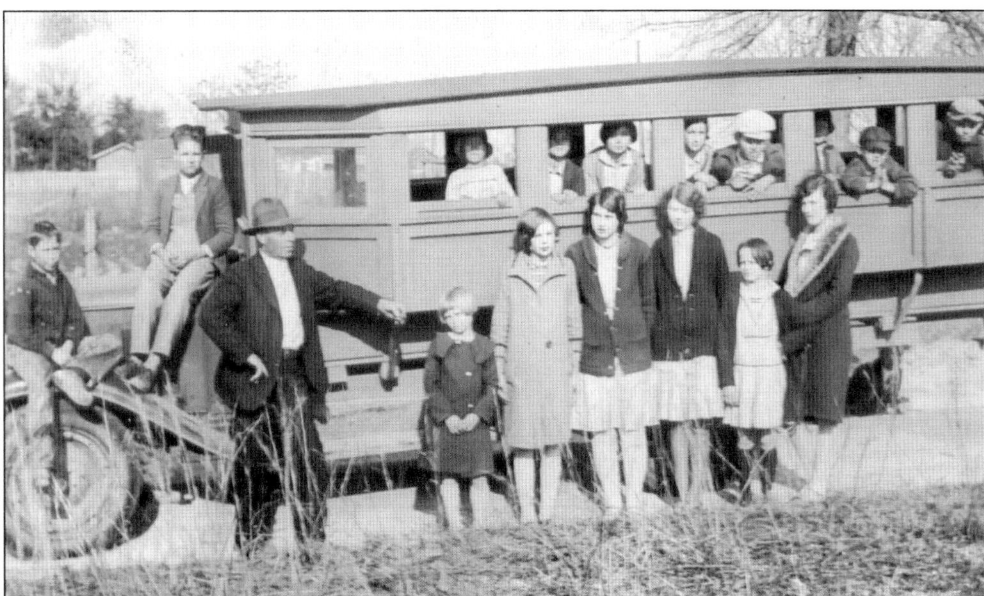

This school bus brought children from Soperton to the Gillis Springs Industrial School in the 1920s. The third child from the right (standing) is Essie Mae Carter, daughter of Columbus C. Carter and Mary Mozelle Taylor, who in 1931 married Leon S. Peebles, son of Thomas Jefferson Peebles and Florence Anderson. (Courtesy of Jones Peebles.)

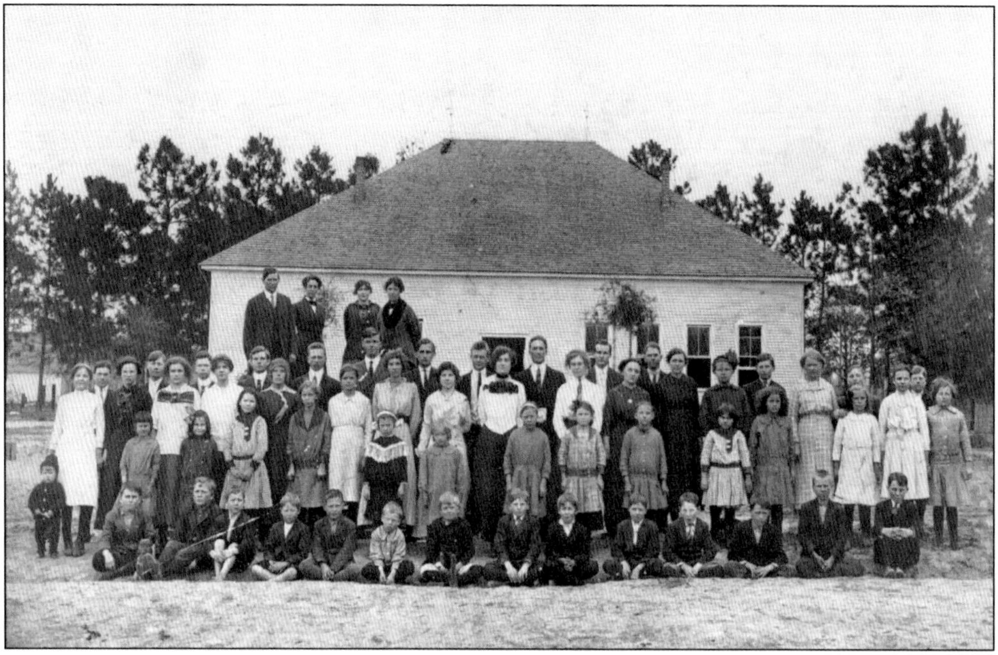

The Gillis Springs Industrial School is pictured here in 1913. This building was later expanded, and more classrooms were added. The only boarding school that was ever located in Treutlen County is still standing on the site and is currently the handsome restored residence of the Tillman Durden family. (Courtesy of Hal Jones.)

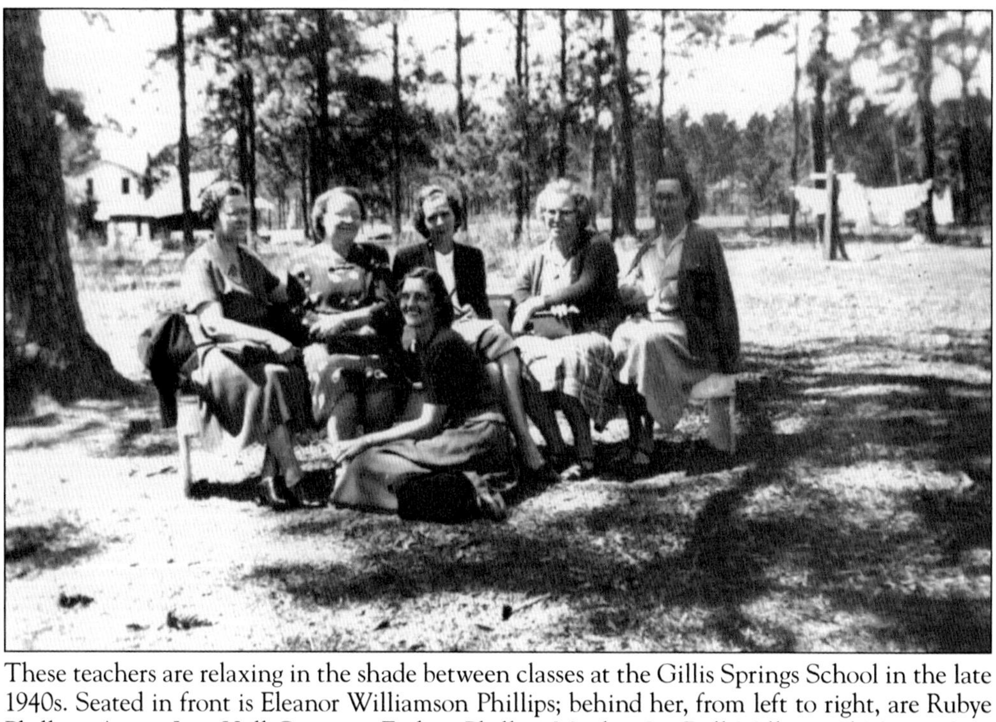

These teachers are relaxing in the shade between classes at the Gillis Springs School in the late 1940s. Seated in front is Eleanor Williamson Phillips; behind her, from left to right, are Rubye Phillips, Annie Lou Hall Courson, Eudora Phillips Moxley, Ira Dell Miller, and Minnie Lou Gillis Raley.

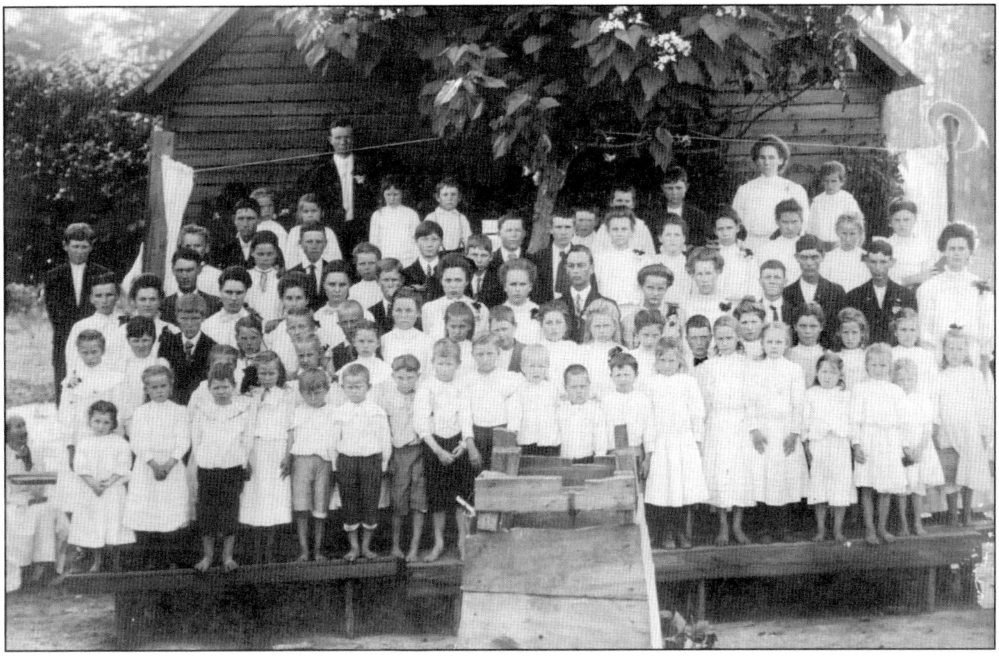

The Hall Tree School was located in Smutt in eastern Treutlen County. Maggie Gillis was the teacher. The Gillis and Herndon families were among the area families who sent their children to this one-room school. Notice the wooden-curbed well in the foreground. (Courtesy of Patsy Meeks Ware.)

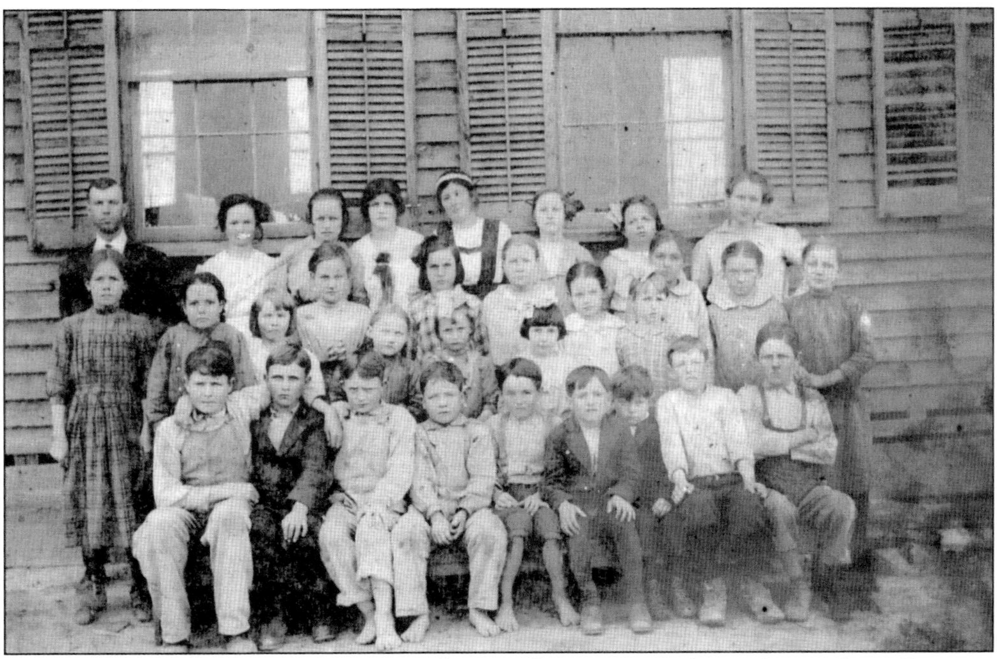

The Hutcheson School was located on the Merida Norris Hutcheson home place. Shown is Bunion Chastain, the schoolmaster. Among area children attending this school were those of the Hutcheson, Stewart, and Brinson families. At one time, this building was also used as a meeting place for the Advent Christian Church. (Courtesy of Norris Hutcheson.)

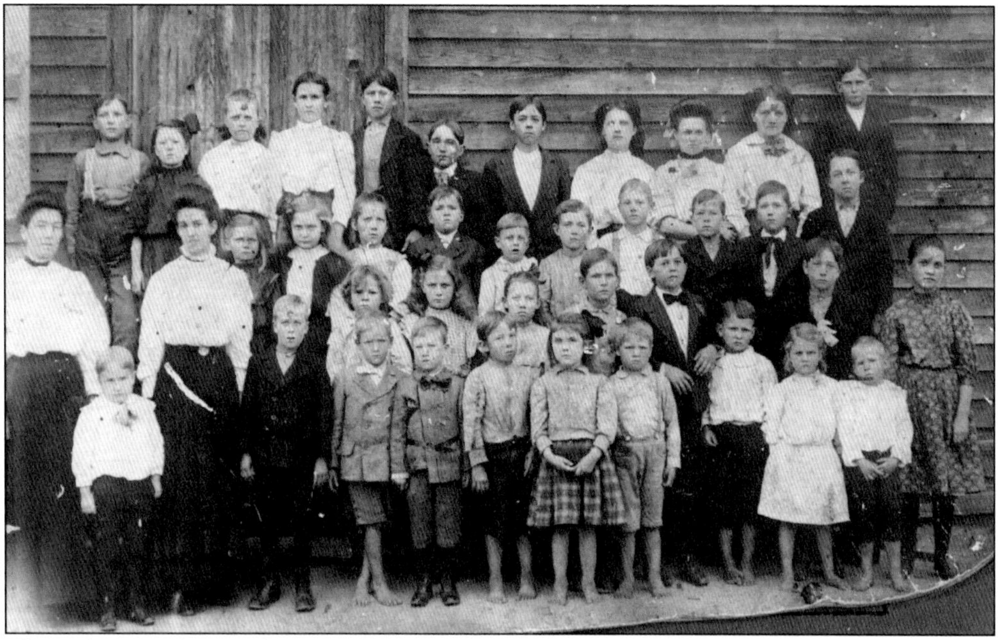

The Lothair Academy is shown in this 1908 photograph. In the first row are the teachers, Josephine McCrimmon Jones (left) and Maude McDaniel. Some of the children attending school here were from the Mosley and Miller families.

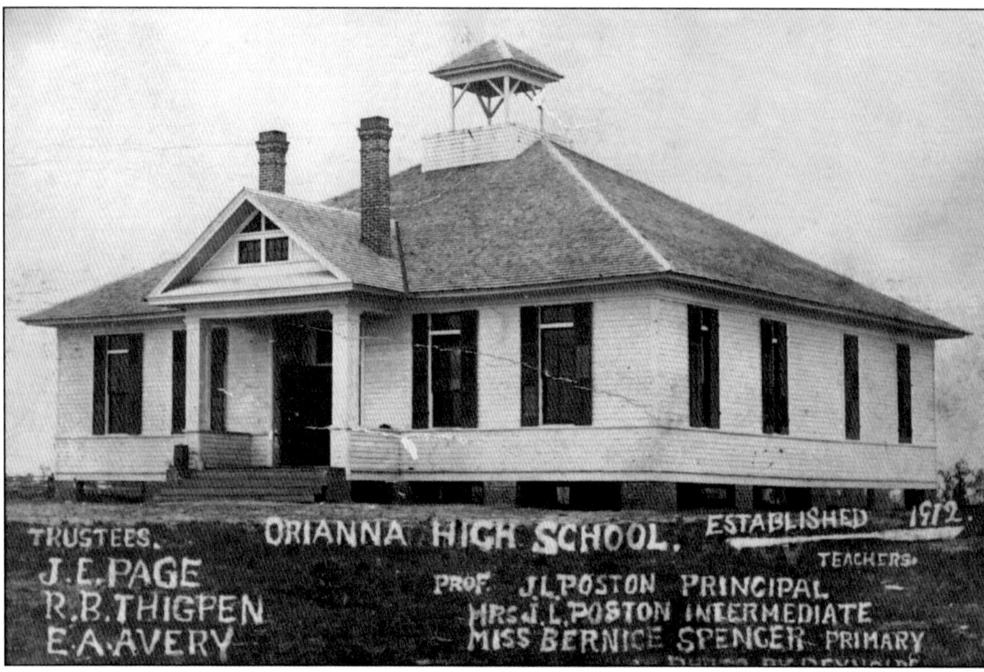

The Orianna School is shown in this 1912 photograph. After it burned in 1946, J. B. Thigpen bought the property from the board of education and built a general store as well as a new home, which was erected on the original foundation of the school's auditorium. The store building is now the Orianna Community Hall and is used for social functions. (Courtesy of Frances Hussey Watts.)

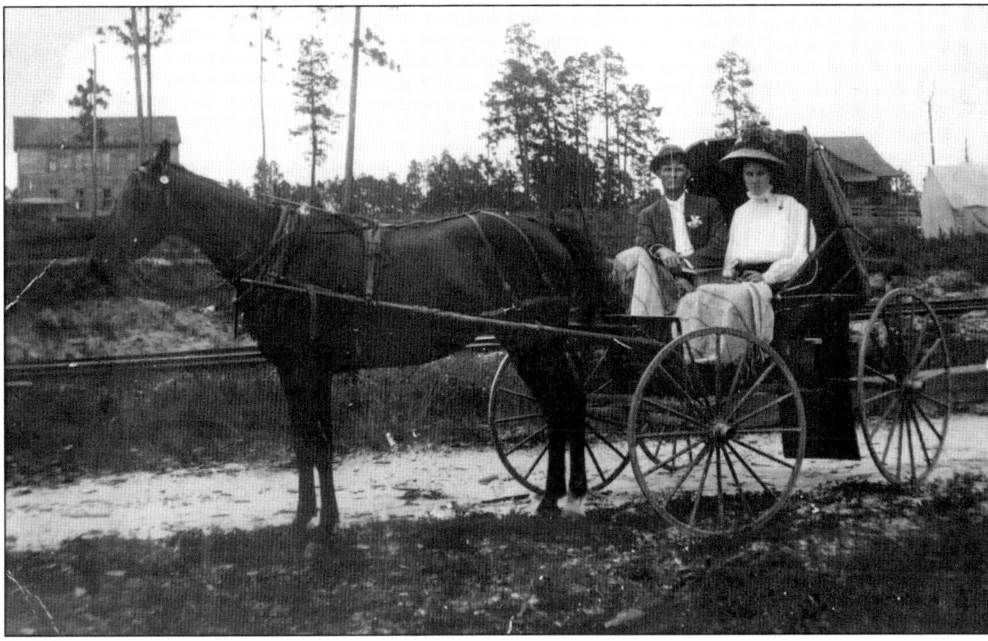

The original Orland School is shown in the background, pictured about the dawn of the 20th century. It was located on the hillside between the present J. C. Pullen Sr. residence and the MD&S Railroad in Orland, and was no longer used after 1920, when the new school was built. The couple in the carriage is unidentified.

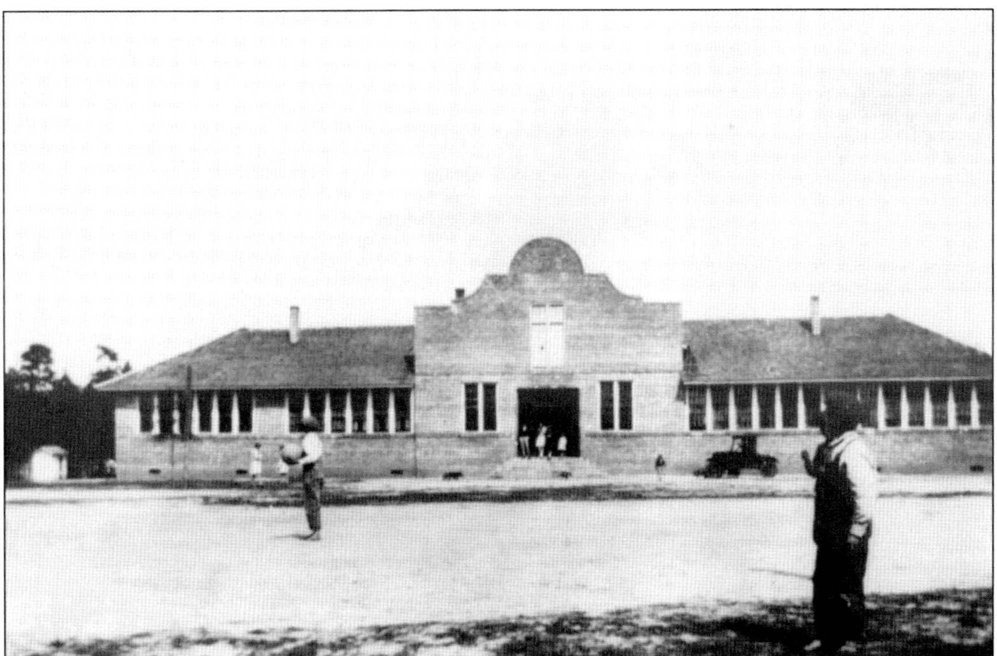

This is the Orland Consolidated School in its newer building, completed in approximately 1921. Notice the Model T pulled up to the side of the building and the outdoor restroom to the left.

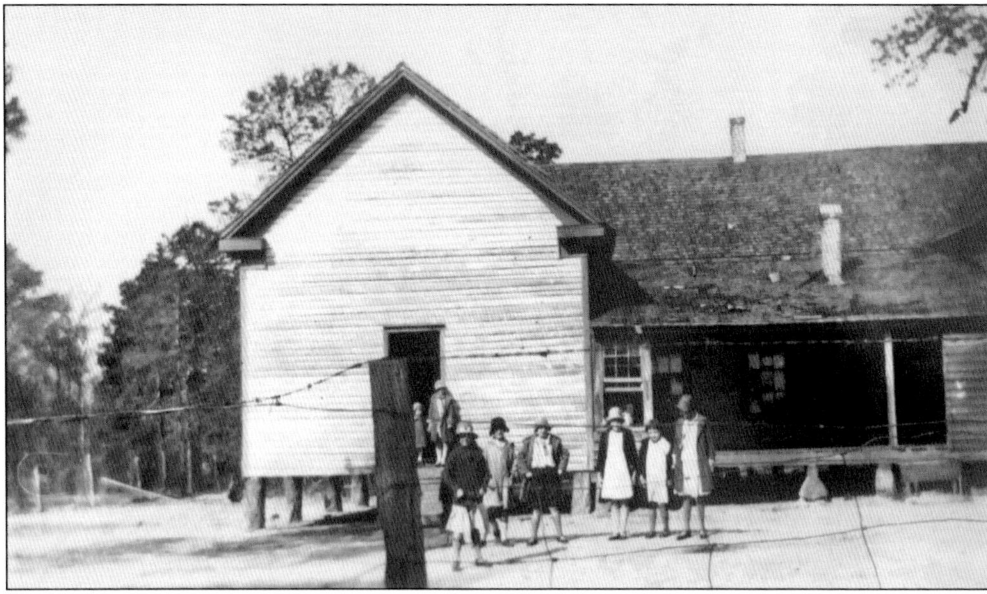

The Rosemont School predates Treutlen County's creation and was located near the site of Troup's Tomb. This picture was taken in approximately 1926. A wire fence with barbed wire at the top surrounds the school campus.

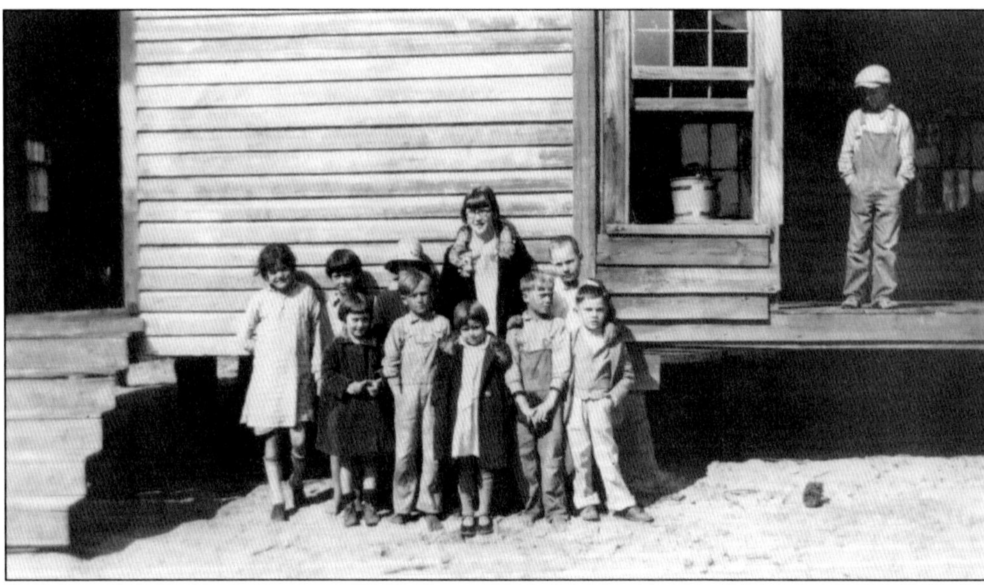

Destroyed by fire in 1931, the Rosemont School was in operation for several decades in the late 1800s and early 1900s. This view shows a group of children posing for the picture while a lone boy stands on the porch watching. The purpose of the bucket in the window is unclear.

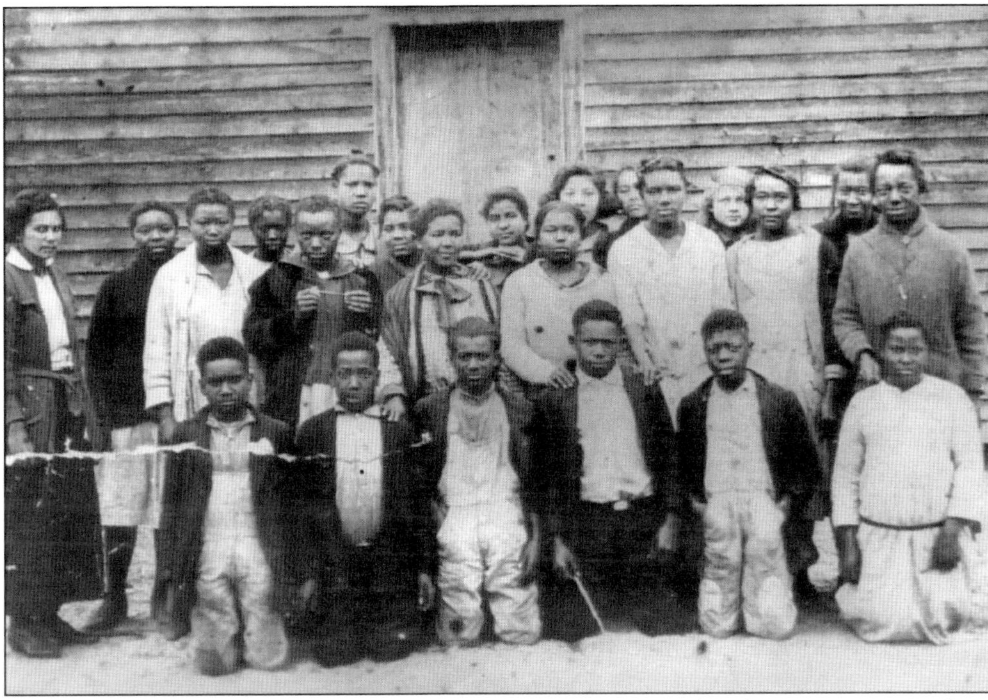

This is the old school for black children beside the Mount Zion Church in Soperton. Students shown are (first row) Beret Moore, Sam Gillis, Alvin "Bud" Outlaw, Buster Collins, Eulis Oatts, and Nettie Mae Burdon; (second row) Leola Gillard, Eldora Kinsey, Annie Pearl Todd, Cathlene Collins, Gertrude Gillard, Susie Sherrod, Marie Milford, and unidentified; (third row) Maetta Wells, Minnie Davis, Ophelia Outlaw, Ruby Todd, Ethel Todd, Sarah Cason, Lillie Mae Tables, and Matt Miller. Alice Durden (far left) was the teacher. (Courtesy of Lester Ricks.)

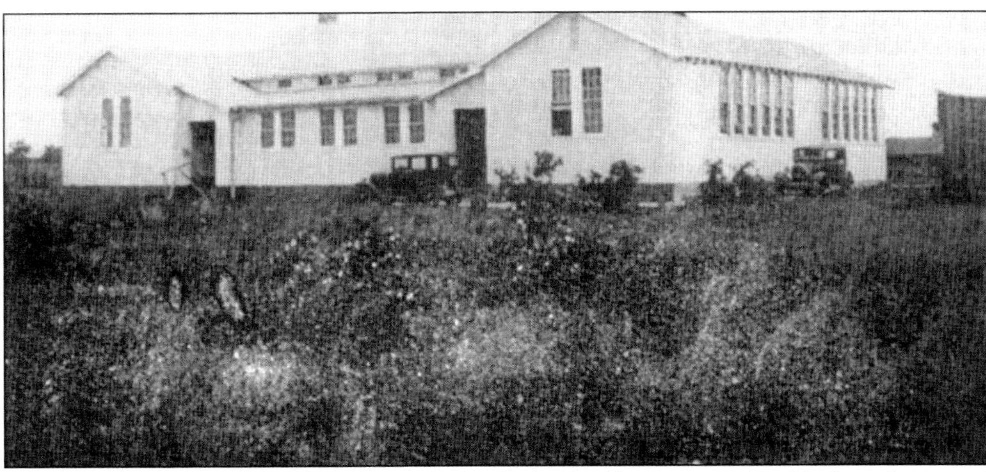

Known as the Treutlen County Training School, this building was used by black students until they moved into new facilities (now Treutlen High School) in the mid-1950s. (Courtesy of Regina Banks Harrison.)

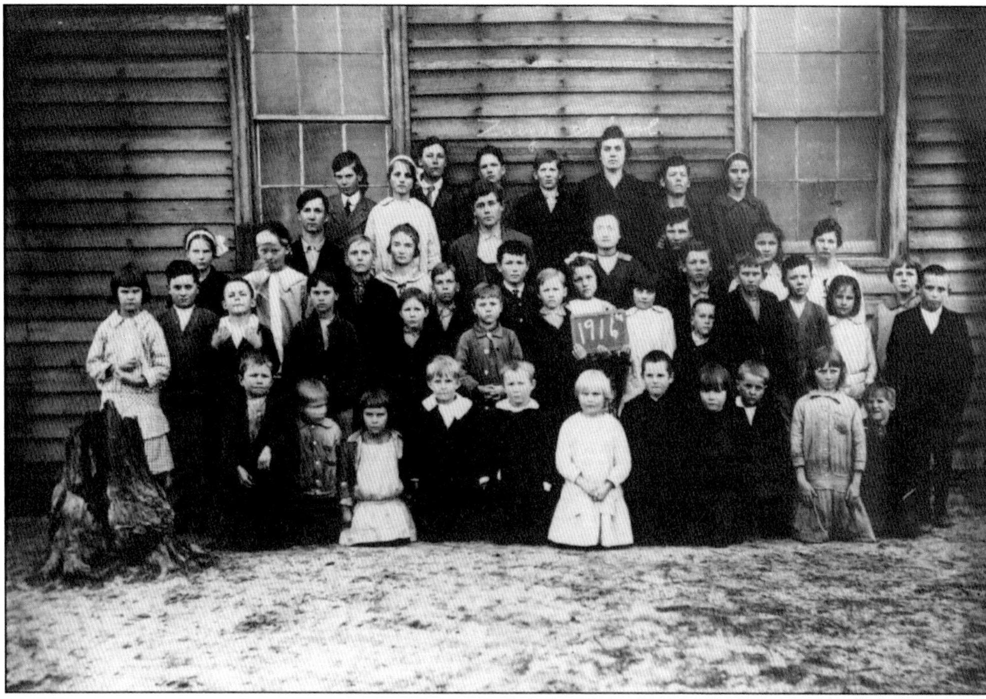

Students from 1916 are pictured at the old Zaidee School. Some of the families of the area who sent their children to school here were Phillips, Herndon, Braddy, Willis, and Moxley. Notice the photographer misspelled the name of the school when he wrote it on the building behind the students.

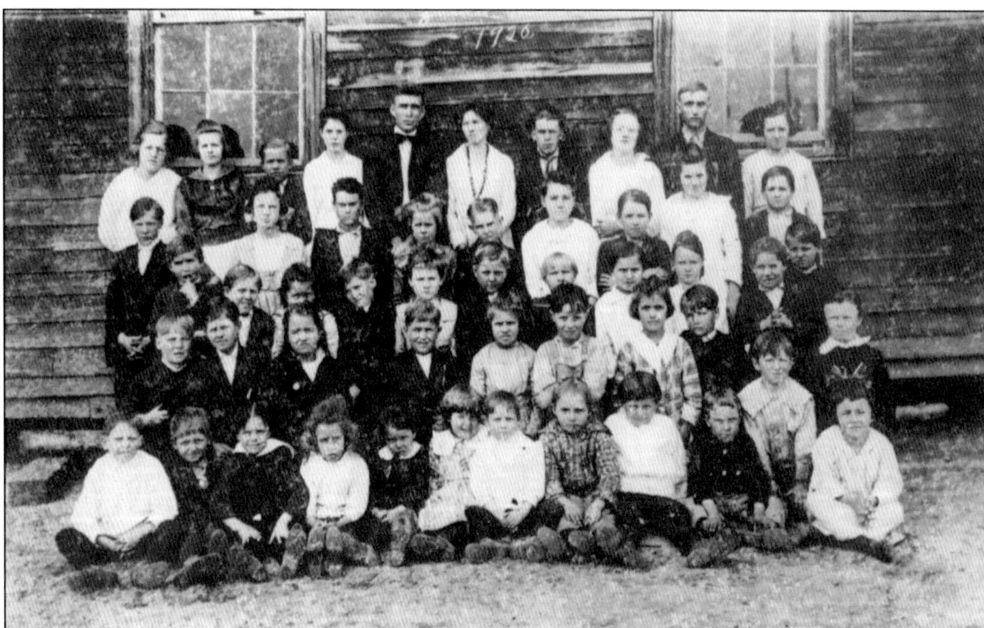

The Zaidee School is pictured here in 1920. The building appears to be resting on log beams lying directly on the ground, as though it was moved onto the site from another location. It is believed that this school building was shared at one time with the Advent Christian Church.

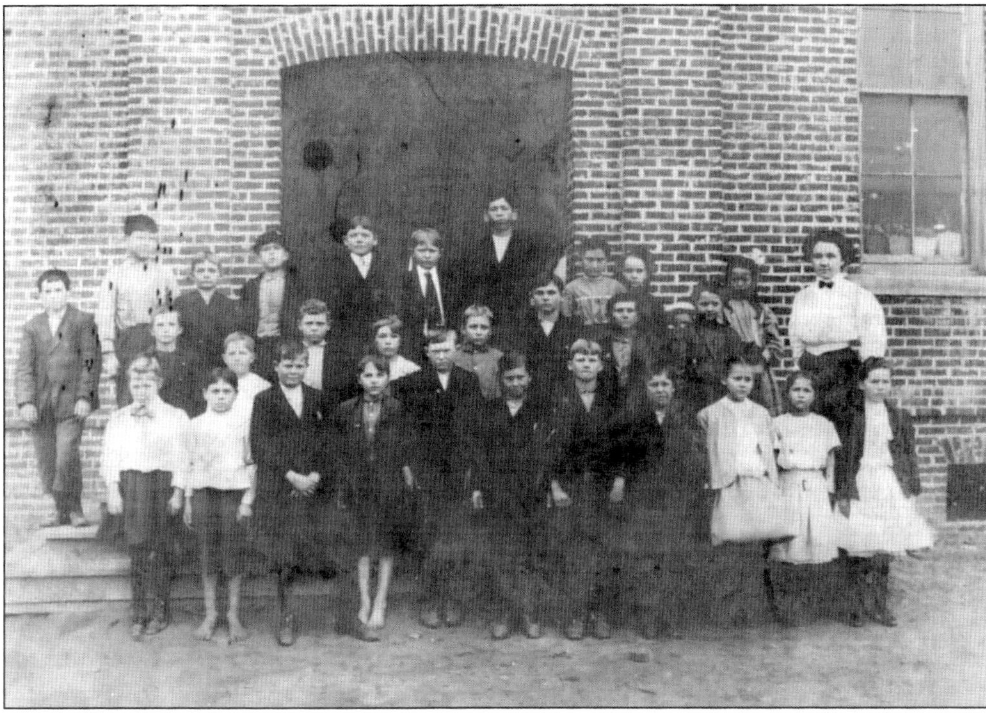

This is an early-1900s photograph of students at the Soperton Elementary School. Soperton was a newly chartered town at this time and was sparsely populated. Many of these students were children of local business owners.

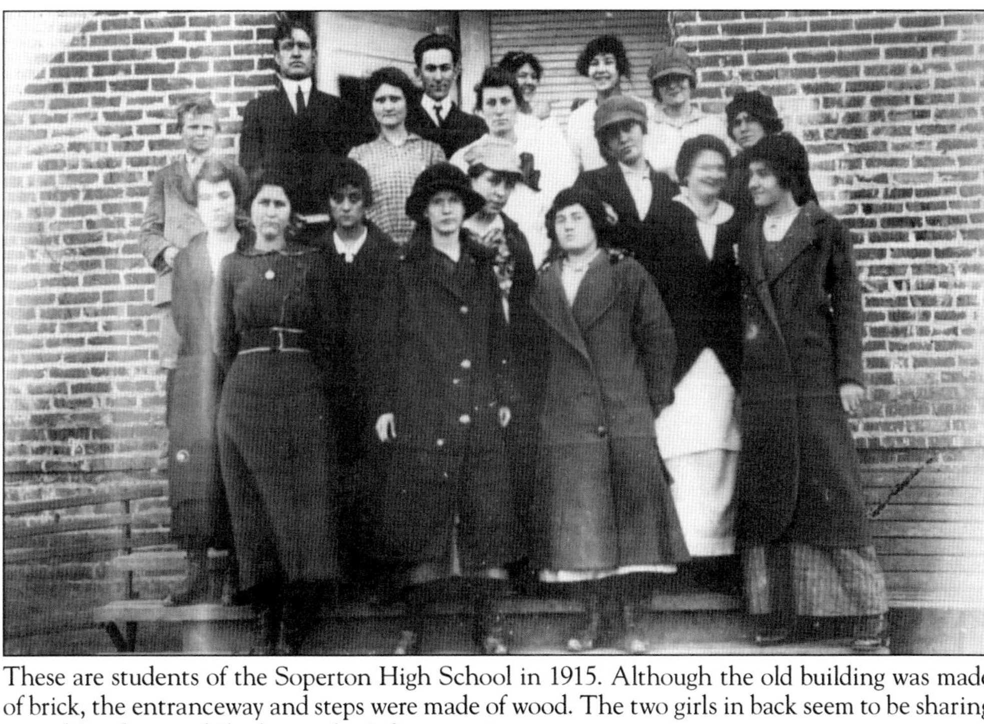

These are students of the Soperton High School in 1915. Although the old building was made of brick, the entranceway and steps were made of wood. The two girls in back seem to be sharing something funny while the teacher's face remains stern.

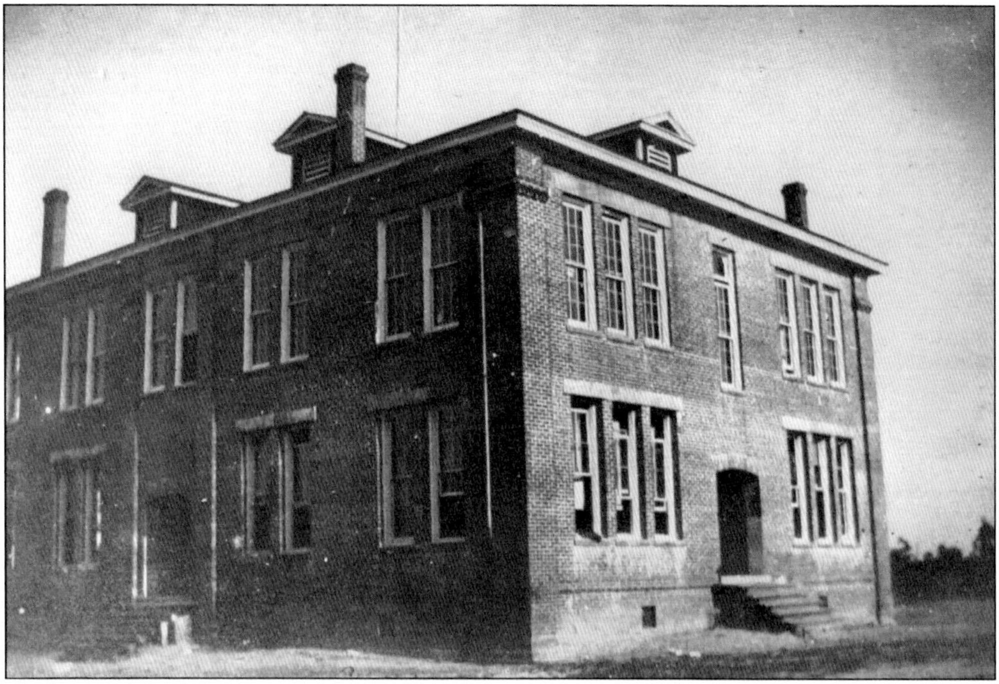

Shown is the old brick Soperton High School. This two-story building stood on the primary school grounds in the early 1900s. It has been said that a piano was once shoved off the second floor by a group of students who wished to avoid music lessons, but another piano took its place the next day.

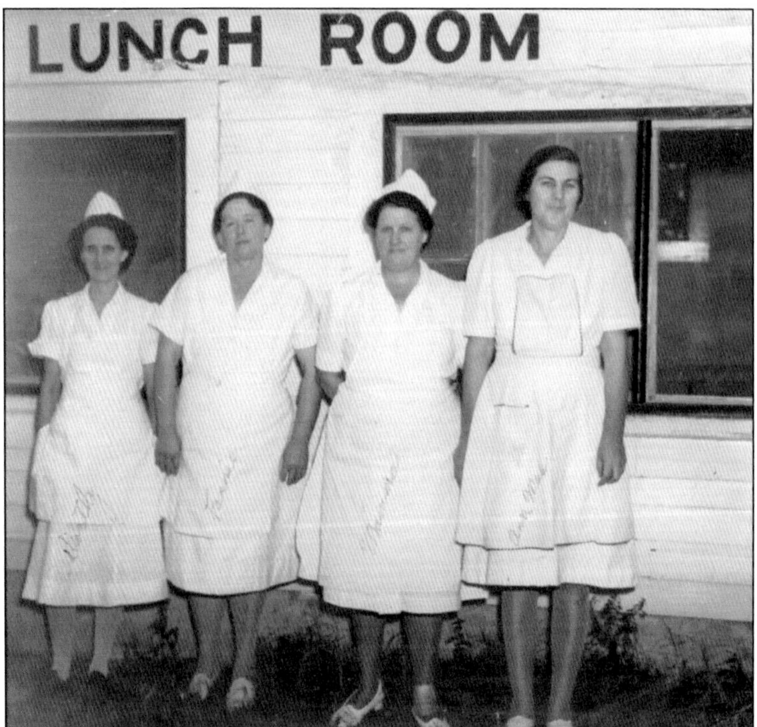

Pictured are lunchroom workers at the Soperton School in the 1950s. From left to right are Audrey Gillis, Fannie Dukes, Dorothy Odom, and ? Blaxton. (Courtesy of Sandra Calhoun Odom.)

These six young ladies appear to be members of a club or organization at Soperton High School. The picture was made about 1920, and headbands were in vogue during this period. The girls are unidentified.

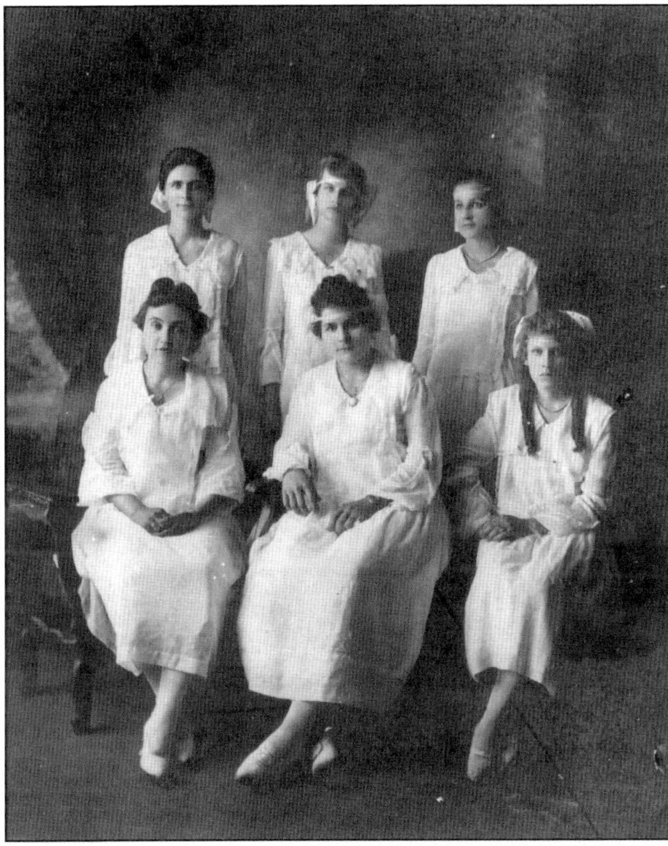

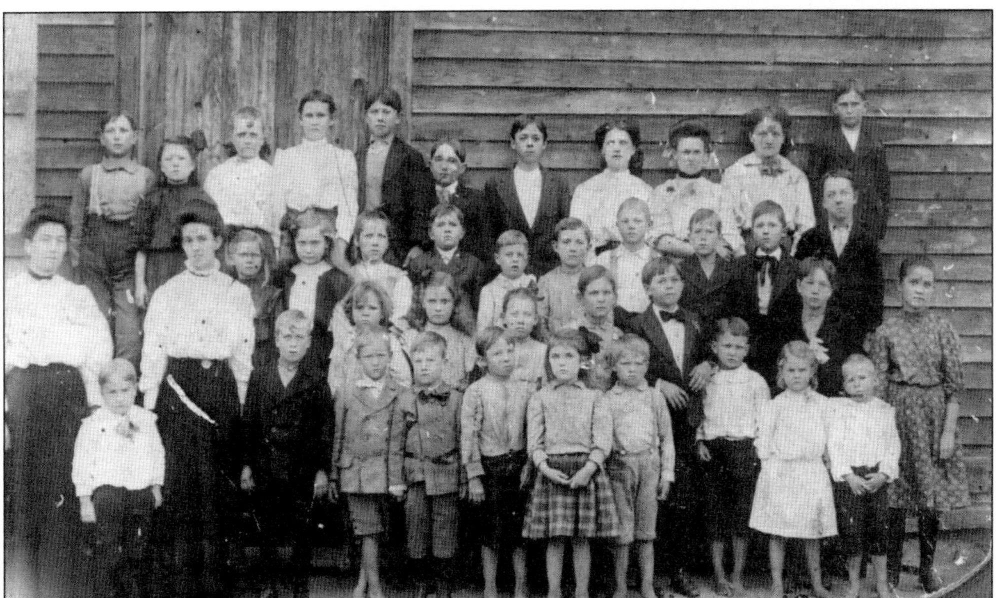

This is a picture of a group posing at an unidentified old school in the county. Taken in approximately 1910, it shows that many children once went without their shoes almost everywhere, even in inclement weather.

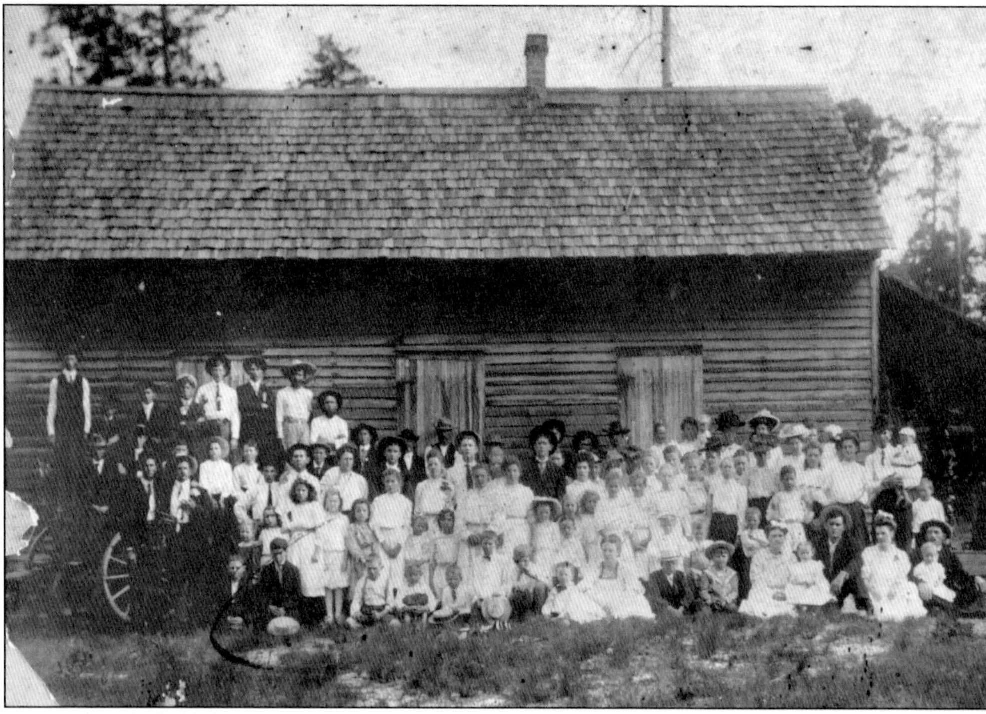

An unidentified old church is holding a meeting in this *c.* 1900 photograph. Perhaps it is homecoming day and "dinner on the grounds." Notice the beautiful hats some of the ladies are wearing; during this period, white was the main choice of color for women's and girls' dresses.

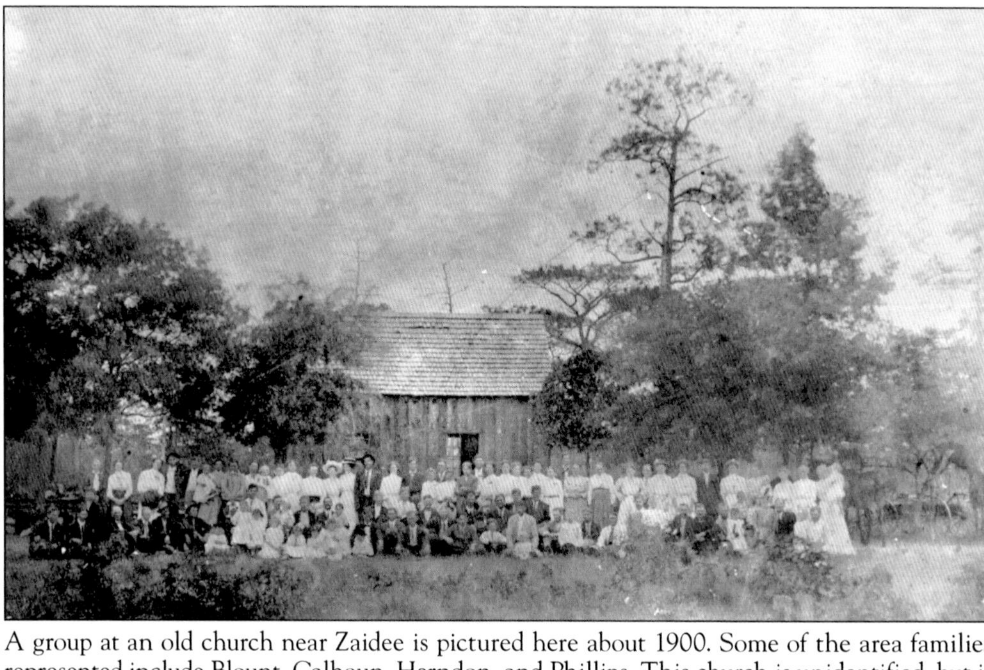

A group at an old church near Zaidee is pictured here about 1900. Some of the area families represented include Blount, Calhoun, Herndon, and Phillips. This church is unidentified, but it is possibly the old Zaidee Baptist Church, which was organized in the 1890s and is no longer in existence. (Courtesy of John Herndon.)

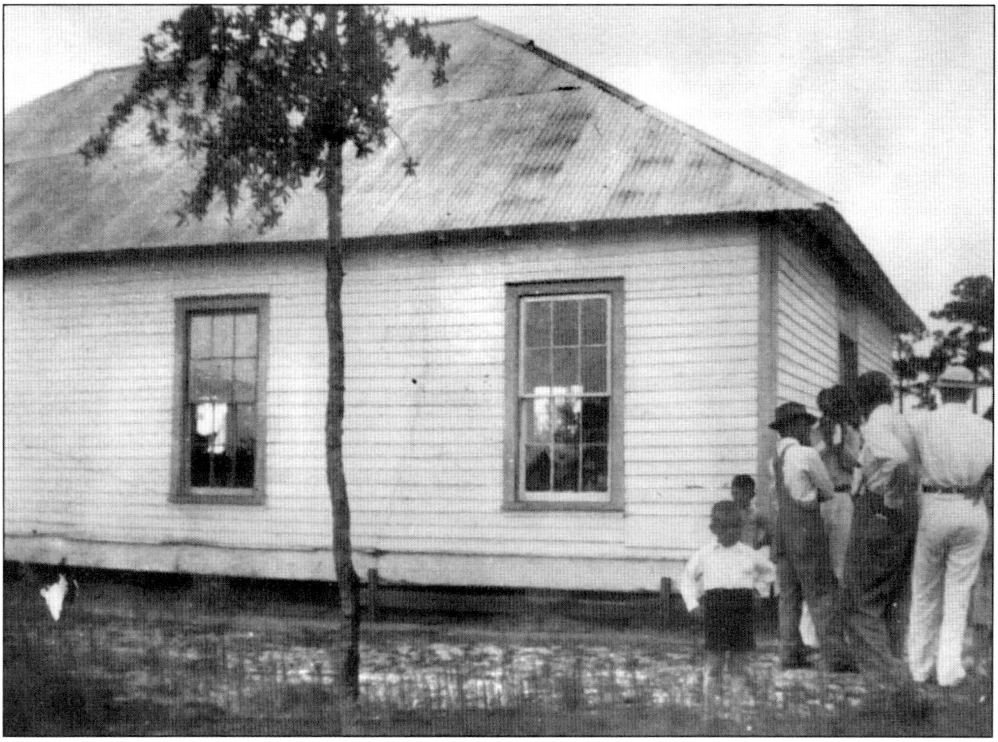

Above is the old Johnson's Chapel as it appeared about 1940. It was originally an old school building bought by J. W. D. Johnson and moved onto his property. Services were held in this building from 1926 to 1948, at which time a new church building was erected. (Courtesy of the Hall family.)

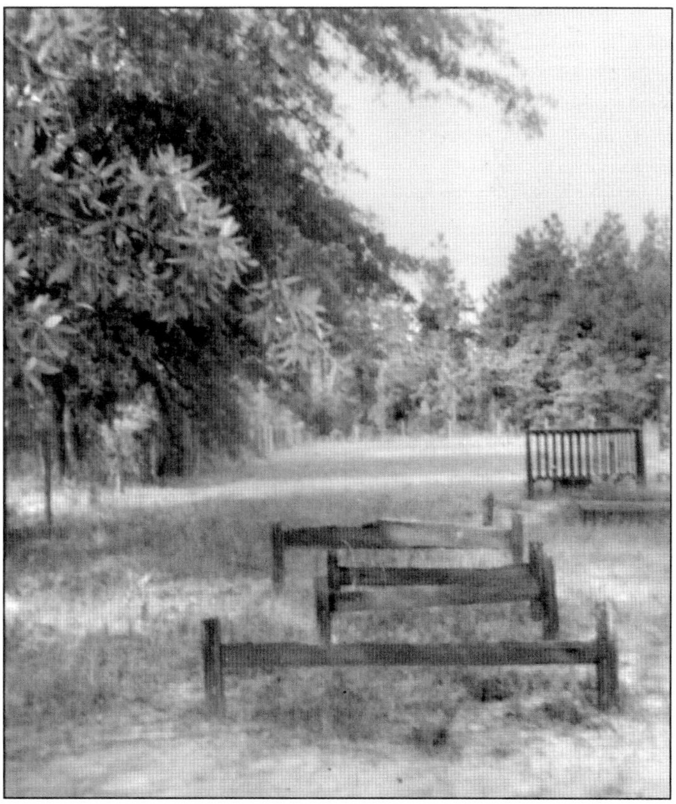

Shown at right in this old photograph are the original "fat lighterd" (lightwood) grave markers that were at the back of the cemetery at the Boiling Springs Baptist Church. In an effort to make the cemetery more attractive, the markers were destroyed in the latter part of the 20th century. Because of their removal, the grave sites have been permanently lost.